Passionate **Work**

RENYI HONG

Passionate
Work

Endurance after the Good Life

DUKE UNIVERSITY PRESS
Durham and London
2022

Project editor: Lisa Lawley
Cover designed by Matt Tauch
Text designed by A. Mattson Gallagher
Typeset in Adobe Caslon Pro and Helvetica Neue by Typesetter

Library of Congress Cataloging-in-Publication Data
Names: Hong, Renyi, [date] author.
Title: Passionate work : endurance after the good life /
Renyi Hong.
Description: Durham : Duke University Press, 2022. |
Includes bibliographical references and index.
Identifiers: LCCN 2021031438 (print)
LCCN 2021031439 (ebook)
ISBN 9781478015598 (hardcover)
ISBN 9781478018223 (paperback)
ISBN 9781478022831 (ebook)
Subjects: LCSH: Job satisfaction. | Job satisfaction—Social aspects. |
Quality of work life. | Social networks. | Self-employed. | Gamification. |
BISAC: SOCIAL SCIENCE / Media Studies | SOCIAL SCIENCE /
Sociology / General
Classification: LCC HF5549.5.J63 H664 2022 (print) | LCC HF5549.5.J63
(ebook) | DDC 650.1—dc23/eng/20211006
LC recordavailableathttps:// lccn.loc.gov/2021031438
LC ebookrec ordavailableathttps:// lccn.loc.gov/2021031439

Cover art: Tetsuya Ishida, *Cell Phone Robot and Laptop Boy*, 1996.
Acrylic on board. 103 × 145.6 cm (40½ × 57¼ in.). Courtesy of
Michiaki Ishida/TETSU Inc.

DUKE UNIVERSITY PRESS GRATEFULLY ACKNOWLEDGES THE
WILLIAM LIM SIEW WAI FELLOWSHIP, WHICH PROVIDED
FUNDS TOWARD THE PUBLICATION OF THIS BOOK.

CONTENTS

ACKNOWLEDGMENTS

Passion binds people and things together to make up a world. This book is a product of this binding, a collaborative effort of the many mentors, friends, colleagues, students, and strangers that I have been fortunate to encounter on both sides of the Pacific. My mentor Sarah Banet-Weiser was the one who seeded the germ for this project and who supported and encouraged its creative development. More than just a mentor, however, Sarah was also there when I had to juggle caring for a newborn and writing. You have left an indelible mark in my life, and I hope to channel your intellectual rigor, generosity, and care in all that I do. Other outstanding mentors—Henry Jenkins, Larry Gross, Mike Ananny—were keen readers of my work, providing the histories and leads that shaped the arguments of this book. My thinking and work would have suffered without you. Several of my chapters began in classes with Andrew Lakoff, Josh Kun, and Manuel Castells, and their advice was invaluable in improving my early drafts. My deepest gratitude to all of you for your honest feedback and the freedom to slowly work out the contours of this project.

I am also fortunate to maintain friendships with many wonderful comrades at the University of Southern California (USC). I am indebted to Tisha Dejmanee for setting up and inviting me to her writing group. She and Kelly Song, Samantha Close, Raffi Sarkissian, and Diana Lee were among the earliest to read my drafts and offer thoughts that were always kind and sharp. Several others also deserve special mention: I deeply appreciate the friendship of Zhang Lin, who continues to be someone with whom I can commiserate about life's problems. Komathi Ale-Valencia and Mina Park were also wonderful friends and meal partners who went through some of my challenging periods. Charlie and Paula Brown and Dominic Goh generously lent their homes when we needed a space and helped us with all the logistical niggles of moving from Los Angeles to Singapore. Many others have helped and touched my life in some way. I apologize for lapses in my memory: Aaron Trammell, Cynthia Wang, Flemming Schneider, Josh Clark, Nikita Hamilton, and Ritesh Mehta. In ways subtle and profound, each of you has contributed to the possibility of this book. Please stay well, and may we meet again in better times.

Passionate Work traveled across the Pacific halfway through my writing and benefited enormously from friends and colleagues at the National University of Singapore (NUS). I couldn't have asked for a better mentor than Audrey Yue, who provided wise counsel on so many different aspects of this book. I am also grateful to Irving Goh, whose sharp observations refined my ideas, provided new leads, and kept me feeling excited about my project. Colleagues in the past and present have also provided support in navigating a new academic environment: Alex Mitchell, Elmie Nekmat, Iccha Basnyat, Jack Qiu, Lonce Wyse, Raka Shome, Shaohai Jiang, and Taberez Neyazi. The graduate students of my department, Communications and New Media, and the Cultural Studies in Asia program also provided feedback on my drafts. I would like to specially mention my research assistants, Aloysius Raja Sekar, Changwen Chen, Rashmi Mehta, and Sarah Lim, who helped with different parts of the editing process. Thanks also to Wong Shu Yun for the initial round of copy edits. It is my great fortune to have met all of you.

I would like to also give special thanks to Courtney Berger, my editor at Duke University Press, for seeing the potential in my book and approaching it with infectious enthusiasm and encouragement. Thanks also to Sandra Korn for facilitating the publication process. The three anonymous reviewers were amazing in the ways that they encouraged and pushed my ideas. Their feedback has had immeasurable impact on the final drafts.

This book would also have been impossible without the fellowship and funds provided by USC and NUS. I was fortunate to be awarded grants from Annenberg that went toward the fieldwork for the chapter on coworking spaces. Much of the revisions later drew from grants that were generously provided by NUS, which also provided me time to refine my work. I would like to specially thank Corlizz Ang, who fielded my incessant queries with patience. Thanks also to Elmie for covering me during my absence at NUS.

I cannot thank my family enough for all that they have generously offered during the period I was writing this book—a total of seven years, all included. My parents, Ang Beng Chin and Ng Swee Lai, expressed unwavering support for my decisions throughout my life; without both of you, it would have been impossible to even contemplate taking on a book project like this. My three daughters were born during the time when I writing the book, and Jilly and Jolly Koh were always ready to help me care for them, so that I could dedicate myself to writing. Thanks to everyone for braving the phobias and inconveniences of a nearly twenty-four-hour flight. I love you all. And to my brother and buddies, Zhiyi, Kelvin, and Jia Jie: this book is inspired by the many different accounts of your experiences.

To Ariel, Esther, and Kayla: Thank you for bringing so much joy into my life. I cannot be more proud to be a father of three girls. This book is also written for you.

Finally, to Jinny Koh, my best friend and spouse: words cannot express my gratitude. I see you there supporting me in everything that I've been through, and I want to do the same for you. This book is dedicated to you.

Introduction

Passionate Work and the Good Life

Among the 47,361 employees surveyed in 120 countries worldwide, 25% report life ratings high enough to put them in the thriving group. Among engaged workers, however, the figure rises to 45%, while among those who are actively disengaged, just 13% are thriving.... There is much that managers and leaders can do to help employees around the globe feel like they have good jobs—and therefore good lives.

Steve Crabtree, "A Good Job Means a Good Life" (2011)

Finding passion for one's work is often described as a positive ideal. It is commonly held in relation to the "good life," something that hinges on the uncomplicated desire that work might provide human life with purpose, financial well-being, and success. Richard Sennett has described this as an instinct, or as an ethos of the artisan or craftsman, whose "desire to do a job well for its own sake" is "an enduring, basic human impulse."[1] Such longing stems from a longer lineage of intellectual thought, of which one influential figure is the young Karl Marx. Commenting on early works of Marx, Thomas Henricks notes that "in the Marxian vision of the good life, people participate together in communities on terms of relative equality."[2] *Equality* carries the meaning of laboring according to the human will; in such a world, labor "expresses the special privilege of human beings to transform freely the conditions of their existence."[3] Like Sennett's, Henricks's notion is built on the model of the craftsman and artist: "The objects we create and the tools we use not only reflect the human abilities we share with others but also provide the basis for our public lives together."[4]

These humanist visions describe the ennobling possibility of labor: the view that work executed in line with one's passions will realize our creative capacities and contribute toward building a better world. Certainly there are qualifications as to what Sennett and Marx would endorse as passionate work. Neither, as a general overview of their scholarship suggests, would support a model of craftsmanship that obtains passion at the cost of exploitation and a precarious existence.[5] Both also produced highly influential and critical accounts of capitalism. Yet their visions, rooted in the notion of an authentic inner life expressible through labor, indicate the persistence of passionate work as a cultural imaginary for how the intricacies of everyday life are to be negotiated.

This vision of passion should be familiar to the contemporary reader. After all, as Miya Tokumitsu relates, the media are replete with images that project work as an object of bliss.[6] A cursory search on a search engine would yield an assortment of strategies to find your passion. It is also the case that celebrities such as Oprah Winfrey, Steve Jobs, and Jeff Bezos have been ardent evangelists of the passionate work ethos. The commencement speech delivered by the late Jobs at Stanford University, which exhorted listeners to "do what you love," remains one of the most popular inspirational talks on YouTube, having accumulated over 36 million views at the time of writing.[7]

On the corporate front, companies have become more involved in attracting and developing passionate employees. In the 2000s, companies such as Zappos and Google created the position of a chief happiness officer, the newest entrant to the C-suite responsible for the mission of organizational happiness.[8] Others, such as Amazon, have initiated "pay to quit" policies, a scheme that offers a nominal sum for unpassionate employees to resign voluntarily.[9] Those uncertain about their passions may also enroll in colleges such as the Wayfinding Academy, a program that prioritizes the discovery of passions. Customizing the curriculum to the interests of each individual student, the Wayfinding Academy claims to empower students to "live life on purpose," helping them find the kind of work that can help them "thrive" and "grow" throughout their lives.[10]

Post-Fordist Trade-off

Concerns arose in the late twentieth century that the shift toward post-Fordism had engendered a different logic of oppression.[11] Writing in the 1970s, Harry Braverman associated the monopolization of technical and scientific knowledge with the accumulation of social power by the technological and managerial classes. The separation of conception from execution polarizes knowledge, forcing the working class into performing simple tasks that erode the relevance of their craft skills and intensify their estrangement from the production process. For Braverman, workplace alienation materializes class warfare at the structural level; alienation and deskilling have become the mechanisms by which "workers would sink to the level of general and undifferentiated labor power" and be subject to the weakening of their bargaining power and the cash value of their labor.[12]

But by the 1990s, a different work ethos had emerged around the New Economy. Corporations in the growing creative and technology sectors had co-opted the resistance to work as a corporate philosophy to engineer a workplace that refused distinctions between traditional boundaries of work and leisure.[13] Instead of denying workers their autonomy or swamping them with bureaucracy and hierarchy, these companies forged a post-Fordist work ethos that encouraged workers to freely express themselves, build team relationships, and blur spheres of leisure and work. Work strove to be a space for pleasure, intimacy, and personal identification, where companies believed that those qualities would best draw the human capabilities most valued in those industries: creative, intellectual, and communicative skills, as well as the worker's emotions and relational capital.[14]

By now there exists a considerable body of work that has addressed the problematics of this postindustrial work ethos. Studies of cultural workers, in particular, have highlighted how autonomy is exchanged for short-term precarious work contracts, lengthy hours, pressures to keep one's skills relevant, and the need to juggle multiple jobs to make a decent wage.[15] The consensus—as David Hesmondhalgh and Sarah Baker have found in interviews across different creative industries—is that the freedom of this work ethic is at best "complicated" and "ambivalent" and at worst blatantly exploitative.[16] While many creative workers do enjoy a certain degree of autonomy and creative pleasure in their work, many are also subject, willingly or unwillingly, to the problematics characterized by post-Fordist work. The individualistic drive for fulfillment through work comes at the cost of fair wages and organized labor, and work culture is said to drive such exploitation through an array of bohemian symbols that makes its adherence cool and exciting. "The humane workplace (with its feel-good simulation and its tests of mettle)," Andrew Ross writes, "has taken precedence over the just workplace (with protection for all, democratic control over the enterprise, and assurances of security beyond the job)."[17] And development of the technological capacities of crowd-sourcing and videocasting and the normalization of entrepreneurialism, internships, and hustle culture have made this work ethos common and its exploitation pervasive.[18]

The salience of these problems has prompted critiques of passion on platforms such as the *Atlantic*, *Jacobin*, the *New York Times*, the *Washington Post*, and the *Harvard Business Review*.[19] The call to follow one's passion has been publicly denounced as an alibi for overworking employees, producing a host of bodily, psychological, and relational ailments that make for a "bruising workplace."[20] It has been accused of downplaying the fact that craftsmanship can be difficult and painful, rather than exciting and stimulating.[21] Most of all, however, passionate work is attacked for its fallacious promise. Jonathan Malesic, for instance, has described the popular *ikigai* model of job fulfillment, which locates the "dream job" within four overlapping qualities (passion, wage, purpose, and skill), as a dangerous lie. Labeling a quadrant covered by passion, purpose, and skill, but short of a wage, as "exploitation," Malesic indicates the problems that exist in the zones of partial exclusion. He writes, "Even in the best of economic times, people rarely find remunerative work that they also love," and high-paying dream jobs have become even rarer after the recession.[22]

These accounts share the assumption that people have, to varying degrees, been seduced into the fantasy of passionate work. The problem, following the shift from Fordism to post-Fordism, is that people have "traded" their wages, time, and job security (ideals assumed by Fordism) for a fantasy of passionate work or self-exploitative pleasure. Terms such as "aspirational labor" (Duffy), "hope labor" (Kuehn and Corrigan), "venture labor" (Neff), and "glamorous labor" (Rosenblat) assert this dynamic, informing the ways that affect is directed toward the capture of labor power, usually through the production of false hopes.[23] Certainly, the trade-off is more nuanced in its variations. The expressed love for the job may be more of a rhetorical strategy than an internalized belief, and the want for autonomy is not always absent a demand for justice.[24] Yet, despite these differences, it remains clear that the shift to post-Fordism has normalized the cultural intelligibility of the trade-off. Tiziana Terranova's influential diagnosis of digital labor—that such work tends toward being "simultaneously voluntarily given and unwaged, enjoyed and exploited"—reflects a key characteristic of post-Fordist work: its capacity to tolerate and harness contradictions between pleasure and a fair wage.[25]

The heuristic of the trade-off serves a powerful explanatory function, but this book argues that the transparency of its exchange has obfuscated yet another ideological purpose in passionate work: its use in dictating how life is to be led happily and well *despite* economic hardship. To explain the cost of corporatist autonomy, trade-off theorists have typically centered their arguments on the false allure of passion. People are driven to chase their passions through false impressions, believing that it will bring them happiness and a better life, but end up being exploited of their wages, time, and creativity. This perspective provides analytical clarity, and its resonance in public discourse reflects how it taps into a contemporary state of affairs. Still, this argument is limited by its assumption—in the logic of the trade-off, the subject exploited is one who *desires* passion and who takes steps to pursue it. Passionate work is a trap laid for subjects "tricked" into its fantasy.

My contention is that this approach obscures the organizational logic that passion serves for capitalism. It also imposes the meaning of passion on certain professions—usually middle- and upper-class, creative, and cultural workers, and entrepreneurs—as indicative of what passion means for work culture at large, narrowing its usefulness and span as an organizational logic of work today. Passionate work, this book argues, does much more. It is not simply a feeling but a logic to labor that informs the governmentality of work.

Affective Structure

I came to examine passionate work because I am interested in and dismayed at how contemporary forms of labor have become more affective and exploitative at the same time. But as the study proceeded, I noticed something else: a different language for passionate work has emerged, where *people are asked to follow their passions precisely because of the existing problems of the economy*. Indeed, what has become clear is that the dynamics of passionate work are not simply centered on a conventional passionate subject—someone who "follows their passion"—and neither does passionate work operate only at the level of a trade-off, an exchange of love for exploitation. Instead, passion is increasingly mobilized as a shield, a means of attenuating the psychic drain of economic uncertainty and income scarcity. This changes the relationship between passion and exploitation: if exploitation is commonly seen as a *cause* of passionate work, then passionate work is now made a *reaction* to exploitation, a panacea for the marginal subject at risk of falling out of the "normal" system of economic personhood.

Passionate Work embarks on the inquiry on those terms, seeking to understand what passionate work does even when the subjects of its address do not feel passion as it is conventionally understood. Instead of focusing on subjects of the "passion economy"—those who have woven their passions into their labor—I gravitate toward subjects and contexts that do not typically conjure impressions of passionate engagement: newly retrenched unemployed individuals, call center workers, and those forced into the precarious work of freelancing.[26] Passion emerges in these spaces as a means of endurance, a way of cobbling a veneer of normalcy amid protracted economic disenchantment. This approach expands on what Kathleen Stewart calls the "contact zones" of analysis, capturing the purposes of passion as it swerves and relays through the circuits that make up a world.[27] Consequently, *passion* is best apprehended not as a self-evident term with clearly defined boundaries in meaning. Rather, its enduring usefulness and relevance must be understood through its fluidity, its capability of joining itself to a range of objects, emotions, discourses, and histories to bring out imagined qualities of the passionate subject.

For this reason, I theorize passionate work as an *affective structure*, a zone of orientation that clusters a variety of affects and circulates them in a way that would make passion matter differently for different subjects. Passion clusters not in the sense that it is an emotional "blend," as cultural historian Fay Bound Alberti puts it.[28] Alberti uses emotional clusters to explain the repertoire of feelings found in emotional states. Loneliness, for instance, can include feelings of rage, sorrow, jealousy, and resentment. Similarly, passion can feel like many things. My interest, however, does not primarily lie with the range of sensations that passion can arouse, although it does have many facets; nor does it center on the ways that the term has gained vernacular use, although that remains important to the contextualization of the affect.

The aim is more specific: I seek to understand the politics of passionate work by examining how it forms an interpretive schema, such that access into the good life through work is made thinkable in a condition of structural violence. Feelings, Sara Ahmed writes, "do not reside in subjects or objects, but are produced as effects of circulation."[29] The more an emotion is associated with an object, the more the association is solidified and naturalized as how things are. I extend this associational proposition by suggesting that affective structures also influence what is recognized within circulation. The more we come into contact with an emotion, the easier its recall in other sites; the more it is used, the more elastic the emotion becomes, structuring how the world comes to gain meaning. Emotion is nonsubjective in this sense: learned emotional vocabularies and conditioned emotional dispositions, Rei Terada writes, influence the terms that we come to recognize and naturalize the sentiments we encounter.[30] The cultural salience to passionate work, coupled with its fluidity of meaning, has allowed it to tinge and enter a variety of contexts that influence the ways that work is transformed, governed, and encountered.

This approach has influenced the methods undertaken for this project. To chart the elasticity of passionate work, I have stitched an array of materials together. The chapters that follow are centered on the fields of managerial ideology (chapter 1), unemployment (chapter 2), gamification (chapter 3), and coworking (chapter 4), but the objects they assemble range from historical managerial texts to contemporary career guides, from social scientific work on unemployment to networking advice, from software protocols to descriptions of office furniture. This wide overview reflects, in part, the saturation of passionate work in our worlds, but it also serves the strategic purpose of bringing its dynamic into focus. As an example, I piece social scientific texts from different disciplinary fields in chapter 2 to illustrate the entanglements that exist between passionate work and unemployment. *Marienthal,* a sociological text influential for insisting on the psychological necessity of employment, shows us how apathy can be used as a label to pathologize unemployment, rendering it a condition uninvestable with any meaningful human interest. This argument is pulled through into happiness and policy studies on optimum unemployment insurance—showing the effort spent in orchestrating a world where joblessness is *made to be* "rationally" painful. This example shows how passionate work is regularized as an affective structure through the sedimentation of ideas, norms, and attitudes. As a rubric for an ideal, it magnetizes a distributed effort to shape work to proximate a particular form.

To capture these tendencies, I attend to the connections in my materials, revealing the often surreptitious collaborations that disparate actors have in making their claims. For instance, I was led to the theory of flow, a psychological theory of concentration and engagement, while examining the case of gamification in chapter 3. At that point, I was engaged in a critique of the compassionate impulse of gamification—its argument that gamified software protocols could yield better lives for low-value information workers—and I thought that flow would simply be another data point. But upon looking deeper, I was struck by the resonances of passion and compassion in these separate accounts. The flow experience (typically described as that of passion) is modeled after the psychological resilience of prisoners who were able to survive war untraumatized, and its theorist, Mihály Csíkszentmihályi, was driven to deploy this quality of psychological engagement to ease the boredom of factory line workers. From line workers to information workers, these similarities show the ways that passionate work can congeal a world.

Understanding passionate work as an affective structure allows us to attend to it as its logic gets stretched out and pulled from the center into the margins. It reveals an expanded utility and highlights the many kinds of compromises and violence that it exacts through its differentiated worldmaking projects. Some might dispute the accuracy of understanding passionate work in this broad sense, of reading it as culture rather than feeling, structure rather than state, and of associating negative affects with the hip "do what you love" movement characteristic of passionate work. I draw my conceptualization of the term from Raymond Williams, who describes culture as neither isolated nor static. Feelings, he points out, can exist as "structures of feeling," "a pattern of impulses, restraints, tones," which have a general organization but which can vary in specific experiences depending on the lived condition that people find themselves in.[31] Similarly, *affective structure* is used here to reference the many forms of recognition that passion affords. It highlights variation in discourses, institutional arrangements, and intended outcomes, while maintaining that a central tenor and logic determine how people are expected to relate to their labor.

At the same time, an affective structure does more than describe a continuum of experiences. The mode of recognition it provides is itself a politics, a means of assuming sameness and difference in feelings, a tool to produce the terms by which unvalued workers in mundane occupations are to be pitied and rescued from their predicament. The idea that passion can be recognized in different ways allows for calls for change while keeping workers relegated to their place. It enables passion to be issued in compromised terms—where excluded subjects can yet experience a semblance of what it might feel to be a valued passionate worker—while bypassing the challenging politics needed to truly engineer fairer conditions of livelihoods.

This description of passionate work as recuperation and endurance may appear contradictory. After all, the ethic of passionate work has largely been critiqued as being the cause for normalizing the characteristics of "bad jobs," whether for wage, job security, or the ethic of overwork. So how has passion continued to be offered as a solution? One reason, I submit, is that as passion becomes a normalized post-Fordist affect, it also subtly shifts ideas about what the good life should encompass and the priorities that people should hold. And within this shift, it has become possible for passion to be presented as an affect that can bring people closer to an idealized selfhood in late capitalism: a resilient subject capable of managing economic disappointment and endurance of a precarious order. Lauren Berlant writes that the Great Recession marks an economic-affective turn, where "the promise of the good life can no longer mask the living precarity of this historical present."[32] The good life has become frayed, and ideas of steady progression—fantasies that hard work can lead to home ownership, a progressively secure future for the family, and an improvement in job status—have become fragile, prone to damage. The affective structure of passionate work is contextualized within this particular milieu as a form of repair and reassurance. Addressed to the postrecessionary realities of joblessness, class anxiety, and precarity, passionate work nonetheless maintains that work can lead to some kind of a good life.

I describe the promises clustered around passionate work to be *compromises*, meaning that they are at once more minor and phantasmic than what the good life is traditionally assumed to be. These new icons of the good life promise much less, but because they promise less, they seem more adequate, easier to achieve, and less likely to hurt if they end up being unachievable. In a scene of anticipated damage, compromised promises are more affectively investable because they allow for pivoting and shifting to different investments of hope. In a milieu of damage, "the hope is that what misses the mark and disappoints won't much threaten anything in the ongoing reproduction of life, but will allow . . . a kind of compromised endurance," Berlant offers.[33] Adaptation to this future takes the form of damage control, and anticipating how the failure to achieve one's ideal can nonetheless enable some measure of continued existence.

This style of navigation carries pragmatic consequences in the everyday. It eases hardship, producing what is called resilience in the vernacular. We cannot downplay relief. Faced with the pressures of life, relief may be what remains to cohere a world. But it is also critical to examine the shape that relief takes, for relief does not simply normalize the damaged, precarious future of work; it can intensify the norm of work and make work the very site of relief. In its most extreme form, passionate work would have us investing more into work to find relief from the precariousness of work itself. This perverse logic deserves greater scrutiny. Ahmed offers that recovering can indicate how we feel structural injury; to recover may be to re-cover, to cover over and write out an urgent diagnosis of something that needs resistance and refusal.[34] Tackling rather than masking hardship, passionate work shapes our encounter with the grim conditions of labor, channeling disappointment toward resilience, sapping it of its potential for radical change. But what can we say to an apparatus that affords survival even as it continues the norm of a workerist society? The book explores this condition to clarify the politics of compromises offered.

Energetic Attachments

To further this discussion, we might first inquire into the specificity of the term. Why focus on passion as opposed to feelings such as happiness or engagement? For one thing, *passion* in the vernacular encompasses the meanings of alternate terms—such as *happiness, engagement, love, bliss, purpose*, and *calling*—that communicate the optimistic view that work can be a source of fulfillment. At the same time, *passion* references something specific about energetic expression. In *Cold Intimacies*, Eva Illouz describes emotions as "the 'energy-laden' side of action, where energy is understood to simultaneously implicate cognition, affect, evaluation, motivation, and the body."[35] Illouz would call all emotions energetic if not energy giving—emotions provide the "mood" to an action by coloring the style of how we act.

But even if emotion were to influence action, it would be passion that takes form as one of the most energetic affects. Passion is defined in the *Oxford English Dictionary* as "an intense desire or enthusiasm for something; the zealous pursuit of an aim." Passion is intense and zealous: if it were to color an act, it would do so energetically, forcefully, persistently. We might imagine a passionate person talking quickly, gesturing excitedly. Passion is spirited, and as Reynold Lawrie offers, it cannot be expressed by anything other than pure energetic expression. It describes "intensity," "fire," and "urgency," states that would urge activity and force: "It would be inconceivable to have a passion for something, and not desire to pursue the object in some way or another."[36]

Thinking of passion as a form of *energeticity* connects the affect to a longer cultural imagination of human energetics. Anson Rabinbach notes that motors and machines have historically served as metaphors for human labor power because they provide a language for the expandability in the capacities to labor.[37] Automata were invested in as ideal laboring bodies in the eighteenth century because they were assumed to be perpetual motion machines, able to function without limit and continue operations forever without complaints of fatigue, discontent, and aversion. Obviously this was never realized, but the hope for inexhaustible labor power continued well into the nineteenth and twentieth centuries with inquiries into the efficiency of energy conversion in human bodies. Ergonomics and time-motion studies, for instance, share similar claims of societal uplift: inducing motivation in workers, reducing their fatigue, and uncovering the precision of movements that can minimize waste have all been described to optimize the production and expenditure of energy, help workers reach their potential, and, in the process, bring forth a better society.[38]

This history reflects the long-standing preoccupation with human energetics and the desire for its extension. Passion offers a scene of this, stretching human vigor in a context of enervation. Like the perpetual motion machine—an animating model of human labor—passion seems unassailable in its conjuration of inner fortitude. In chapter 2, I elaborate on how passion is repeatedly turned to for its capacity to provoke action in the face of adversity. A quality of obsession embedded in passion is imagined to extend the human capability of pursuit, offering a model of driven action that provides fuel beyond what is reasonably possible, which enables extreme expressions of human perseverance and grit. Here, passion coincides with the idea of a well-managed self. The promise of doing more, taking more, *achieving more* is undivorceable from the fantasy figure of the strong, capable, independent man of Western individualism. And in this sense, passionate work might be better characterized not by an inclination for work but by a wanting for the energetic attachments implied by the term. Objects of our passion are things we pursue relentlessly; passion is a relation of force between things that urges activity, often without restraint. This relation of force is central, for regardless of the objects of investment, passion can allow the conjuration of energy, motivating someone who is spent into action.

We might take this to mean that there is a minimal distinction between the affect and object of passion, the former referring to a passionate personhood and the latter to the thing that one is passionate about. In the mid-twentieth century, psychologists such as Abraham Maslow and Mark Lepper developed ideas of selfhood that stress the innate drive of humans to action.[39] Maslow's concept of self-actualization and Lepper's theory of intrinsic and extrinsic motivation point toward the common denominator of a latent passionate species—a being that is naturally desiring and which, when properly attuned, would express these desires in healthful ways that would promote learning, well-being, and self-determination.[40] As Maslow famously related, self-actualization can occur only when an "individual is doing what he, individually, is fitted for."[41] In his view, people who do not fulfill the rule, who lead "stupid lives in stupid jobs," regress with bodily aliments and malcontent.[42] Passionate personhoods will make passion inherently good, for even a wrong object of passion will not make passion bad in and of itself—it merely reveals passion to be incorrectly directed, with the fix found in redirecting passions to something better. Passion, as we inherit the term, evinces this recursive structure to desire: we are passionate for passion, wanting the energetics that an object of desire can provide and believing that it offers the apex of fulfillment and well-being.

Passion opens inquiry into desire and energetics, but when examining it, we have to ask not just about the objects that people are passionate about but also where the passion comes from, who speaks for it, and the attachments that it displaces. The very history of the term *passion* shows the importance of this question: the Latin root of *passion*, *passio*, has a diametrically opposed meaning to how it is used today. For much of our history, passio has been described as a passive form of suffering, an external force imposed on the body that leads one to involuntary acts that needed to be struggled against.[43] Susan James, for example, remarks that Aristotle considers passions to be passive because they are "responses that have to be provoked in us by external things and as states that we suffer. We do not have the power to experience passions unaided, but must wait on circumstances to excite them."[44] When insulted we feel angry, despite our wish to feel otherwise. Anger becomes registered on our body, with flushes and heavy breathing. Even if we adopt countermeasures to calm ourselves, anger still displays its powerful effects on us. Like maladies that come upon individuals, Aristotelian passions are affects that hinder people from acting according to their will.

Beginning in the seventeenth century, however, the word's meaning changed to convey signs of a person's authentic inner motivations. As Amélie Oksenberg Rorty writes, "Instead of being reactions to invasions from something external to the self, passions became the very activities of the mind, its own motions. So transformed they become proper motives, and along with desires, the beginnings of actions."[45] This shift generally corresponded with the displacement of *passion* from popular use, replaced by the secular category of *emotion* to reference the transformed nature of the Western modern subject: a subject who is self-contained, interiorized, possessing an autonomous will.[46] The Latin word for emotion, *emovere*, which indexes movement, captures this new identity of the interiorized subject: feelings are seen as stemming from the inside and migrating out as an expression or act.[47]

The qualities ascribed to passion today may be traced from this new emotional landscape. By the late eighteenth century, the meaning of passion would be influenced by the Romantic ethic, a post-Calvinist theology that embraces sentiments as drivers of moral volition.[48] The Romantic worldview sees spiritual value in the richness of emotional experience. Inner feelings are guides toward appreciating beauty in the divine and intuitive hints that lead toward a transcendental way of being. This view would even invert the relationship assumed in passio, where emotions are understood to be subordinate to reason. James Averill writes that the Romantics saw passion as something that needed protection from reason, lest reason befoul the otherworldly creativity that the purity of the passions aroused.[49] With Romanticism, therefore, passion would take on its full modern meaning. The interiorized qualities of passion, with its strong drive and desire, would no longer be resisted. Instead, people are to use passions as models for action, to produce good-willed behavior and to develop into what they are divinely ordained to be.[50]

From outside affliction to interior authenticity, the somersault history of passion tells a story of naturalization, a tale which legitimates the disappearance of desire from critical inquiry. Ahmed reminds us that our emotional contact with things is "shaped by past histories of contact, unavailable in the present."[51] An instance of emotional experience is a pressurization of dense affective contacts, sedimented historically. Passion extends this proposition, for it shapes the terms by which those historical contacts can be explained, even if it is turned to analytically. The turn from passio to passion, Teresa Brennan notes, produced the "self-contained individual," a subject who is made to trust in his desires, seeing them as coming "from nowhere other than the history embodied in his genes."[52] Structural ways of explaining our feelings are to be placed aside in favor of autobiographical explanations.

The injunction to "find your passion" showcases this fantasy of self-contained interiority. Someone reflecting on this question, for instance, may describe a liking for fiction as a unique attribute of the self. They might recall the time they first felt overjoyed writing a story, the pride they felt when they were commended for their effort, and the affirmation provided to them. The question then becomes a source of reflexive selfhood, a moment where emotional knowledge is both sourced and verified as a basis for genetic identity.

These accounts would necessarily have to forsake a more complicated history of struggle that had to be in place for the valorization of energetic attachments to be made commonsense. Erased is the political history that grounds the "good" in the energetic exercise of human capacities. There is a mutability to desire that is important to consider in passion: the history of passionate work is characterized by that of transposition—the tendency toward naming one population's desire as another's—and the suppression of this relationship as passion becomes imputed as personal want. This naturalization of passion determines the terms by which desire is made sensible: as natural want, it urges both an uncritical examination of passion and a willingness to use it as a source of motivation and drive. Unpacking passion requires us to resist this interiority to passion: Who gets to claim what people should be passionate about and what happens when this history is erased? From there we can ask: Why do some objects inspire passion so easily, while it remains nearly impossible for others to spark the slightest interest? And finally, given the strong relations between passion and work, what are the openings that can be afforded to rethink how passions should proceed? These questions guide the inquiry of the book.

Struggle in a Moment of Disenchantment

I began this book in 2015, at a moment where I sensed a cultural contradiction between the circulation of passion and an indignation expressed toward the exposure of economic inequality and hardship. A Pew report published a year later notes that belief in the American Dream had changed significantly since the Great Recession: "In 2009, nearly 4 in 10 Americans said they felt it was common for a person to start poor, work hard, and become rich. Five years later, that number had declined to 23 percent."[53] This is not surprising given the strong discussions about wealth inequality and the harsh economic realities faced by many. But passionate work continued to remain a strong cultural discourse in the public sphere. This trend emerged again with the pandemic, four years after I began the research. As with the recession, the virus has presented a space where people turn to passion as unemployment skyrockets and their livelihoods are threatened.

We are advised to take the quarantine with a "growth mindset," to find our passions so that we can come out of the lockdown with a stronger sense of what to do with our careers. More people are also encouraged to join the "passion industry," to create small digital businesses out of their passions as unemployment stretches on. Even children are not exempt and are entreated to find their passions to grow up with more grit so they can better survive in a world that is getting ever harsher.[54]

The repetition of these accounts highlights the cultural significance of passion in a moment of disenchantment. Writing in the shadow of the Great Recession, Italian philosopher Franco Berardi concludes in *The Soul at Work* that the "crash in the global economy" burst the "work bubble"—the abrupt loss of jobs made brutally apparent the "abandonment of vital social functions and a commodification of language, affections, teaching, therapy, and self-care" caused by an ethic of overwork.[55] Widespread disaffection, he speculates, would then incentivize people to look for alternatives, "extra-economic networks of survival" that would reclaim the freedom and joy of life. He writes, "In the days to come, politics and therapy will be one and the same. The people will feel hopeless and depressed and panicked. . . . Our cultural task will be to attend to these people and to take care of their trauma, showing them the way to pursue the happy adaptation at hand."[56]

A crisis need not be negative if it can be directed toward new subversive imaginaries. In line with other autonomist Marxist theorists, Berardi's manifesto urges for revolution from the angle of social reproduction, arguing that the processes involved in the reproduction can produce the alternative subjectivities and organizations of life that can oppose the workerist norm. This represents what Paolo Virno has called the "neutral kernel" of disenchantment, the lines of political potential to which disenchantment can be directed.[57] Such an effort is essential, Peter Fleming offers, because the most insidious aspect of the ideology of work is not its "love thesis"—the lie that corporations care for workers—since most people are already aware of its hypocrisy.[58] Instead, it is the possibility that awareness drives no corrective action because alternate possibilities are unthinkable. This argument dovetails with what scholars such as Eric Cazdyn, Fredric Jameson, and Mark Fisher suggest: that late capitalism continues not because of a lack of knowledge about its problems but because its alternative has become impossible to envision. Fisher's account of "capitalist realism," for instance, points to the preemptive formatting of human desires that renders capitalism the only viable economic and political system that people can imagine.[59] Seeing problems but left without a solution, then, we willingly cede ourselves to amnesia regarding the harms that capitalism can do. [60] Intervention thus takes on the critical purpose of building substantive alternatives to the cruel optimisms of the conventional good life.

Yet, the recuperation of abandonment does not always originate outside capitalist imperatives. Social reproduction is a terrain of struggle open to different kinds of intervention, each offering rationales for how life is to be organized, invested, or disinvested in the ongoing precarious order. Since the late twentieth century, autonomist and feminist theorists such as Michael Hardt, Antonio Negri, Maurizio Lazzarato, Cristina Morini, and Paolo Virno have described social reproduction as a crucial component in the chain of post-Fordist value creation. The reliance on intellectual, creative, and affective qualities in modern information industries has made the subjectivities, social cooperation, and relationships of workers more important. These cannot be extracted simply with more hours of work—they have to be paired with a variety of services and contexts that can extend such capacities for labor. Hence, recuperative practices of meditation, therapy, and yoga, for instance, have become some of the more popular methods to increase the mental capacity for creative labor.[61] Likewise, surrogate pregnancy, corporate egg-freezing perks, and commercial childcare facilities show how commodified life-providing services have tapped into reproductive science and the global care chain to create alignment between reproductive choices and the temporal rhythms of labor, an effort to draw the maximum from the worker's most intellectually productive and creative years.[62]

But while these accounts tend to focus on the relationship between social reproduction and its effect on increasing production, we need to see social reproduction as important in the ways it screens cost in production, too. As Silvia Federici grasped during the Italian *operaist* struggles, the "social factory"—a provocative term used by Mario Tronti—describes more than just the entry of capitalist relations into a pristine terrain of social life. The private sites of social life—"the kitchen, the bedroom, the home"—have already historically been part of capitalist relations used to produce and maintain commodified labor power.[63] What is happening with the social factory is more an intensification than the emergence of something new, and the suppression of this historical relationship from view is what allows the masculine realm of commodified labor power to be imagined as self-replenishing rather than dependent on the feminized labor of child raising, caring, and household maintenance.[64]

The fact that social reproduction is, as Nancy Fraser writes, "an indispensable background condition for the possibility of economic production in a capitalist society" alerts us to the problems of its invisibility.[65] As many feminists have argued, writing off social reproduction from accounting books has provided a tremendous concession to capitalist economic development. It fetishizes the replenishment of the labor power, allowing it to be left to the workers' seemingly natural ability for self-preservation, and poses the sphere of production as an autonomous domain, unentangled from unpaid feminized labor. Not only does this hide the labor of social reproduction; it also makes routine production seemingly undamaging to the human systems that it extracts from. Thus, production can be made into an object of fantasy—able to continue endlessly without harm.[66]

As a result, the struggle for making capitalist relations of domestic and reproductive labor visible and a priority has taken on a particular political efficacy.[67] The politicization of reproduction relates to a larger goal: if reproduction is the originating point of labor power, then its politicization should destabilize and send reverberations down the circuit of labor, providing for new possibilities of resistance throughout the entire circuit. Demanding wages for housework, for instance, is not only aimed at addressing the sexism involved in economic relationships; it also hopes to challenge the social relations of capitalism at a fundamental level. Federici writes, "Capitalism requires unwaged reproductive labor in order to contain the cost of labor power . . . and a successful campaign draining the source of this unpaid labor would break the process of capital accumulation."[68] Focusing on social reproduction can foreground what is often read as an "externality" to production, bringing to light the costs to production that are often ignored and dismissed.

The political significance to social reproduction explains why it is necessary to reconsider the conventional perspectives of passionate work. While commodified labor power has characteristically served as the source of critique for passion, I find its relationship to social reproduction to be more disturbing, because it threatens to appropriate the futures that disappointment opens. Passionate work has become an important site of recuperation, applied anticipatively as a way of allowing subjects to be stretched out in their capacity to be worn down.[69] Whether through career advice, gamification, or coworking, the idea of passion is already deployed to prepare for economic fallout and disappointment, such that workers can be cushioned and encouraged to pick themselves up and reattach themselves to the compromised fantasies of the good life made accessible through work.

The act of screening damage, however, is not equivalent to its removal. Part of this book's effort is directed toward revealing the compromised forms of living that passionate work endorses and the stakes involved in returning to optimism in work. We see the violence of passion, for instance, exercised in states of awkward exuberance, where temporary zeal is expressed at the risk of humiliation, or numbness, where passionate actions are made to continue without the feelings of tedium and fatigue. Most apparent, however, is the fragility involved in keeping a facade of undamaged calm. Left in a world of diminishing substantive sources of support, one's push to show resilience also means that cracks can occur more easily, suddenly, and without warning.

This conceptualization means that passionate work is fundamentally about an aspect of capitalism at a historic juncture. Its analysis shows how capitalism is recuperating itself amid a protracted period of transformation—a time of stagnant wages, precarity, and heightened inequality—and, in the process, soothing the revolutionary affects that economic disappointment can raise. The ambivalence lies in that endurance is being urgently required for many of the populations addressed within this discourse, who need to conceive a different way forward. But it is also clear that the endurance endorsed here fails to provide the substantive change needed to challenge work as a necessity. And by directing energies toward the reattachment of work, alternative imaginaries are stifled.

Connecting passionate work to the good life is my way of beginning a conversation about a political impasse: attachment to work is at once necessary for survival and problematic for flourishing. We need to focus on the dynamics of this process, to understand how it traverses into many different aspects of the social world. A seemingly obvious answer to the conundrum of passion is that our attachments need to change, that the problem of passionate work would be resolved if the range of our attachments could shift to pursue the structural transformation desired. This is a tempting proposition, but I hesitate to proceed too easily with it. It is true that a different "mattering map," as Lawrence Grossberg puts it, would open our affective horizons, but it remains true also that passionate work does not simply produce an attachment to work; it also recalibrates our conditions of life, making certain kinds of lives unlivable and attachments impossible.[70] Finding new attachments, therefore, cannot be done in situ. It is not merely about pivoting from one attachment to another, as the dominant ideology of passion suggests. Enabling certain attachments would require struggle: one needs to challenge the conditions for certain kinds of lives and possibilities to be made viable. Furthermore, it is important to consider the terms by which work has shaped our understanding of *passion*. To fashion worlds more amendable to care, we might need to change how the meaning of passion is understood. The book proceeds with this hope in mind, believing that a change in the inquiry into passionate work can shift the ways that we have come to recognize the problems of work culture today.

Organization of Chapters

This book embarks on this argument through four chapters. Chapter 1, "From Happiness to Passion," sets up the context by denaturalizing passion as ordinary desire, asking who it is that speaks for this desire. If it is indeed passion that is desired, then how is this desire made historically consistent and biologically natural? The narrative pivots around the shift from happiness to passion as the ideal emotional state in the twentieth century. Starting from the 1920s, I examine how happiness in work took shape as a promise of the good life within the field of human relations. This field gathered all members of administration—foremen, managers, and supervisors—to push the agenda of happiness to line workers, who were believed to be incapable of recognizing the cause of their persistent dissatisfaction. Such rhetoric, however, encountered a backlash by the mid-twentieth century. Concerned about the conformity of American workers, the human relations movement condemned the once-lauded idea of happiness as manipulative and inimical to the development of individualities.

The emphasis on self-actualization and unique individualities that followed laid the foundation for the late twentieth-century ideal of the passionate worker. In one aspect, the notion of passion that emerged in this period carried on the argument of managerial theorists: under the right conditions, workers would voluntarily commit themselves to work. However, in naturalizing that as ordinary desire, academics, management professionals, and popular writers also contributed to erasing the conflictual history that precedes passion, presenting the desire for passion as a historically consistent demand articulated by workers themselves. From an affect that managers struggle to impose on workers to a demand that workers seemingly issue themselves, the narrative shift from happiness to passion reflects on one of the most successful corporate ideological projects of the twentieth century.

Chapters 2 to 4 follow with contemporary accounts. Chapter 2, "Jobless, Undamaged, Resilient," focuses on the very present space of serialized unemployment, a condition where unemployment is normalized and where social welfare is in retreat. The first of a two-part argument centers on apathy, an affect commonly understood to describe a damaged motivational structure encountered after a job is lost. I trouble this view, however, through a close reading of *Marienthal*, an influential social scientific text on unemployment. Curiously, in *Marienthal* apathy is not used to signal depression or listlessness as much as to highlight an adaptation to material lack. The text describes the jobless who found contentment and optimism that removed them from the motivation to seek reemployment. This development—a threat to the ability of capitalism to control its workers through desire and survival—then played out in unemployment policy over the next few decades, emerging especially through policy attempts to make unemployment more painful, such that the drive toward reemployment could be made rational and compulsory.

Ironically, though, the more punishing unemployment becomes, the more passionate the unemployed have to be. In the second part, I consider how passion can be rendered a modality for resilience, a way for the serialized unemployed to persist in a brutal marketplace by presenting themselves as undamaged. Passion here is imagined to spur the human qualities of tenacity and positivity, affording the capacity to take on damage without revealing its signs. Reading a range of career guides, I show how this demand for resilience diffuses the burden of its exercise into a variety of domains—from the effusive techniques of networking to the protective realm of fist pumps and meditative chants—entering also into the social, with the forced participation of family and friends.

Chapter 3, "The Compassionate Imagination," pivots on the argument of resilience by turning to another group of workers: those who would like to act passionately but are unable to because of their poor conditions of work. I address this through the gamification movement, a community that utilizes a humanitarian imagination to justify how familiar gaming tropes may be used to transform the experience of banal, mind-numbing work. Gamification here is imagined as a play technique that can be embedded into software, ensuring that unvalued information workers can return to the fold of passion and appreciate its meritocratic possibilities of career progression. Of course, such an argument is easily dismissed as a corporate ruse, but embarking on two case studies, I argue that gamification reflects a more complicated and troubling politics, germane especially where behavioral conditioning has become the norm in big data and surveillance industries.

This argument starts with Csíkszentmihályi's theory of flow, an influential theory of concentration used in game design and positive psychology. At first glance, the theory would seem to describe a conventional application of industrial psychology. Applied to production line labor in some of his earliest 1970s research, Csíkszentmihályi's theory provides a seemingly trite argument of how workers in banal jobs may yet develop excitement by making work more of a game. But within this account exists a more complicated politics. According to Csíkszentmihályi, flow is modeled after the psychological resilience of survivors of war, people who were able to disconnect from the trauma of their situation and come out of it psychologically unscathed through play. Understanding this leads us to an insight of what flow can achieve—this feeling of engagement can be defined in both an additive and a subtractive sense. Not only does it potentially indicate creative pleasures; it can also afford a state of suspension, a condition that enables action while shielding subjects from negative states such as boredom, fatigue, and fear. "Open Badges," the second case, materializes the context for hopefulness to suspension by seeking to perfect an ambient form of human capital development. Each task here, no matter how banal, holds the potential of yielding points and badges—signifiers of one's capability, which can be used as currency for advancement. Hence, by ceding themselves to the algorithmic flow of the gamification program with the dopamine hits of points and badges, workers are promised a record of human capital accretion and career progression.

If chapters 2 and 3 are centered on regaining the passions that workers have been denied or which they have lost, chapter 4, "Urban Preserves," turns its attention instead toward the preservation of passions that workers are assumed to possess. The central figure here is the middle-class lonely freelancer, a subject forced into a precarious economy, placed on the edges of superfluousness, who lacks the social capital to remain confident in herself. Loneliness constitutes a nebulous experience that captures this sense of middle-class melancholia, a state of abandonment that threatens the ability of subjects to engage with the world passionately—that is, with the hustling qualities of boldness, spontaneity, and creativity.

Coworking represents an attempt to address this need, by seeking to dispel the deep sense of abandonment and risk that middle-class freelancers face as they lose the security of their traditional jobs and workplaces. Assembling a range of coworking objects and discourses—from the ordinary fear of losing one's seat in a café to the aesthetics of office interiors and events such as work sprints and "fuckup nights"—I show how coworking represents an attempt to build a space for attunement to the rhythms of capitalism, where workers feel "right" and affectively aligned to how they ought to be feeling about their work. This is done by making work a tightly bound concern— for example, by creating an atmosphere that allows workers freedom to cultivate their passions while protecting them from the sense of precarity and abandonment that freelancing entails. In this way, investment in work can continue unimpeded, made possibly even more authentic as workers share and build communities untethered to corporations.

In the conclusion, I tie together the various openings found in the previous chapters to offer a different way of understanding passion. Passion, as it is currently understood, comes in the last instance. It is invoked in crisis as an improvisational way of taking control over the insecurity of the situation. This does not, however, need to be the only way that passion can be considered. Visiting the varied historical meanings of passion, I explore how passio can lead us to a different understanding of passion. If passion is conventionally about forcefulness, energetic intensity, and interiorized authenticity, then moving toward "passio passions" offers an alternative. It leads us to return to a politics that stresses holding back and delayed contemplation—the ethics of being a nonsovereign actor involves a deeper intent, locating oneself in vitalizing flows of affect, allying with and adding to it rather than claiming it to be one's own. Passion needs room for ambivalence, the space for us to be comfortable even in the absence of wanting. Written as critique, diagnostic, and provocation, *Passionate Work* takes a tentative step toward locating passion's politics and possibilities, imagining a different path that can unsettle the lasting hold that passion wields over our worlds.

1

From Happiness
to Passion

In *The Human Condition*, first published in 1958, Hannah Arendt relates a problem of political action to the distinction between labor and work. Labor, she writes, refers to the state of the *animal laborans*, a slavish mode of being that focuses on survival and subsistence. Unlike the *homo faber*, who "works" by producing things that are stable and of lasting consequence to the world, the *animal laborans* is "imprisoned in its metabolism with nature," her energies spent on the sustenance of everyday life.[1] Relentless concern over self-preservation suppresses awareness of the potential within productive activity, causing the *animal laborans* to be deprived of the drive to ethically contemplate how productive action can influence the state of generational and collective life.

This contrast between labor and work was directed in part as a corrective toward the perceived pessimistic stalemate of Marxist theory. As Margaret Canovan points out, "Though Marx spoke of making, using the terminology of craftsmanship, Arendt claims he understood history in terms of processes of production and consumption much closer to animal life."[2] In Arendt's opinion, Marx's perspective renders it difficult to locate a site of optimism within productive action; all work is potentially labor subsumed into the capitalist system.

Dissatisfaction with the bleak state of human labor at the time, however, was not unique to Arendt. In the same period when *The Human Condition* was written, management professionals and academics were engaged in a similar debate over the debased quality of industrial work. Theorists such as Peter Drucker argue that people are primarily motivated not by material incentives but by the recovery of meaning and pride in their jobs. In *The Practice of Management*, published four years before *The Human Condition*, Drucker fights against the dehumanizing nature of industrial work, urging managers to tap into the entirety of the worker's skills, "his ability to make a whole out of many things, to judge, to plan and to change."[3] Hired hands, he insists, want to be treated not as automatons but as people with the capability to "drive themselves," so that they may cultivate a personal attachment to their jobs.[4]

Like Arendt, management theorists wove a language of morality around work. In doing so, they actively evoked an image of the good life that work could provide, but the impression as to what that constituted differed. For Arendt, the ideal of work refers to political action. Craftsmanship serves as grounds for fostering an ethical commitment to production for the betterment of the world. For management theorists, work centers on personal job satisfaction, feelings of success, and industrial harmony. Such disparity was, in fact, nontrivial to Arendt. As she clarifies, the "goodness" that work offers should never primarily be centered on human psychic experience.[5] Even if human labor is made less painful, it does not naturally follow that it will induce the kinds of affective attachments necessary to foster ethical thought in production. Though lives may be made less difficult, human beings may still remain trapped as *animal laborans*: unable, or even unwilling, to engage in the thinking and discussion crucial for deeper insight into the purpose that making should serve.[6]

Still, Arendt's philosophy has been primarily appropriated through management discourse to deplore unsatisfactory human psychic states. For instance, *Work in America*, a federal report in 1973, references Arendt in the introduction but reduces the difference between the *animal laborans* and the *homo faber* to self-worth. "Self-esteem is so deflated" for some workers, it laments, "that the distinction between the human as worker and the animal as laborer is blurred." The report continues, "What workers want most, as more than 100 studies in the past 20 years show ... [is] to feel that their work and they themselves are important."[7] The slide from ethics in production to ethics in feelings reflects an imagined consensus in the cultural idealisms of work. The wanting of psychic rewards from work is communicated here as an uncontroversial, historically consistent mode of emotional desire, which sets as orthodoxy and common sense the importance of feelings in work. Such portrayal does not only simplify what people want out of work. Framing psychic satisfaction from work as the norm of the human want also makes it difficult to recognize other possible ways in which work can serve the good life.

In taking passion seriously, we need to question the seemingly natural association between passionate work and the good life. Capitalism seeks to convince us that work can be a site of true meaning if passion can be aligned with labor. Luc Boltanski and Eve Chiapello, however, remind us that the frames of the good life that capitalism provides will always attend to its logics of accumulation: "No market operator wants to be the first to offer a 'good life' to those he hires, since his production cost could thereby be increased . . . [but] on the other hand, the capitalist class as a whole has an interest . . . in overall measures that make it possible to retain the commitment of those on whom profit creation depends."[8] Class interests contribute to the sway of things in the good-life promise. Even though the worker's economic welfare has the most direct relationship to labor, it is also the aspect least appealing for employers to highlight, because it chips away at the bottom line.

The cost of labor under capitalism, Marx suggests, will always have the tendency to be forced toward zero. Although the zero of labor cost is "always beyond reach," capital "can always proximate more and more nearly to it."[9] Thus, in the cultural ascendance of passionate work, it is not uncommon that corporations repudiate the importance of wages even as they affirm the deeply fulfilling life that work can offer. Problematizing feelings may not only be more cost-efficient than increasing wages; it may also be more effective in stimulating productivity, getting workers to put more of their energies into their working hours to accommodate unpaid and overtime work and to curb threats to the smooth functioning of business. Leaning into the normal, happy fold of corporate life aligns with capitalism's relentless search for profits.[10]

A Genealogy of Passion

Still, regardless of how effective the manipulation of emotions may be, we should not assume that it is either historically consistent or internally coherent as a corporate strategy. To denaturalize passionate work, it matters that we understand how our demands from work are structured across historical time. Who speaks from this demand? Have our demands been different? And how, even if we understand such emotional manipulation to be exploitative, has such exploitation varied? My suggestion is that passionate work represents a particular kind of affective engagement that is derived from a longer genealogy of emotional attachments, of which a significant one is "happiness." The point is not that workers have felt differently across time or that emotional states can be reduced to terms such as *happiness* or *passion*. Feelings, after all, do not describe a fixed phenomenological reality, but they represent, following Brian Massumi, "an idea of the idea of the affection"—cultural models that prescribe commonly held meaning to physiological affects experienced.[11] The complexities of emotional lives mean that workers have certainly experienced more than just happiness and passion in the past and present. What I am concerned with is how the change in the terms from *happiness* to *passion* matters for the constellation of meanings behind idealized models of optimism about work: the normative expectations people have of its outcomes, the goodness these results offer, and the paths by which these outcomes are to be attained.

Happiness and passion represent distinct affective structures; at different historical conjectures, happiness and passion have taken form as conceptually separate, normative emotional subjectivities filtered into corporate rituals, programs, regimes, and practices. Again, this is not a claim for a standardization of sentiments. Affective structures describe zones of affective tendencies. They are inductive landscapes where bodies are attuned to a circumscribed field of affective life without enforcement of homogeneity in experience, interpretation, and reaction. "Bodies can be inducted into, or attuned to . . . the same affective environment," Massumi writes, "even if there is no assurance they will act alike in that environment."[12] Both *happiness* and *passion* describe a container of varied emotional states and practices, but they also congeal differences through unifying rationales of why emotional orientations are deemed more valuable, useful, and even moral, prescribing models of behavior across different social classes with the promise that adherence to them will lead to a life of true fulfillment.

William Reddy's concept of "emotional regimes" conveys a similar notion of how emotions can take on historical specificity.[13] Individuals in every society, he explains, navigate emotional regimes to arrive at "the proper end point or ideal of emotional equilibrium."[14] These emotions are primarily achieved through emotives—performative speech acts that facilitate interpretation of affective states, instructing on the emotional sensibilities to attend to and strive toward. For Reddy, emotives delimit the emotional repertoire of emotional life, coloring the interpretations of everyday affects and privileging certain emotions over others. Barbara Rosenwein explains, "Emotives are choices—automatic choices, for the most part—made from a huge repertory of possibilities. Most of those possibilities will never be explored because most are not recognized, or hardly recognized, by the society in which an individual lives and feels."[15]

But is the diversity of emotional life always constrained by a normative structure of affect? As a study of emotional pedagogy, emotional regimes are primarily repressive—they center on how particular emotions are cultivated at the expense of others, leading to the partial interpretations of complex feelings.[16] But the affective structures of happiness and passion in managerial discourse are productive in their modes of emotional subjectification. Control over the distribution of emotional subjectivities requires an intensification of emotional recognition and scrutiny: "surly" supervisors need to be identified and dealt with, "charismatic" leaders need to be cultivated, and "pessimistic reveries" need to be uncovered and given release through therapeutic interviews. The affective structures of happiness and passion not only intersect with ideas of the good life in the form of prescription—pointing to the emotional states that people need to cultivate in order to achieve success in work and life—but they also designate different roles for subjects based on perceived emotional capacities and point to a life that is outside the good-life imaginary: templates of emotional life that require correction if they are to be fitted within the normal fold of good corporate living. Far from limiting emotional life, an affective structure expands and transforms it, creating ever more nuance in emotional recognition, with the goal of increasing the range of problematizations possible to develop an idealized emotional character to social life.[17]

While historians have done the important work of detailing the various managerial philosophies that have been influential in America and elsewhere, management history has seldom been analyzed through the frames of affect and its instruments of optimism. Two important works need to be mentioned here. Nikolas Rose has done a similar genealogical analysis of "the productive worker" in the twentieth century, where he identifies shifts in subjectivities of workers over time.[18] Using examples from Britain and the United States, he argues that the psychological sciences (derived from research of the Second World War) are crucial to the construction of productive subjectivity and that such governmentalities have produced varying subjectivities across time. Similarly, Boltanski and Chiapello have studied management texts to examine shifts in what they call the "spirit of capitalism," the individual and collective justifications which serve as "ideology that justifies engagement in capitalism."[19] These scholars highlight similar changes to subjectivities across time: the steady move from the rational, peaceful human relationships stressed in mid-twentieth-century human relations discourse—which offered a fixed path to personal development—to one that emphasized spontaneous self-discovery, genuine autonomy, and the setting of freedom that organizations offered employees in the 1990s, so that the latter might blossom through their labor.

My work is indebted to theirs in many ways, but while I am also interested in the construction of productive subjectivities, my attention lingers on the discourses that structure our optimistic transactions with work and the ways in which our emotional lives are made to intertwine with the subject of our productive activity. I suggest that reading the notion of happiness—from its emergence in early twentieth-century management texts to its rejection in the mid-twentieth century and the shift to the norms of passion by the late twentieth century—opens the important potential of disturbing, as I reference *Work in America* again, "what workers want most."[20] It reveals the politics of our affective structures, allowing us to understand which group speaks for the human want, how one group's interest is made the desire of everyone else, and how even challenges to our good-life fantasy cannot detach themselves from the optimistic transactions with work.

To be sure, there is a panoply of entry points available into the discussion of work cultures and their influence on emotional subjectivities. Historians such as Andrea Tone and Nikki Mandell have traced the management of emotions to welfare work in late nineteenth-century America.[21] In contrast to the dominant managerial ideology of Taylorism in the same period, which assumed workers to be mindless brutes interested only in economic gain, welfare advocates attended to the feelings of workers and sought to implement a variety of workplace amenities to boost morale and loyalty. However, these attempts were met with derision from their working-class beneficiaries, who resented the paternalistic quality of these policies. Others, such as Paul Willis and Michael Burawoy, have taken the resistance of workers as their analytical focus.[22] They highlight how, in being unwilling to assimilate the good-life imaginaries offered by schools and factories, the working class may adopt alternative emotional habits associated more with rebellion and mischief, engendering practices that range from coping to creative resistance to direct antagonism.

My analysis of happiness and passion contributes to these works by beginning with the human relations movement in the early twentieth century.

The field of human relations is particularly significant because, as Reinhard Bendix points out, it contributed to a shift in the conception of work and the worker.[23] Before this period, workers were primarily framed in terms of virtue; virtuous workers were thought to be able to climb the corporate ladder to success, while those steeped in vices reaped poverty and hardship. The entry of the psychological sciences into the industry, however, reconceptualized workers as psychological beings with unfulfilled needs that work would meet. In this schema, "work was praised," Bendix notes, "for the satisfactions arising from it rather than for the success to which it might lead."[24] Work's good-life promise no longer relied on outcomes from other spheres: it did not need to frame itself as offering a comfortable life of consumption, nor give a spiritual promise of redemption.[25] Rather, the rewards of work may proceed from itself; the psychological pleasure of work is reward enough.

In the following sections, I trace the affective structures of three different historical moments, with each period describing a particular understanding of the nature of workers, their emotional needs, and the practices necessary for those needs to be fulfilled. I examine how, from the early twentieth century, happiness in work took shape as the fantasy of the good-life promise. Human relations professionals emphasized the importance of emotional welfare and gathered members of administration—foremen, managers, and supervisors—to construct a happy atmosphere for line workers, who were presented as being incapable of recognizing the cause of their persistent dissatisfaction. Management tried to convince workers not only that happiness in work was possible but that happiness was something that they should desire and reasonably demand. However, by the mid-twentieth century, such rhetoric encountered a backlash. Concerns about the conformity of American workers arose, and the happiness that had been lauded by those in human relations was portrayed as manipulative and inimical to the development of individualities. Such happiness caused workers to suffer from a damaged structure of desire, which made them apathetic and passive toward their job. Dissatisfaction was then reframed as a sign of healthy individuality—a model for the self-motivated employee who is unfulfilled because of the lack of opportunity to properly demonstrate his worth to the corporation.

In the late twentieth century, the idea of the self-motivated employee began to take root, and numerous texts during this time argued that the many indications of worker dissatisfaction were a sign of a healthy desire for fulfillment that remained frustrated. In one aspect, the ideas of passion that emerged during this period carried on the argument previously made by managerial theorists about how, under the right conditions, workers would voluntarily commit themselves to work. However, academics, management professionals, and popular writers who discussed passion also erased the conflictual history that preceded passion and presented this desire as a demand from workers themselves. And with this new source of demand, it became possible to position passion as a right that workers had won, which needed defending from unenlightened labor leaders.

My analysis of managerial discourse is primarily derived from a reading of books targeted at managers, executives, and aspirational workers. They constitute two main sources: management texts aimed at the professionalization of managers and popular texts targeted at the public that address management thinking.[26] Unlike academic articles, these books are explicit about the need to fit the practical concerns of audiences. Most writers of these books employ a language that is accessible and compelling, and the content is carefully organized into sections and subheads to facilitate easy reference. Though academic knowledge is sometimes alluded to in the texts, it is not uncommon to see intuitive reasoning, religious views, observations, and personal experience. This mixture of authoritative science, common parlance, and conventions on management knowledge produces a particular mandate to this genre: popular management texts translate new management ideas into practical uses, prescribing the normative good-life fantasies of work agreed on by the management community.[27] Analyzing these texts thus foregrounds the shifting trajectories, exclusions, and practices of the good life, revealing how the relentless search for "true" fulfillment has invested and reinvested optimism within the emotional rewards of work.

Producing the Happy Good Life

A 1938 manual titled *How to Be a Leader*, directed toward managers, prefaces that "there is probably no one other thing which can contribute to the attainment of a well-rounded, successful and happy life than an ability to understand and influence people."[28] Happiness is espoused as means and end: to get at happiness, one needs to make others happy. Influence, it continues, can be gained by following the Golden Rule: "Always take every honest opportunity to say and do those things which make people feel bigger, better, more important."[29] This account shows how happiness serves as a connective bond between two figures—the manager and the worker—who are glued together by an interdependent want for happiness. Creating happiness for the lay worker will grant happiness to the manager, and so a frictionless class society will depend on the successful induction of workers into this happiness discourse.

This "mutually beneficial" social relationship, historian Daniel Wren writes, defined the managerial philosophy known as human relations in the 1930s.[30] Departing from the Taylorist style of management, which stressed the physiology of workers and the organization of the workplace, human relations turned to psychology during this time to suggest the importance of social relationships and emotional well-being. The advice is simple at its core: human beings are social beings, and if managers want to keep workers happy, then they need to address not just their want for wages but also their psychological needs for recognition, esteem, and community. Achieving these would produce a happy workplace that would bring forth more productive and harmonious enterprises.

This philosophy of management is deeply influenced by Elton Mayo's participation in and interpretation of the Hawthorne plant experiments from 1928 to 1931. In the bible of human relations, *The Human Problems of an Industrial Civilization*, Mayo writes that the common focus of industrial ailment—"fatigue" or "monotony"—is inadequate in accounting for the true reason for inefficiency in labor.[31] He compares repetitive work between two plants and notes that while workers in one plant became bored and unproductive, workers in the other had "a real interest in work" and even experienced "an accumulation of it as the day wore on."[32] Mayo attributes this contrast to the emotional states of the workers and the human relations of the enterprise, such as the small-group relationships that the workers shared and the intergroup relationships that existed with their supervisors. Hence, he argues, the emotional well-being of a workforce and its constitutive human relationships are no small factor in governing corporate productivity and profits.

Mayo would bring his training in psychotherapy to this theory of management. In his conception, work and society function in mutual, organic entanglement not only at the surface of actions and rationale but also in the unconscious drives of subjects.[33] Problems in one sphere will invariably emerge in another, just as repressed frustrations in the home can surface on the shop floor as maladjustments, producing misdirected complaints, resentment, and poor work behaviors. Mayo litters his book with examples, explaining, for instance, how an employee's anger toward a supervisor is attributed to the latter's resemblance to a hated relative and how the poor work attitude of another worker stems from a bad relationship with her mother.[34] According to Mayo, these ailments lower productivity, but they also introduce an opportunity—if ailments can be brought to the workplace, then the workplace can serve as a clinic for social ills. It can relieve the deep, unconscious tensions of industrial society and lead to a healthier, more emotionally balanced citizenry. Having this notion, Mayo brought a range of psychotherapeutic techniques into the Hawthorne plant, using nondirected interviews, for instance, to bring out "industrial adaptation" in the belief that it would relieve the repressed tensions of industrial society and lead to a more productive, compliant workforce.[35]

Over the next few decades, many came to dispute Mayo's seemingly commonsense interpretation of the Hawthorne experimental findings. The absence of strict controls in the experiments made for many plausible alternative explanations for productivity improvements—for instance, the group of participants changed midway through the experiments, financial incentives were introduced and tied to the productivity of experimental subjects, and managerial discipline was tightly enforced in the small experimental room, which could have led to coercive pressure.[36] And yet, what is significant is not necessarily the truth of what occurred in the experiments. As Fritz Roethlisberger, his protégé, notes, Mayo was more "an adventurer in the realm of ideas," a sower of "seeds to be cultivated," than a systematic thinker.[37] Mayo has provided what Abraham Zaleznik calls the "big picture" to the managerial profession; his contribution centers on his paradigm-shifting conception of the role that management plays at the level of the workplace and society.[38]

The title of Mayo's book, *The Human Problems of an Industrial Civilization*, is suggestive. It implies that the commitment of human relations is not to industrial productivity but to the health of society. Drawing from Émile Durkheim, Mayo argues that the displacement of workers from traditional ways of life caused them to suffer from "anomie," a "planlessness in living" that is disruptive to happiness.[39] Therefore, industry has a moral obligation to reforge the social relations of society, providing workers with the empathetic human networks to relieve themselves from the unhappiness of industrial alienation. Such an interpretation of Durkheim's work, James Dingley observes, is at best partial—Mayo appropriates Durkheim's concerns without adhering to his moral philosophy, which is critical of the capitalist system.[40] Regardless, the piecemeal understanding of Durkheim has the important effect of giving human relations a tint of moral legitimacy, allowing businesses to become the savior of an alienated society.

This notion accentuated the already highly uneven differences in authority within industry. Human relations has taken the conceptual core of Mayo's ideas and transposed the hierarchical relationship of the therapist and the patient to that of the manager and the worker.[41] In this framework, workers are irrational beings unable to articulate the source of their unhappiness, who rely on a class of trained administrative elites to help them uncover and release these negative emotional states. Managers, on the other hand, are tasked to act like therapists, to relate to others but also to exercise self-control, especially withholding themselves from the influence of emotional states that workers exhibit. This idea of the irrational worker-patient and the rational manager-therapist has brought industrial relations into the constitution of personhood in public life. As Richard Gillespie notes, Mayo's psychoanalytic framework had allowed even him, at an early stage, to turn "any challenge by workers of managerial control into evidence of psychiatric disturbance."[42] The wide adoption of this belief would extend its influence: any complaint could be dismissed, any demand disregarded as confused, once workers are assumed to be lacking in their capacity for self-expression.

These new roles came to exert significant influence on the ways that industrial strife was treated. Management texts of the period increasingly suggested the irrelevancy of the views of lay workers, especially where it came to demands for wages and benefits. For example, in a section titled "The Worker Has No Word for It," David Houser in *What People Want from Business* suggests that workers are fundamentally unable to articulate the cause of their dissatisfaction, because they lack the capacity to identify the source of their true unhappiness.[43] Drawing from surveys, he points out that even though most workers describe pay and advancement as the most important factors contributing to their unhappiness, what workers "really" want are things that cater to their dignity and self-worth, such as recognition from supervisors for a job well done. From Houser's perspective, workers suffer from a problem of misrecognition. They may give "good reasons" for their unhappiness—complaints that seem culturally appropriate, such as a low wage—but fail to name the "real reasons . . . [which are] deeper and undisclosed."[44] Such studies that "show" how workers do not have a good grasp on what they "really" want have provided management with the ammunition to dictate the "correct" things that workers want.

Unsaid but central to this claim is how the good life is reframed from a context of structural justice to one of psychological justice—an issue of whether desire coheres with idealized emotional states. There is no reason to suppose that the fight for wages, security, and job promotion, advanced by unions and workers, has been aimed at emotional progress; rather, it would be more accurate to describe this struggle as directed toward the power differentials inherent within the capitalist system. In making feelings the telos of the good life, however, managers and psychologists have changed the conversation around work and shifted the normalized objects of proper desire. Workers' demands can now be disregarded as coming from an undeveloped will, a structure of desire that fails to tap into the reality of their psychic needs. As Houser points out, "The employee cannot say: 'My sense of personal significance is constantly offended; my craving for decent consideration is consistently defeated.' He does not think or speak in such abstractions."[45] This dismissal represents a long-standing strategy of managerial dispossession: workers need to be convinced that it is in their best interests to be managed, because managers themselves are impotent in the direct processes of production. Management historian Gerard Hanlon notes that managers do not have the skills, inventiveness, and tools that workers do, and so their control over workers depends on the elimination of their independence in the production process.[46]

Claims to happiness have been weaponized on these grounds, and the paths to happiness, which now depend on right and wrong desires, have become tied to the subject of strong and weak wills. As Sara Ahmed notes, deviation in the will is largely understood as a matter of pathways, not goals: "Those who will wrong," she writes, are still assumed to "will happiness."[47] The common will for happiness has endowed the rational, male, managerial class with the mandate to fulfill needs that weak-willed workers are unaware of. On the subject of leadership, for instance, George Halsey argues that the main purpose of leaders is to "show the way" by bringing to light the deep desires of workers.[48] "All voluntary action springs from the desire of each person for certain things, tangible and intangible, the possession of which he believes will bring him satisfaction or happiness," he writes.[49] If workers perform poorly, it is because they have the wrong orientation to happiness: their visions of the good life do not conform to the correct paths of happiness. Leadership involves expertise in altering the structure of desire—or what he calls "the organization of the will"—such that employees will be harmoniously integrated in wanting the right things that will proximate happiness.[50] As Ordway Tead reiterates, the art of leadership should involve "modification in the desires and purposes of those being managed and of himself that, over a period of time, what he wants and what they want comes to be much the same."[51] Such convincing is to come not through enforcement or manipulation but through enlightenment and uplift. The true paths to happiness have to be "convincingly interpreted [by workers] as for their own good"; leaders have to bring these deeper desires to light, showing workers the objects they want that will provide them with true joy.[52]

The delineation between all-knowing managers and unknowing workers captures how human relations has construed the will as a matter of ownership. Ahmed explains that right and wrong wills can be used as placeholders, forms of social power that designate certain bodies and populations as prone to willing wrong and therefore, by default, already willful: "It is the depositing of willfulness in certain places that allows the willful subject to appear as a figure, as someone we recognize, in an *instant*."[53] Problems of the will are not necessarily ascribed to bodies based on actions; for some populations, the defective will is already assumed—what remains is finding the contrarian instance to this negative norm. We see this reasoning at work in a training manual designed for hiring managers. When warning managers of "psychopathic personalities," psychologist Donald Laird forwards such a large range of possible mental weaknesses (over twenty categories, including the "queer guys," "disturbers," "negative," "conscientious") that it would make most workers, by default, psychologically unbalanced in some sense.[54] Laird reminds hiring managers that they are not meant to look out for the "normal," since such a character would be hard to find. Instead, managers need to carefully evaluate the extent of deviations, accommodating those whose "temperamental defects" are minor and "amenable to proper care."[55] In other words, it is not identification that an anomaly needs as much as an assessment of its variance, its extent, and the amenability of its deviance.

Yet, human relations understands fundamentally that altering the desires of workers is more easily said than done. Workers have ways of thinking that are historically sedimented, and persuading them to change would require effort. Therefore, even though human relations has prided itself as a scientific enterprise that stresses rational thought, its advocates have emphasized that its implementation needs to be affective to speak to its lay audience. In line with historian Roland Marchand, who notes that the corporate communicative style of the 1930s largely emphasized "the language of ordinary people," management texts advised managers to address their workers' hearts rather than their heads, believing that this style of communication would suit the purpose of humanizing the administrative elite and be made more persuasive to a public that tends to be simpleminded and incapable of grasping difficult arguments.[56] As one text offers, a manager needs to be careful not to show himself as "superior, paternal, or patronizing" to his subordinates; instead, he should try to speak in the vernacular, convincing them that he is "one of the group," a friend rather than a sermonizer.[57] The executive, another offers, is "entitled, if not required, to invest his cause with some excite and glamour" because workers cannot just be convinced in their minds; they need to feel "aroused, attracted, and energized."[58]

The demand for emotional appeal would saturate the linguistic, behavioral, and material codes of the workplace. Most management texts coach readers about the importance of smiling, of being a good listener, of remembering first names; they also call for restraint in public reprimand and threats.[59] The new junior administrator, for example, is advised to learn about colleagues promptly, to remember little things about them because "friendliness is a good outer sign of something more fundamental, namely, respect for the individuality of others."[60] Several texts go even further, reminding managers not to embarrass workers by asking questions that they cannot answer, warning them not to grow mustaches in a way that could be associated with anger, advising them to smile *with* rather than *at* workers, and encouraging them to dismiss employees in a way that is kind and gentle.[61] One text even asks managers to "measure the timing of each individual's contact with others" so that an "objective, numerical appraisal of each person's relationship to others" can be derived.[62] These scattered targets of emotional modulation ensure that humans relations appears at the reality of the workplace in the smallest details, emerging as an unmistakable change in how a workplace is not just to feel but also to look and sound.

And though workers and their emotional lives are the focus of intervention, the administrative class has been just as much a subject, and perhaps even more so. Before administrators can be ambassadors of this new good-life promise, they themselves need to internalize its system of belief. In one of the best-selling self-help books to date, *How to Win Friends and Influence People*, Dale Carnegie opens by trying to convince readers of the importance of human relations. He advises readers to repeat to themselves "over and over" the mantra "My popularity, my happiness, and my sense of worth depend upon my skill in dealing with people."[63] To convince others of this good-life philosophy, managers need to first internalize the value of human relations and change their affective dispositions. Relationships, management texts warn, are not something that ambitious managers can simply manipulate to advance their interests. Ultimately, success in forging happy relationships depends on the sincerity of the manager's feelings. The art of good human relations, Erwin Schell writes, is "dispositional" in nature.[64] These positive relations do not simply constitute certain phrases or acts but "form an atmosphere or background" to the words and acts themselves.[65] An executive seeking to convince workers of the significance of their work, for instance, needs to feel equally enthusiastic about it: "He appears excited; he is confident and assured; he waves his arms and uses gestures . . . he feels the way he talks and acts."[66]

Management texts do not assume that the alignment between desire, feeling, and action is easily achievable. As a means of governmentality, the good-life fantasy has been normatively built into the evaluative mechanisms of institutions. Many management texts of this period bundle up a series of checklists, surveys, and questions. Some of these are reflexive in quality; managers are expected to reflect on their skills of emotional conduct and work on them if they are found lacking. Schell, for instance, asks readers to ponder various dispositions, such as "enthusiasm," "cheerfulness," and "calmness." In these sections, executives are tasked to consider how they might best incorporate these emotions as a lifestyle. In a section on cheerfulness, for example, they are asked to consider if "cheerfulness is something that you can . . . discard when your work day is over, or is it a quality which must become habitual"?[67] In other texts, emotional competencies are presented in the form of checklists (see figure 1.1). A section in *How to Train Supervisors*, for instance, tells executives to look out for a range of attitudes in workers and foremen, ranging from "interested" and "energetic" to "surly," "antagonistic," and "irritable."[68] The binarization of good and bad emotional attributes is common in texts of the period, and these checklists subtly show management the extent to which their emotional competencies will be surveilled and appraised by their superiors.

Paradoxically, the greater the emphasis on happy relationships, the more important monitoring became. While the disciplinary actions themselves became more considerate of the feelings of those chastised, the need to quickly spot and address cracks in happiness grew more pressing. This is because management discourse at this juncture began to understand happiness, fundamentally, as a fragile emotion in conflict with class interest. As one text notes, even if a happy atmosphere is successfully cultivated, "thoughts, suggestions, ideas are pouring in continuously from all

A SUGGESTED PROGRAM

RATING IN LEADERSHIP

Scale to be Used in all Ratings

9.5 Exceptional	8. Good	6.5 Below Passing
9. Excellent	7.5 Fairly Good	6. Poor
8.5 Very Good	7. Just Passing	5.5 Very poor

I. *Rating on Possession of Leadership Attributes*

Review carefully the rating made earlier (see page 64). Read again all of the questions, and make any revision you think should be made. Put this revised rating in the self-rating column. Put the rating by others in the columns provided.

	Self-Rating	Rating by Others
1. Integrity, Sincerity, Honesty		
2. Fairness, Impartiality		
3. Initiative, Courage, Self-Confidence, Decisiveness		
4. Tact, Ability to Make and Keep Friends		
5. Enthusiasm, Ability to Arouse Enthusiasm		
6. Curiosity, Observation, Open-Mindedness		
7. Judgment		
8. Thoroughness		
9. Resourcefulness, Ingenuity, Originality		
10. Coordination, Strategy, Execution		
Rating on Leadership Attributes (Average of all ratings given above)		

Attributes to work on first...

Plans...

Attributes to work on next...

Plans...

(181)

1.1 In his 1938 book *How to Be a Leader*, George D. Halsey included this rating program for the emotional skills deemed to be required of "leadership." Such apparatuses were common in texts of the period. (From Halsey, *How to Be a Leader*, 181.)

sides, and any one of these may supplant the idea we have so carefully planned."[69] Managers, therefore, always have to be alert to protect the happy facade; they are even advised to be suspicious and to look out for the absence of malcontent, because "silence is a sign of danger," a boiling dissatisfaction that is left unarticulated.[70]

The happy atmosphere of the workplace in the early to mid-twentieth century came about from this complex amalgamation of discipline, fantasy, and seduction. To be sure, human relations was not entirely successful in convincing workers and managers of this new good-life fantasy. Yet, as Bendix points out, human relations left an influential "new vocabulary of motivation," which fundamentally reframed the idea of human desire.[71] It replaced traditional objects of demand with psychic desire and cultivated an optimistic possibility in work. Rather than seeing work as a site of struggle and toil, it positioned work as a pathway into the good life, a sphere able to grant happiness. However, by the early 1950s, the facade of happiness was starting to show cracks. The roles that human relations relied on—the irrational worker and the agreeable manager—were now repudiated for their manipulation of human affect. Happiness came under attack for being a mask, producing the unfeeling smile of the "cheerful robot" deprived of individuality and will.[72]

Conformity and Apathy of Happiness

America experienced a major cultural transition in the mid-twentieth century that implicated the human relations discourse on happiness. Particularly, the notion of charismatic leadership, which was influential in the Mayoist period, came under significant suspicion in the wake of the Second World War and the Cold War. As Fred Turner offers, postwar intellectuals primarily attributed the atrocities of the war to a fascist "authoritarian personality," a personality type that assumes a model of unthinking docility.[73] Those with such a personality type lack a reasoned mind, are prone to rhetoric that sways emotions, and have a tendency to look to others for affirmation and direction.[74]

This concern coalesced in the concept of "conformity" for writers of organizational culture in the 1950s, such as C. Wright Mills, William Whyte, and David Riesman.[75] Whyte, a writer for *Fortune* and the author of a best-selling text, especially offers strident critiques that have had a significant influence on managerial discourse. In *The Organization Man*, Whyte pointedly questions Mayo's belief in the "social ethic," the hypothesis that the "ultimate need of the individual" is to find a sense of belonging in the place of work. Not only does Whyte doubt the purported importance of social belongingness; he also attacks the foundation on which this argument rests. He observes that by dismissing the worker as "a nonlogical animal incapable of rationally solving his own problems or, in fact, recognizing what the problem is," human relations has effectively made it impossible for the views of workers to be taken seriously. Therefore, human relations would not want true belongingness for workers but instead demand that "the individual sacrifice his own beliefs that he may belong."[76]

The attack on human relations made the purported promise of happiness suspect as well. "How good is 'happiness,'" Whyte continues, if the price for it is voluntary self-repression?[77] To be happy, he notes, the individual "must not only accept control, he must accept it as if he liked it. He must smile when he is transferred to a place or a job that isn't the job or place he happens to want. He must appear to enjoy listening sympathetically to points of view not his goal."[78] Unhappiness masquerades as hollow smiles and empty cheery gestures under the norm of coercive happiness. And if that is not bad enough, writers such as Riesman warn, the repeated portrayal of false happiness can permanently blunt the proper expression of emotion. "White-collared workers cannot so easily separate coercive friendliness on the job from a spontaneous expression of genuine friendliness off the job," and so the mimicry of superficial happiness at work carries the more serious consequence of thwarting the development of deep relationships and true joy in life.[79] Far from being an authentic mode of self-expression, happiness began to be presented as an instrument of deception and manipulation, a tool to suppress the individuality of workers and to produce docile yes-men for the insecure egos of corporate leaders.

Yet, repudiation of happiness did not do away with the fantasy of the good-life imaginary in work, nor was it antithetical to the changing landscape of corporate America. In *The Conquest of Cool*, Thomas Frank observes that conformity was never quite celebrated by corporations in the ways that critics presented it to be. In fact, shifts to capitalism in the 1950s and 1960s toward an economy based on information and creativity made clear that conformity would be a drag on the profitability and growth of businesses. "Old values of caution, deference, and hierarchy," Frank offers, were increasingly made obsolete. At best, they added unnecessary bureaucracy to organizational functioning; at worst, they stifled the qualities of creativity and flexibility essential for the increasingly competitive business landscape.[80]

Therefore, the term *conformity* condensed a cultural zeitgeist, but it repackaged rather than broke with the management thought of the early twentieth century. Countercultural texts that paint corporate life as a "technocracy"—a meaningless, bureaucratized system that robs people of spontaneity, joy, and freedom—are not as adversarial to business objectives as the arguments first seem to suggest.[81] Management elites of this period did not dispute the bland view of work presented by counterculture. Instead, they absorbed the criticism to produce a new, revitalized image of working America. By admitting to the disappointments of work, these management elites strove to implant new ideas as to what constituted "true" happiness and unhappiness, so that new worker subjectivities might take root. The critique against happiness became an opportunity to advance a different affective structure that would insert work deeper into society.

Consider, for example, how the unhappiness involved in conformity differs from that caused by anomie. The model of unhappiness in human relations took the shape of a belligerent but misguided worker. Industrial maladies, it was argued, were rooted in a general dissatisfaction with life; the loss of one's bearing in society causes industrial strife when workers misdirect their unhappiness toward their supervisors, peers, and jobs. By contrast, unhappiness for the conformist may not look or feel unhappy at all. Conformist corporate culture has taught workers to repress their desires, to bottle up unhappiness, and to seek a compromise by turning to superficial sources of pleasure. Chris Argyris, an influential management theorist at the Harvard Business School, writes about how workers are forced to change their psychological expectations when they learn that their work is unable to provide the deep satisfactions they require. In upholding the dogma of happiness, conformist corporate culture "blocks the expression of inner needs and emphasizes the expression of peripheral or skin-surface needs," causing an artificial disruption in the structure of desire.[82] As illustration, Argyris describes the concessions that a hypothetical employee would have to take if he chose to stay in an organization that does not speak to his needs: "One way for Dick to defend himself is to reduce the psychological importance of the work situation. He may say (unconsciously) in effect, 'To hell with it; I am not going to permit myself to become involved. Why should I pressurize myself to leave and to stay? Why should all this mean so much to me? I'll do just enough to get by. I'll block up my need for self-actualization until I get out of work. Then I will live!'"[83]

The happiness that human relations provided is not just insubstantive; its biggest problem is that it warped the human want and detracted workers from the paths of the good life. Management texts equate happiness to passivity and apathy; workers who have given up hope for a fulfilling job are said to have given up hope for a fulfilling life, having learned to find contentment in a bland but secure ordinary existence. Argyris, for instance, is surprised to discover that the "apathetic, uninterested worker on the assembly line" has become the model employee, "adapted and adjusted" to factory work.[84] Such workers are punctual and give little trouble to management but are otherwise inflexible and uncommitted to the quality of work performed. Happiness has taught workers to settle for a life of apathetic compromise; they no longer demand interesting, rewarding work but have psychologically accepted the exchange of mundane existence for secure, superficial contentment. The push to change the nature of work continued to be ethically charged during this time; it involved the need to produce truly satisfying work so that workers would not just be passively contented but would find authentic, driven joy.

Management elites such as Douglas McGregor, Frederick Herzberg, Peter Drucker, and Chris Argyris, as well as popular writers such as William Whyte and Abraham Maslow, created ground for this affective structure by diverting attention from organizational groups and human relationships toward the individual and her personal sense of fulfillment on the job. Maslow's hierarchy of needs, published in 1954 in *Motivation and Personality*, has been particularly influential in providing a framework that management elites use for supporting their argument of a profound human need for work. For Maslow, the highest need of Man was self-actualization. Unlike other needs rooted in belongingness or esteem, self-actualization—defined as a need for the individual to be "doing what he, individually, is suited for"—is inherently tied to the exercise of physical, psychic, and creative labor. Maslow states this concept unambiguously in the context of creative production: "A musician must make music, an artist must paint, a poet must write." His argument—that self-fulfillment can come only when the individual is "actualized in what he is potentially"—enshrines and constructs a unique productive potentiality in each human being that needs enactment to inspire sustained fulfillment.[85]

In positioning doing as crucial to the good life, the hierarchy of needs offers a powerful metaphor for managerial elites to promulgate a new selfhood. Herzberg and his colleagues incorporate this idea into their influential dyadic scheme that separates the factors of "satisfiers" from those of "dissatisfiers."[86] They argue that dissatisfier factors, such as wages, are necessary only up to a point; they can prevent workers from feeling negative about their work and can make work tolerable, but they cannot produce the satisfaction that people want. True happiness, they believe, can be engendered only by catering to "the individual's need for self-actualization." However, the need cannot be fulfilled by the dictates of the manager. In a manner completely at odds with Houser's argument two decades before, Herzberg and his colleagues present studies demonstrating limits to the managerial capacity for empathetic knowledge. Attempts to have managers "predict the needs of the worker" have largely "shown that management is unable to make valid predictions."[87] Individualities, they note, are far too varied and complex for paternalism. Hence, the solution must center on the restructuring of work: giving individuals more control over their work process so that they "may realize their ability for creative achievement."[88]

The concept of "individuality" has been described as essential to the success of corporations and workers. As one text argues, older methods that stressed conformity for groups produced a "dull and discouraged" workforce that removed an organization's "zip and spontaneity."[89] "The individual is the source of creativity, spontaneity, flexibility, initiative, variation—all the things that keep institutions vital and growing," and it is important for the administrator to believe in the power of his workers' "free will," developing his employees to the fullest extent in their uniqueness rather than forcing them to conform to a particular type that would serve his own ends.[90] All workers, another text offers, need to be considered as unique, rounded wholes, complete with "particular traits," "special sensitivities," and "deep-seated needs and feelings."[91] And while human relations would ask to carefully guard and amend negative traits, the managerial philosophy of the mid-twentieth century increasingly demanded managers to work with the inborn individualities of employees, to "help them to be the individuals that nature intended."[92] This advice carried over to managers: even undesirable traits that managers discover in themselves should not be too critically evaluated and controlled. "Try to accept yourself as you find yourself to be; do not emphasize either the 'good' or the 'bad' as you unearth them in your make-up," advises a text; true self-mastery can come only when one works *with* what is naturally assigned, rather than working *on* it.[93]

Many aspects of this philosophy were popularized through Douglas McGregor's influential Theory Y concept of management. In his book *The Human Side of Enterprise*, McGregor upends the traditional view of human desire, explaining that contrary to popular opinion, people do not naturally dislike work, nor do they want to be directed or to avoid responsibility. The flaw of human relations, he argues, is that it has taken on these assumptions in its Theory X model of management, which, while well-intentioned, is autocratic at its core. Instead of trusting workers to develop their own efficient objectives, work processes, and standards, human relations provides only hypocritical modes of employee autonomy that require workers to adhere to the ideas and principles directed by management.

McGregor sees inner needs as biological drives that can only be actualized, not manipulated—and doing the latter would produce deep-seated resentment that cannot be easily resolved. This view forms his strongest basis for the rejection of human relations—a Theory X philosophy that could manipulate workers so cleverly that they would "come up with the answer which the manager had in the first place, but believing it was their own."[94] "It is important to note the distinction between making people *feel* important and *making* people important," he writes, because the former would likely destroy the integrity of the manager and produce revulsion among his subordinates.[95] Managers need to treat their workers as adults, not as people whom they are trying to placate for temporary harmony: "The manager who perceives staff members as flunkies to carry out orders will never obtain *professional* staff help."[96] Workers perceived as children will deliver slipshod work at best, anger and resentment at worst; they will never offer their "imaginative, creative effort" to their employers.[97]

To cultivate creative, professional employees, managers should rely on a Theory Y mode of management, which has a fundamentally different view of workers. In this mode, managers need to have "a relatively high opinion of the intelligence and capacity of the average human being"; they must see "most human beings as having real capacity for growth and development, for the acceptance of responsibility, for creative accomplishment."[98] Unlike Theory X, which centers on the dictation of employee goals, Theory Y requires managers to be patient, optimistic nurturers. Managers are exhorted to help workers discover their own goals, to guide workers in aligning those goals to the interests of the organization, and to give them the support and resources needed to develop in the direction they desire.

This view of human nature serves as a backdrop for the transition from happiness to passion. The affective structure invests in a new condition of reciprocal exchange: management texts argue that if provided with an appropriate job placement and autonomy, workers will awaken to their own desires for self-actualization and become self-motivated, responsible, and driven. Passion retains the fantasies of happiness, posing work as a route to the good life, but it revises the subjectivities of entry into the good-life imaginary. In this regime, experiential happiness is no longer made the objective. Even though happiness might be an outcome of passion, management texts now make clear that happiness has a more complex relationship in the overall scheme of passion. After all, the ugly underbelly of happiness is passivity and apathy, behaviors that directly contradict passionate conduct.

With passion as the ideal, negative emotional states such as unhappiness and anger also became transformed. The refusal of passive happiness may be a sign of passionate conduct: an indication of dissatisfaction with the status quo and a possession of an authentic drive to make a difference. Thomas Spates asks readers to project what pacifying happiness would look like: "You can visualize a 'happy' employee at his desk, bench, or machine. He's just happy. In fact, he is so happy with things as they are that he does not want to alter either the pace or the conditions of work."[99] The worker who is "just" happy became representative of a worker so contented that she has stopped searching for self-improvement, becoming even "resistant to change" and unwilling to provide new ideas to the organization to have it improve. By contrast, Spates offers, it is "the 'unhappy' and 'aggressive' employee" who would be "pressing for change, improvements, innovations, better ways to get the job done."[100]

While the affective structure of happiness deplores negative emotional states such as anxiety, unhappiness, anger, and dissatisfaction, the new affective structure of passion regards such negative traits as plausible signs of a healthy relationship with work and even as sparks for radical ideas and change. In that case, these negative states are not meant to be simply supplanted with happiness. Rather, they need to be carefully channeled and managed so that individuals can be motivated to adopt proper practices of economic conduct.[101] Therefore, the shift from happiness to passion has been a complex transformation that does not just involve a switch from one ideal to another. It also details changes to the very idea of what the good life represents: no longer exempt from moments of anxiety or dissatisfaction, the good life in fact understands these negative states as components that can induce the motivations necessary to produce true fulfillment.

The affective structure of passion continued to gain ground in the late twentieth century as the issue of work satisfaction entered the public arena, framed as a want articulated by workers. As Harold Sheppard and Neal Herrick note, by the early 1970s, discussion of "blue collar blues" and "white collar woes" was no longer confined to an elite managerial group. As the unmet want for good work bled into public consciousness, it became recognized as "a major area of societal concern" that required the attention of the government, intellectuals, and the public.[102] During this period, newspapers, magazines, and other popular publications described dissatisfaction as an ailment that afflicted the American working population, especially its youths, who had come to demand more from their jobs. Judson Gooding, a writer for *Fortune*, indicates that while people used to accept "the necessity of working unquestioningly," they now insisted on discovering meaning in their work and would even terminate their jobs if they found them unlikable or uninteresting: "A job is no longer for life, but is just for as long as the worker likes it and it satisfies him."[103]

While texts of the previous periods had argued that workers could not grasp the psychological significance of work, texts in the 1970s reframed the desire for self-actualization as something that workers were cognizant of and which they actively demanded. Gooding, for instance, describes as "striking" the "uniformity about the demands being made" when he talked to "hundreds of workers, foremen, and managers in every part of the country for months on end, focusing on what is wrong with their jobs, and what should be done to make them better."[104] Their dissatisfaction did not come from wages; rather, they complained about their lack of passion, indicating that work did not cater enough to their aspirations and talents. Academic research funded by the federal government lent scientific credibility to this view.[105] Studies conducted by the Survey Research Center at the University of Michigan, which used large sample sizes, were often marshaled as evidence of the innate need for self-actualization. One report of the period, which was based on interviews with over a thousand workers, stated that workers themselves had reported wanting to find more meaning in their jobs and that their satisfaction at work primarily depended on whether their talents were tapped into and whether the job was interesting.[106]

These self-reports presume transparency in the self-knowledge of desire, as if desire is an object located within the individual, uninfluenced by circumstances outside, and as if it is individuals themselves who can assess and rank what they want most objectively. However, if the prevailing corporate belief is that a good job corresponds to good feelings, then the response to the question of what you want is necessarily already imbricated into ideas about what you *should* want. Assumptions about what leads to the good life constitute the value-laden categories that influence what we describe as our desire. Besides, studies during this time did not just measure the wants of workers; they also interpreted the findings as evidence of the innate need for passion, providing grounds for *Work in America* to claim that "what workers want most, as more than 100 studies in the past 20 years show, is to . . . feel that their work and they themselves are important."[107]

The depiction of passion as historically consistent, a revelation supported by "more than 100 studies in the past 20 years," erases the conflictual history of desire, the struggle over its construction, and the consequences of its articulation. Passion is made natural and uncomplicated to human nature, which suggests that in discovering and pursuing our organic desire, we may experience the good life and find meaning, recognition, and other elements that constitute conventional fantasy. It is thus possible to portray passion as something that needs defending, an attachment that necessitates protection from the forces of mechanization or unwise managers who refuse to acknowledge individual talents and personalities. Ralph Nader, for instance, overlooks a long, complex history of desire when he writes that "the quest for meaning in work—as distinguished from the quest *for* work—is one of history's least chartered courses" and advocates more research in motivation studies.[108] The suggestion is not just that the attention to the psychological want is new but also that its newness is indicative of a long-fought victory for workers, an important element that corporations and society have refused to attend to.

This position renders passion a moral right, a point not exaggerated given how texts in the 1970s had illustrated the social consequences of dissatisfaction. As the introduction to *The Quality of Working Life* reveals, consensus about the psychic importance of work must be understood socially; it is critical to consider how "working life affects a worker's outside life, and vice versa."[109] Studs Terkel's influential best-selling book, *Working*, published in 1974, popularized this view by using vivid oral histories to give the hardships of work an intimate veracity uncharacteristic of the discourse of the periods before. Terkel is candid in his critique of work: "The book, being about work, is, by its very nature, about violence—to the spirit as well as to the body."[110] Assembling 128 interviews across numerous occupations—including a sanitation worker, service staff, and sex worker—he built nuanced, colorful images of the challenges experienced in everyday working life, showing how they affected not just the interviewees' immediate work situation but also the entire quality of their lives: "It is about ulcers as well as accidents, about shouting matches as well as fistfights, about nervous breakdowns as well as kicking the dog around."[111]

A key figure of *Working* is the American worker who is bereft of fulfillment at work but is nonetheless desirous of it. Difficulties on the job, Terkel notes, do not inhibit the search for "daily meaning as well as daily bread," because the former is what distinguishes "between a sort of life rather than a Monday through Friday sort of dying."[112] The drearier a job is, the stronger the impulse becomes to escape into fantasy and play, so that work might feel more interesting and meaningful. Terkel's identity as a political liberal indicates confluence in the demand for psychological fulfillment expressed by both the political right and the left. Both sides endorsed such romantic individualism, seeing passion as a hard-won fight for one's personal, deep-seated beliefs.

Terkel's caution about the societal damage of unfulfilling labor also coincided with long-standing critiques of apathy expressed by managerial discourse. In the late twentieth century, management texts continued this argument and expressed that feelings of entrapment can damage the human psyche, leading to social ills. Gooding, for instance, describes "job hatred" not only as sad but "dangerous," warning that it can lead to a "downward spiral" with "grave consequences for the nation's social fabric," resulting in "death threats," "family disruption," "the use of drugs," and "overt sabotage" at the workplace.[113] Another text confirms the psychological damage that work can do, using the example of a normative family to illustrate the attritive damage of an unpassionate job: "To go to work each morning is to face a daily beating of the ego. The family naturally feels this. A child, whose father expressed deep dissatisfaction with his job, said: 'Daddy is cranky all of the time. He used to take us to the movies, but now he doesn't anymore.' His wife remarked: 'He is very unhappy with his job and it naturally reflects in his attitudes and conversations at home. His naturally happy-go-lucky attitude is disappearing.'"[114]

Institutionally, these ideas contributed to the quality of working life movement, a program that enlisted corporations to reengineer work by providing job enrichment and enlargement opportunities.[115] The movement called for organizational policies such as rotated work roles, autonomous work teams, and an expanded job scope, with the hope that such policies would enable workers to discover the areas that they are most passionate about. But while these efforts were applauded, their limits were recognized. Passion assumes that workers have unique sets of aspirations and talents, and a general corporate scheme cannot fully address such complexities. The fostering of passion, Clair Vough advises, needs to be personal.[116] It requires the alignment of work responsibilities with workers' identities, so that work may become a source of pride. Successfully doing so would produce passionate involvement even in low-status work positions. Vough relates the story of a janitor who complained that nobody recognized his contribution to the cleanliness of the office. To resolve the problem, the janitor asked that he alone be responsible for one section of the plant, adding, "All I'll ask is that you look at my section every morning and compare it to someone else's section. I think I can do the best job on the crew and I want to prove it."[117]

The discourse on passion is democratic in its scope. While it acknowledges differences in satisfaction among jobs, it nonetheless positions as common the human desire for fulfillment in work. The janitor is as likely as the executive to demand self-actualization, and corporations are tasked equally to provide for both. But there are costs involved. When passion is prioritized as the want of workers, other ethical responsibilities are made invisible or neglected. Vough, for instance, emphasizes psychological justice at the expense of considering other factors, including wage differentials between the janitor and the executive, the extent to which job motivation could translate to higher pay, and the security and welfare provided by these different positions. Sar Levitan and William Johnston's warning in 1973 about the naivete of assuming that workers would willingly "sacrifice much of their pay for 'better quality' work" is important to consider, for it shows how the discourse on passion involves a politics of attention—to what is important and to what is not.[118] Even though managers would not claim that pay is unimportant, the norm of passion provides new grounds for dismissing traditional concerns about work. It allows, among other possibilities, the criticism of union leaders who downplay passion and stress the importance of wages. These leaders, Gooding suggests, are out of touch with the realities of human wants and proceed with their demands only as a desperate attempt to feel needed in a changed economy.[119] Worse, unions that continue to push for wages may be dismissed as a hindrance to the reengineering of work, holding back new workplace policies due to their skepticism about corporate intentions.

When psychological fulfillment is made the goal of work, those things that hinder the achievement of passion become obstacles to be removed. Richard Irish's wordily but aptly titled management text, *If Things Don't Improve Soon I May Ask You to Fire Me*, illustrates the productive dynamics of passion. In Irish's unambiguous view, passion should be everybody's goal: "Work is what we want to do, not what we must do."[120] However, he also believes that not all job situations that are considered "good" in the conventional sense are helpful in the cultivation of this emotion. Asserting that people have the natural tendency to "lie low in a bad situation . . . and die the slow death of the occupationally dissatisfied," he argues for a new, positive view of layoffs.[121] Firing unpassionate workers "puts an end to this on-the-job charade" and creates an "enormous growth in self-esteem," because workers are finally rid of their unhappy jobs and have regained the freedom to reembark on the paths of sourcing for passion.[122] Placing importance on psychological fulfillment, therefore, supports the dismantling of job security and the production of precarity; in so doing, it can provide the most human freedoms necessary to find passion.

The dismantling of obstructions to passion would also make a new pathology for those who refuse to identify with the want for passionate work. While earlier managerial texts warned of a warped structure of desire produced by conformity, texts in the 1970s took to pathologizing those who continued to refuse passion in the face of corporate benevolence. One management guide, for instance, noted not only that "there are people content with repetitive and externally imposed controls" but also that these individuals are fundamentally defective in their motivational structure; they refuse to seek self-actualization in the workplace *and* on the outside.[123] Their "motivational level may never rise to the self-actualizing plateau" and will remain forever "apathetic, noninvolved, and noncommitted."[124] This typification suggests the coercive function of the passionate norm. As self-actualization becomes biologized, it becomes easier to pathologize workers who continually refuse the passionate norm suggested by managerial discourse. Framing problems of work resistance first as industrial alienation in human relations and then as conformity in the repudiation of happiness, managerial discourse finally, in the 1970s, made the refusal of coercive passion a problem of individuals with inborn defects in their desires. The passionate conduct of working life thus becomes a barometer of a healthy psychic life and an indicator of one's full ability to participate socially and civically.

The Illusive Search for the Good Life

The good life can be thought of as an orienting object: it directs our agencies based on its utopian promise of where it resides, even closing off possibilities as it directs us away from paths that would lead us astray. This explains why impressions of the good life are deeply political. Ideas about what we want—what brings us happiness—can, as Kathi Weeks offers, close off "possible futures" with "ready-made visions and predictable outcomes," restricting even imaginations of the utopia that could be envisioned.[125] Ideas about the good life ground investments in the conceptions of our future and magnetize a field of positive affects around it. When an object is said to lead to the good life, the object *itself* becomes good, magnetizing energy and positive affectivity. Management discourse has, over the decades, made passion that good object, stressing that it fulfills the need for self-actualization that is common to all human beings. And by doing so, the good life of work has also prioritized psychological justice, making fulfillment the main achievement of work.

Charting the contingent optimisms of work allows us to unsettle this history. The swerves in happiness and passion reveal the disappointing history of our desires: the condition where the provided frames of the good life repeatedly turn out to be less than satisfactory, requiring revision. What does it mean when the good life has failed to satisfy and keep its place? When what we are said to want from work actually disappoints? For one thing, it may highlight the mutability of the human want, as management texts have done by insisting on the new desires of countercultural youths. Or it may also, as Sara Ahmed suggests, signal a more fundamental problem in the conception of the "good," where limits to our beliefs about work and its rewards cause us to misrecognize the cause of our persistent dissatisfaction.[126]

The illusive search for the good life illustrates the cost involved in the larger enterprise of passion. When passion is thought of as being necessary or good, an innate human need, we make the goodness of passion a fact rather than a tentative proposition.[127] This fact is also bundled with models of behaviors and beliefs that privilege the interests of capital. It is not just that right feelings in right jobs lead to a good life; people are also told to transform themselves, to actively seek out the means of experiencing those right sentiments. The shift from happiness to passion illustrates the political qualities of this demand; it reminds us that it is important to consider who articulates the demands from work, how one group's demands are made the demands of everyone else, and the effects such demands have.

Our contemporary discourse on passion obscures the longer struggle that exists around the rights to articulate desire; it muddles the reasons why a rejection of passion might make sense as a claim for agency, a claim to rights to a different world that might hinge less on work and its necessity for survival. My aim in this chapter is to start this process by creating room. To provide space for critique, it is necessary to first create room to discuss what we want from work. There is no need to assume that that dissatisfaction is bad, that it needs to be quickly fixed. Withholding judgment to consider the different stories that dissatisfaction can tell may produce different optimistic relationships, different imaginative possibilities of the good life. The following chapters continue this discussion of bringing the passionate demand to contemporary work culture.

2

Jobless, Undamaged, Resilient

We were in one of the worst recessions on record. . . . So what started out as a story of a man who simply fired people for a living . . . became a movie about a man who was trying to figure out who and what he wanted in his life. And in addition to that, I had to cut out all these kind of satirical firing scenes that made sense when I first started writing the movie, but in this moment, don't make any sense.

Jason Reitman in an interview with Terry Gross
on his film *Up in the Air* (2009)

Witnessing the mass unemployment during the Great Recession, Jason Reitman, director of the film *Up in the Air*, decided to replace satirical scenes of corporate firing with authentic vignettes of retrenched workers reacting to news of their layoffs. A striking scene early on provides a glimpse of the film's original direction. In it, Ryan Bingham, a professional downsizer, delivers a cliché on passion to a newly laid-off worker, only to quickly seize his key card while the latter is momentarily placated. Bingham's line—"Anyone who has ever built an empire or changed the world sat where you are right now, and it's because they sat there, they were able to do it"—is meant to mock the genre of trite career advice, the stereotype that unemployment can present a positive moment where one rediscovers passions and pursues a better life. But in light of the recession, Reitman worried that the satirical tone would make the film sound "fake" and disrespectful.

As remedy, Reitman included in the film reenactments of the shock and anguish that real laid-off workers from St. Louis and Detroit expressed when receiving news of their layoffs. Critics reacted favorably to these scenes, calling them an "amazingly prescient" display of national suffering and the "truer tragedy" of the hardship that many Americans were forced to face in the recession.[1] Reitman himself experienced the depth and authenticity of this national hurt: he states that he had to do little to get these workers to reveal the pain of job loss. During shoots, subjects reverted to their "sense-memory" almost immediately upon being told they were fired. Reitman says, "Their body language would change, their shoulders would fold, their eyes would turn, one girl broke into hives."[2]

Somewhat ironically, then, passion transforms from the subject of satire to the film's redemptive object. By the film's end, enlightened by familial and romantic relationships, Bingham starts pondering the meaninglessness of his life and career.[3] This transformation, Reitman tells us, relates to the subject of purpose: "Where do you find purpose in life and what do you want in your life?"[4] This direction was also inspired by his interviews with the unemployed. Reitman explains that the loss of income "rarely came up" during those conversations. Rather, "what people said, time and time again, was: 'I don't know what I'm supposed to do. . . .' It was really about a lack of purpose."[5] Purpose was thereby not only impressed as something that workers once had but lost; it was also framed as the primary cost of job loss and the main crisis of the recession.

Up in the Air illustrates how the recession transformed the narrative of passion into a social good, an object that animates recovery for those laid off, who are experiencing a "lost" sense of purpose.[6] Bingham's new ambition to chart a purposeful life at the end of the film marks the symbolic usefulness of passion, even as it remains wrongly directed. Having undertaken a process of self-discovery, he is poised to passionately pursue a different life. Instead of channeling his passions to airline miles and a callous job, we see a possibility for him to engage in something more meaningful. And so, where passion might once have been raised as a cliché, its critique is now nullified through acceptance of its necessity. Reitman is unwilling to mock passion because of its significance in molding a purposeful world and a good life. In fact, it is loss itself that makes the cliché of passion powerful and worth circulating: when there is a breakdown that needs rebuilding, we return to ideas of normative family values, romantic relationships, and the purpose found in work.

A Psychological Recession

Though employment has never guaranteed passion, it is often recognized as a prerequisite to a good life. For many, employment remains the main avenue whereby a progressively well-off future of consumer comforts is imagined to be made possible.[7] The Great Recession, however, problematized this assumption by normalizing a culture of unemployment into everyday life and consciousness. Indeed, employment conditions have remained strikingly precarious, despite variations in the extent of unemployment in the decade after the recession. Just months before the coronavirus pandemic, US unemployment figures were repeatedly praised for reaching a "50-year low" of 3.5 percent.[8] This was itself a lackluster achievement, a number attained only years after it peaked at 10 percent in 2009 and was unaccompanied by wage gains for the majority.[9] Even so, the pandemic erased these gains in a few months. By April 2020, unemployment had spiked back up to 14.7 percent, before steadily dipping to a figure of around 6 percent in 2021.[10]

The unemployment statistic, of course, informs only one part of the larger story of unemployment in the United States.[11] For one thing, it does not reflect the inequality in employment. Even during periods of celebrated lows, unemployment numbers understate the disproportionate number of racial minorities unemployed and struggling with poverty.[12] The national rate of unemployment for Black Americans has been at least twice that of whites, and Black Americans have always borne the brunt of recessions, finding it harder to become reemployed after layoffs.[13] This discrepancy is also geographically distributed in what is called the "two American economies," where expensive coastal areas, such as New York and California, experience speedy growth, while other states, especially those in the Rust Belt, continue to be mired in unemployment and poverty.[14]

Further, the commonly used U-3 unemployment figure does not take into account underemployment and long-term unemployment, two issues that have become significant with the rise of self-employment and temporary work.[15] National panel surveys conducted by the Rutgers University Heldrich Center between 2008 and 2015 found that one in five laid off in the recession was unable to find employment in the entire seven-year period.[16] Half of those reemployed spent more than two years searching for a job, and one in four took on jobs of a temporary nature. These trends are again marked by distinctions in race, education, and age. The long-term unemployed tend to be more poorly educated, older, and Hispanic and African American.[17] Those reemployed in the aftermath of the recession were also more likely to be underemployed, working fewer hours than they would have liked or forced into temporary, gig jobs.[18] This compromise appears to carry consequences in the long term. Economists note that those who have willingly moved down the occupational ladder during the recession have found it hard to move back up when the situation improved.[19]

These contemporary issues arise from a longer process of neoliberal restructuring, which took root especially in the mid-1980s as corporations shifted from the "stakeholder" to "shareholder" model, which greatly loosened the assurance of livelihoods for workers.[20] While businesses in the stakeholder model are bound by social contract to serve the interests of their employees and communities, the shareholder model renders the interests of investors their primary responsibility, incentivizing corporate leaders to strive for short-term profits.[21] This ideological shift toward the shareholder model has implicated how workers are perceived. Workers across the spectrum have been increasingly understood as liabilities or costs that chip away at corporate profits and whose removal would garner shareholder approval. Accordingly, businesses turned to a lean and mean strategy of staffing, undertaking initiatives to press labor costs down and keep head counts flexible. Work was routinized and sent offshore to tap into cheaper labor sources, expensive long-term employees were replaced with cheaper disposable ones, and unions were broken down so businesses could achieve maximum control over labor processes.[22]

These trends provide a basis to understand why unemployment has been experienced affectively as an ongoing crisis despite unemployment figures that sometimes suggest full employment. In this chapter, I address the *serialized pattern of unemployment* that has become especially obvious in the postrecessionary context: a condition where workers have to anticipate and cope with repeated cycles of unemployment, even in a normal economic climate. This pattern clearly manifested in the early 2000s through what management theorist Douglas Hall calls a "protean career," a mindset necessitating that workers regard every job as a temporary position within the multiple career tracks that one must undertake in a lifetime. Job changes are now seen as positive and are regarded as an ordinary part of one's career experience as layoffs become normalized.[23] Hence, while interviewing unemployed technology workers in the same period, Carrie Lane noticed that her respondents had largely absolved their employers of blame when speaking of their plight. While they leveled blame at themselves and the economy for their job loss, almost no tech workers that she spoke to criticized their employers for not providing "cradle-to-grave employment." "Modern-day tech workers," she writes, "no longer expected a company to provide such things."[24]

Still, the affective consequences of serialized unemployment are not so easily overcome, especially with the growing stakes and length of unemployment. In the 1970s, the average person spent eleven weeks unemployed before finding a new job. This number increased to seventeen weeks in the 2000s, then to the height of forty weeks in the recession, before dropping to about twenty-three weeks in the present.[25] The increased duration of unemployment comes with a heightened emotional drain. The modern job-hunting process, according to the recruitment agency Randstad, requires an average of four different versions of a résumé, four cover letters, seven applications, and five different interviews.[26] Similarly, career coach Tony Beshara explains that workers should view job hunting as a numbers game that is unlikely to yield results with a single application and which they must be ready to repeat in the future, even after landing a job. Beshara writes, "You are going to be depressed, dejected, rejected, refused, denied, forgotten, ignored, lied to . . . and after all that abuse, you are going to get up and run the risk of its happening again."[27]

The emotional strain results in what Beshara calls a "psychological recession"—a situation where workers worry about their jobs even when they are employed. But while the stress of the job-hunting process might garner sympathy, career advisers argue that the prominence of unemployment in public consciousness should not be deplored and erased. In fact, workers today *cannot afford not* to think about unemployment. The psychological preparedness needed is so significant that the strategy must be to cope and deal with this realistic worry rather than to will it away. The normalization of unemployment thus implies the construction of a different psychological attitude that needs to be implanted in the contemporary psyche of workers. Essentially, workers need to be more psychologically resilient than ever, so they can take on job loss without its full negative emotional consequence.

Apathy and Maladapted Adaptation

How did unemployment come to possess such psychological significance? We might begin with the word *employ*, which is derived from the classical Latin verb *implicāre*, meaning to "entangle, involve, connect closely."[28]

On one level, employment is an entanglement, a contract with an employer often established in return for wages. But the idea of a connection in employment also hints at work's normative imbrication with a social world. To be employed means to be used; it means to have one's time and abilities purposed for a time toward a goal. The *un* in *unemployment* presumes a breaking of this connection, a lacuna that translates into other kinds of lack, starting with the ability to sustain oneself and following into one's social value and mental well-being. This is indicated in the numerous titles of self-help texts—*The Panic Free Job Search, Keeping Your Head after Losing Your Job, Finding Your Career Path without Losing Your Mind*, and so on—where the loss of employment is implied to lead to a deeper kind of absence. The fear is that severing connection with an employer can lead to a series of other breakages—such as from the broader society or of one's self-esteem—that ultimately renders the subject even less employable as she sinks into despair.

In this section, I consider how apathy, or what I call "maladapted adaptation," constitutes this severance, building a link between circumstance (unemployment), subject (the unemployable), and a population deemed a "threat" (the long-term unemployed). Maurizio Lazzarato reminds us that "unemployment, employment, and work are not 'natural' realities that have an objective existence."[29] Unemployment is a concept that has acquired different meanings at different points in time, referencing sets of concerns and ideologies.[30] From there, we might ask: How did apathy come to play an important part in the story of unemployment? And how did passion come to be seen as a solution to the problem of apathy?

Matthew Cole's critical examination of the Marienthal study provides a good entry point to an assessment.[31] *Marienthal*, a book published in German in 1933 and in English in 1971, is a sociological classic that has been described as "foundational in social scientific understandings of unemployment."[32] Its case centers on the industrial village of Marienthal, a community of 478 households twenty miles southeast of Vienna, which was seized suddenly with complete unemployment when the sole textile factory closed down in 1929.[33] As the lead researcher, Marie Jahoda, remarks, Marienthal has provided a rare microcosm to study the effects of unemployment on a community. Because this was "a community that was totally unemployed," it differed from the usual situation of partial unemployment.[34] And so, while Jahoda and her colleagues would go on to qualify importance in the specificity of context, what is implied in *Marienthal* is the objective reality of unemployment as a transformative force—a condition that affects people and things outside class and individual psychology.

The *Marienthal* narrative centers on prolonged unemployment and its influence on the "breakdown of a social personality structure."[35] Decades after the first edition was published, co-researcher Paul Lazarsfeld noted that the book remained relevant in the 1970s, explaining that unemployment during this time had twisted people's normal psychological state. Long-term unemployment, he wrote, was a malaise that afflicted its "victims" with "apathy," causing them to be without motivation and unable to "utilize any longer even the few opportunities left to them."[36] The erosion of their sense of purpose prevented them from pursuing the right behaviors that would lead them back into a happier state. A "vicious cycle," he conceded, then existed between "reduced opportunities and reduced level of aspirations."[37]

This argument is characteristic of the discourse about unemployment in the Great Depression of the 1930s. As historian William Walters explains, the prevalence of long-term joblessness in the period prompted researchers to extend concepts of mental health into a field that had previously been dominated by discussions of Victorian morality and the cyclical nature of labor markets.[38] In this framework, work is deemed to provide a structure that embeds people into communities and offers purpose and status, the absence of which produces "psychiatric disorders" such as "anxiety, stress, and depression," which can leave people "discouraged"—or, in today's parlance, "apathetic"—as subjects drop out of the labor force.[39]

The emphasis on apathy in these accounts allows us to see how passion has come to play a major role in the narrative of unemployment. *Apathy* is defined as the inverse of passion and is commonly expressed as a "passionless existence," a state of indifference toward what is normally calculated to "excite interest or action."[40] The allusion to apathy as an affliction should draw attention to what is understood as psychologically normal: a potentially impassioned self, who is always ready to spring into action through affection from other forces. Apathy signals the muting of this latent potential, in someone whose affectivity is impaired and who has become incapable of being affected by other objects or beings.

This reading makes apathy fundamentally different from other negative affects. While the sad and angry are still affectable and potentially changeable, the apathetic resist influence of all kinds. And so, if formations of affect describe the "meaningfulness of the world," as Lawrence Grossberg puts it, or "the capacities to act and be acted upon," in the words of Melissa Gregg and Gregory Seigworth, then apathy in its technical form would count as a kind of antiaffect.[41] The blunting of affectivity highlights the stakes involved in apathy in capitalist culture. Not only is apathy problematic for productivity; the absence of a potential subject of passion makes human agency something that capitalism is unable to grasp and manipulate. Apathetic masses would "disappear," as Jean Baudrillard puts it.[42] The passionless character of apathy inhibits its subjects from being seduced or threatened into commodifiable labor power.

I will return to the discussion of apathy, but it is useful first to attend to the argument that Cole makes about the normativity of paid work in the *Marienthal* narrative. In *Marienthal*, employment is implied to be necessary for healthy functioning *outside* the instrumental purpose of a wage. This bias is made clear, Cole explains, when Jahoda and her colleagues state that "'a feeling of irrevocability and hopelessness had a much more paralysing effect than economic deprivation itself,' without considering the possibility that the latter may have caused the former."[43] Despite the descriptions of poverty and references to gendered relations of childcare and waged work, *Marienthal* largely assumes paid work to be the "normal, default condition of adult male life," while unemployment is seen as "intrinsically problematic" and demeaning for the identities of adult men, eroding their sense of moral purpose and even causing regression of mental states.[44]

This critique should lead us to question the naturalized association between unemployment and emotional pain. Certainly, the loss of work can lead to feelings of hopelessness and ineptitude. However, the diagnosis of a direct relationship between unemployment and emotional suffering conflates the complex emotional effects of other factors surrounding unemployment with the direct cause of unemployment itself.[45] With factors of emotional effects hidden, we are more likely to advocate employment as a cure for the "suffering" of unemployment as opposed to challenging a dominant social order that has made work a priority and necessity of human existence.[46]

But while insightful, Cole's critique stops short of examining the specificity of apathy, a point especially significant once we grasp the odd way in which apathy is conceptualized in *Marienthal*. Indeed, what would logically follow the norm of paid work—that the unemployed would be sad and languishing—was *not* the condition that the *Marienthal* researchers found. Despite vivid portraitures of lack, the researchers concluded that the "most common basic attitude in Marienthal" was not synonymous with desperation or depression. Instead, a lighter term—"resignation"—is used to convey what the researchers saw, defined as "a relatively calm general mood, and even sporadically recurring moments of serenity and joy." Most resigned families continued to maintain their households, cared for their children, and even had "an overall feeling of relative well-being," but the problem lay in that they had "no plans, no relation to the future." This community was surviving, its members offering some help to each other, but their survival came with a "reduced demand and a lack of expectation" that diminished their motivation to figure a way out of their predicament.[47]

The moral charge of *Marienthal* must be understood in this context. Unemployment was not painful in the sense that it produced depression or sorrow in the community. Any unhappiness, if it did emerge initially, did not stay for long, and the community was able to survive despite their lack. But the successful adaptation to lack, from the researchers' perspective, presented its own problem: in being so well adjusted to their impoverished circumstance, the resigned had also lost the will to change things for the better, which carried dangerous consequences for their future. As the profile of one family suggests, most in Marienthal believed that "they would get by somehow," despite their adversity: "Somehow we will manage to keep alive; it can't finish us all off."[48] But this attitude, the researchers argue, may have been blindly optimistic. By accepting their lot, they had sealed themselves to risks that the future presented. Hence, *Marienthal* concludes with the dire message of "fading resilience," noting that the moment will come when shoes can be no further mended, crockery cannot be replaced, and illnesses cannot be recovered from without medical attention. "At the end of the process," they write, "lies ruin and despair."[49]

Thus, *Marienthal* revises the notion of what constitutes a *proper* adaptation to unemployment. An adaptation that might be considered ordinary—one that ends with making do with poverty and finding contentment despite challenges—is presented as bad, stifling activity and harming existence. This reversal, from adaptation to maladaptation, or *maladapted adaptation*, must be understood as political, as a means of protecting the normative productivist order that Kathi Weeks argues has been key to capitalist culture.[50] In *Marienthal*, the norm of productivity implies structural continuance, with work construed as the only object that can guarantee a livable, worthwhile future. Hence, after the researchers analyzed essays written by Marienthal youths on their hopes for the future, they note that only those with apprenticeships had "specific, individual plans for the future in the context of the trade they were learning." Others were "unapproachable" or expressed only "general hopes" of a "world revolution that would liberate the oppressed, but nothing about their own particular future."[51] Dreams of structural change are thus implied to be fanciful instead of radical, the dreamers afflicted with the same "atmosphere of hopelessness" that was being carried from the old to the young.[52]

Apathy, as such, cannot be reduced to a lack of desire. In *Marienthal*, apathy comes in to inscribe differences between acceptable and unacceptable desires. The label is used to pathologize those who want wrongly and is rationalized through a series of "natural" developments that will come to harm the apathetic subject. We see this enacted especially in a chapter where a variety of technologies are used to denote the maladjustment of the Marienthal men to capitalist time. Records of the number of instances that the men stopped on the streets, of the pace of their walk, and of the demarcation of their day are used to reflect their loss of temporal awareness and, consequently, their inability to hurry, to be efficient, and to refuse idling. "Everything that occurs happens as if it were unintentional," the researchers summarize, going on to describe the general Marienthal man as someone "primitive" and mindless, driven by instinct: "He hears some slight noise outside in the street and goes out; a moment later the noise is forgotten. Nevertheless he remains standing outside until some other trivial impression prompts a further move."[53] Apathy's damage is thus construed to go beyond the loss of income. It enforces the decline into an insipid, passionless life and eventually transforms the unemployed into an animal-like object of apprehension, whose presence threatens public safety.[54]

In the previous chapter, I showed how contentment in happiness can be seen as a negative affect with the rise of passion. Though the contented are satisfied, the passivity of their happiness keeps them from acting in self-enhancing ways that could lead to corporate profits. Similarly, we see how apathy is construed as negative, not particularly because it creates unhappiness but because it blocks the formation of a passionate, purposeful subject, someone capable and *willing* to commodify their labor power in a self-enhancing manner. As David Harvey reminds us, capitalism counts on its workers to possess an ethic of productive consumption, an attitude to life that aligns working bodies to the requirements of capitalism, where voluntary behaviors are cultivated to lead to a seamless insertion of labor power into capitalist development.[55] The capacity to mobilize workers and direct drives to a given purpose defined by capital forms an important appendage of the system. What is threatened is this very system of motivation.

A.M.

6–7	Getting up.
7–8	Wake the boys because they have to go to school.
8–9	When they have gone, I go down to the shed to get wood and water.
9–10	When I get back up to the house my wife always asks me what she ought to cook; to avoid the question I go off into the field.
10–11	In the meantime midday comes around.
11–12	Empty.

P.M.

12–1	We eat at one o'clock; the children don't come home from school until then.
1–2	After the meal I take a look at the newspaper.
2–3	Go out.
3–4	Go to Treer's (the shopkeeper's).
4–5	Watch trees being cut down in the park; a pity about the park.
5–6	Go home.
6–7	Then it's time for the evening meal—noodles and semolina pudding.
7–8	Go to bed.

Accounts such as this daily schedule of a resident of Marienthal   **2.1**
helped to reinforce the idea of idleness in unemployment, as illustrated by the sentence "In the meantime midday comes around."
From Jahoda, Lazarsfeld, and Zeisel, *Marienthal*, 68.

The community already adapted to lack, as seen in Marienthal, has much less to fear from being excluded from capitalism. *Apathy*—and the charge of being passionless that forms this label—is used to problematize the population unwilling to normalize to the dictates of capitalism. In the later sections, I will cover how apathy is used to perversely justify an increase in emotional pain, such that pain can produce the "right" degree of distress to force the continued search for a job. But already visible are the outlines of a biopolitical project, where unemployed populations are to be differentiated between the normal and apathetic, where the latter are a threat to capitalism.

The link between emotional pain and unemployment is more complicated than it initially seems. While *Marienthal* and the Depression naturalized and reframed unemployment as a psychological phenomenon, another important aspect of unemployment is the social process of adaptation—the ability of people to live *with* the reduced circumstances of job loss rather than rebel against them. The state of psychological coping that results from long-term unemployment, surfacing as a calm mood, ironically forms the main problem of apathy, its contentment from adaptation resisting the rise of irascible affects that could motivate change. With this argument developed, a new scene comes into view. The mild outer signs of Marienthal—a community of people who have become contented sufferers of poverty, spending their days sitting at home, walking aimlessly, or standing on street corners attending to meaningless sounds—now stand as a facade that tells the true sickness of unemployment: the nearly invisible condition of apathy that leads to gradual, quiet ruin as the unemployed become unfit for life under capitalism.[56]

Orchestrated Unhappiness

We can now make sense of how unhappiness can be rationalized with unemployment. The legacy of *Marienthal* allows for the orchestration of unhappiness in unemployment while naturalizing it as an inevitable result of the employment norm. If apathy arises because unemployment is tolerable, then measures must be put in place to make the tolerable intolerable, such that the unemployed will take notice and seek to rectify their situation. Unhappiness can take form as a technology of governance, a variable calibrated to preemptively prevent apathy and to spur the unemployed into reemployment. At the same time, however, this approach to governance is suppressed, masked under the employment norm that makes the unemployed "naturally" unhappy.

We see this dynamic in a foundational article on happiness economics written by Bruno Frey and Alois Stutzer. After examining the voluminous literature on the topic, the authors argue for a strong connection between unemployment and unhappiness. Surveys, they write, have shown conclusively that "the self-proclaimed happiness of unemployed persons is *much* lower than employed persons." These results relate to what they claim to be the "pure" effect of unemployment, meaning that the association holds even after factors such as "income loss, as well as other indirect effects" on happiness are controlled for.[57] There are good reasons to mistrust this strong conclusion, given the variegated concerns in the measurement of happiness, the generalizability of results, and the difficulty of operationalizing the many "indirect effects" of unemployment.[58]

Yet a posed consensus can remain powerful even as it remains in doubt. In Frey and Stutzer's case, the commonsense assumptions about unhappy unemployment allow them to extend their proposition, suggesting that the causality could work in the inverse. Instead of having unemployment cause unhappiness, it may be that the unhappy struggle to stay employed: "Unhappy people do not perform well and get laid off. Happy persons are fitter for working life, which makes it less likely that they will lose their jobs."[59] This reasoning reveals how the sign of unemployment can form a heuristic that allows a range of toxic associations. As Sara Ahmed notes, "If we keep using one word with another word, the association between them becomes stronger. . . . Once an association has become strong, one word seems to follow, almost automatically, the other."[60] We can pull this *unemployment* association along: if unemployment causes unhappiness, and if unhappiness makes one perform worse at a job, then prolonged unemployment can easily justify one's lack of suitability for work. The unhappiness caused by joblessness becomes that which explains the loss of employability for the unemployed. This association can be understood as *automatic*, a "natural" result of suppositions pieced together to suggest a logical conclusion.

Indeed, numerous studies on unemployment have described a bias both implicitly and explicitly directed toward the unemployed, exercised without reproach.[61] In random résumé studies, for instance, Kory Kroft and his colleagues found that callback rates from job advertisements decrease by about 4 to 7 percent with each month of unemployment.[62] After the sixth month, industry-relevant experience ceases to matter.[63] At that point, all applicants are pushed to the bottom of the barrel, rarely considered to have any valuable skills.[64]

It is tempting to chalk this up to an exercise in subjective discrimination by employers, but to do so would elide the ways that such discrimination is orchestrated to produce a culture of compulsory employment. I earlier described apathy as maladapted adaptation, a label assigned to those who are too well adapted to unemployment—those who, in surviving, have refused to consider the necessity of employment to their future well-being. In the late 1970s, economists began theorizing "optimal unemployment insurance" through those terms, seeking to preemptively manage what they called the "moral hazard" of unemployment insurance—a process where unemployment insurance benefits subsidize "unproductive leisure" and unintentionally promote adaptation to unemployment and its increased length.[65] Optimality in this context would seek to reduce "distortions" in the benefit system, offering protection for those who become unemployed through no fault of their own while ensuring that the unemployed are urged to find reemployment.[66] To ensure the latter, these economists offered that mechanisms underlying benefits systems must punish workers for continued unemployment. Even with unemployment insurance benefits, the jobless must rationally find it in their interest to head back to work.[67]

Suggestions for the design of unemployment insurance followed from this proposition. Economists Steven Shavell and Laurence Weiss proposed a payout scheme that initially starts higher but decreases over time, with the decreasing rates meant to drive a negative outlook to unemployment, bringing into consciousness a stronger threat of benefit loss that will be suffered if unemployment lengthens.[68] In like manner, J. S. Flemming suggests that mathematical models of unemployment insurance should ideally factor in the valuation of leisure.[69] If leisure is seen to be more valuable than consumption, then a delay of the job search would be incentivized—people would be happier with the increase in free time compared to the partial loss of purchasing power. Studies that follow in this line expand into a panoply of factors—for instance, the effects of monitoring on search efforts, taxes on the wages of the reemployed, and the liquidity of consumption—to refine models based on utility, ensuring that reemployment would continue to be made more attractive than unemployment.[70]

Notice how the "rational" behavior of reemployment is normatively enforced here with unhappiness. Any possible sign of happiness in unemployment (represented in contradiction to intended effects in mathematical models) needs to be *made* irrational and transient through the calibration of punishment. The greater the chance of a moral hazard, the more punishing unemployment needs to become. Optimality implies a condition of a "natural" drive toward reemployment, a rationale made airtight with the preemptive modulation of the large number of factors that could play into these decisions.[71] These efforts would then carry the consequence of suppressing the wage and reducing the bargaining power of workers. As economists recognized early on, minimizing insurance would depress the "reservation wage"—the minimum wage that the job applicant can accept for the job.[72] This happens because the more desperate workers are, the less picky they will be about their wages, and the faster they will find reemployment. Over a longer period, these policies would increase the capacity of firms to push wages down—a surplus pool of labor, constituted through a reserve army of the desperate unemployed, would give firms more leverage over worker pay.[73]

And while optimal unemployment insurance centers on policy governance, its effects easily extend into norms elsewhere. For example, economist Rand Ghayad has speculated that the coincidence of the drastic fall of callback rates for job advertisements and the termination of unemployment benefits—in the American system, at six months of unemployment—may relate to the terms of unemployment insurance. Since most workers would try hard to get a job before the termination of benefits, hirers would assume that those left behind are the least employable. Economic reasoning here substantiates the time sensitivity of reemployment, creating the conditions for discrimination that reinforces the pressurizing drive toward reemployment.[74] With these efforts, unemployment policies would intervene in the central concern of *Marienthal*: that unemployment had failed to provide the proper, corrective signaling to the jobless, making them calm and satisfied rather than motivated toward getting a new job to avoid the steady decline of their lives.

Misery in unemployment thus comes as a collaborative effort in worldmaking. Loosely distributed across the social field, it is made sensible through systemic obstacles that make life progressively harder for the unemployed. One effect is that the newly unemployed experience tremendous time pressure to find employment quickly. Not only do they have to struggle with income loss and the absence of healthcare benefits; knowing that their chances for reemployment will decrease over time also forces applicants to anxiously hurry in their search for jobs. Career guides even advise workers to start looking for jobs the moment they hear rumors of layoffs, so that they can capitalize on their employed status to negotiate for a better position.[75] Those unable to get back into the market quickly are recommended to find creative ways to disguise the conspicuous unemployment gap. Mary Gray and Siddharth Suri, for instance, have noticed that microwork platforms are sometimes strategically used by the unemployed to produce impressions of an independent, productive subject.[76] Similarly, the free work of volunteering may be picked up to produce a narrative that can explain away the stigma of "unproductive" unemployment spells.[77] We can see here how exploitation is substantiated by the loss of bargaining power that unemployment culture forces workers into.

But as problematic as these practices are, they are predicated on subjects assumed to be rational. Rational choice theory assumes a calculating subject, someone who can be driven to act based on utility produced through incentives and disincentives.[78] This is a population that can be mathematically modeled and hypothetically driven into action. This assumption, however, does not work for the apathetic, whose motivational structure is deemed incomprehensible. For this "irrational" population, the argument of governance would take a much more painful and coercive tone.

We see this development raised in the second relationship that Frey and Stutzer pose with unemployment. Here, they argue that unemployment affects the happiness of not only the unemployed themselves but the general citizenry; people can become unhappy with higher unemployment rates even if they are not themselves out of work.[79] In this second instance, unemployment is positioned as a factor that unravels the good life that employment seems to foster: perceptions of job security, a good economy, appropriate use of tax contributions, and low crime. A shared horizon of the good life can create a collective moral principle that aligns the interest of the individual with that of the community.[80] But this binding principle also puts pressure on the actions of individuals. If unemployment makes others unhappy, then the choice to remain unemployed would no longer remain personal—it would become a subject of public health and concern.

This proposition completes the leap that the "moral hazard" of optimal unemployment insurance did not do. It justifies the reduction of welfare for a population in need, significantly reducing their ability to collect benefits.[81] The withdrawal of the US Aid to Families with Dependent Children (AFDC) program in the welfare reform legislation of 1996 provides such an example. As Marisa Chappell notes, the AFDC program was primarily withdrawn on the grounds that it incentivized recipients, often nonwhite single mothers, to be lazy, dependent, and promiscuous.[82] This follows the long-standing "perversity thesis" that welfare had caused dependency instead of betterment.[83] Lawrence Mead, whose views were influential to the reform, argues that such programs encourage poverty, allowing the poor to behave in inappropriate ways without holding them accountable: "Although the poor feel defeated, society has allowed them ways to avoid functioning that other people lack. . . . It no longer tells the poor clearly what they are expected to do."[84] Welfare and its encouragement of "dependency," Mead charges, enable recipients to be psychologically unaligned from the right orientation toward work, threatening the good life of society at large.[85]

The derivatives of *apathy* used in this discourse—words such as *defeated*, *discouraged*, and *demoralized*—should remind us of the backdrop that passion serves with maladapted adaptation. Perhaps it is not that Mead expects the unemployed to be passionate about work. Nonetheless, passion forms the normative backdrop for the expectation of the "right" attitude: a concept of the active will. For Mead, as with the researchers of *Marienthal*, the problem with welfare is that unconditional handouts promote adaptation to poverty. Welfare recipients are permitted to be passive about work—to see it as voluntary rather than as a social obligation— which allows them to be apathetic and inconsiderate of general happiness, which in turn squanders taxpayer dollars.[86]

Hence, the solution would come in the shape of "tough love."[87] The Temporary Assistance for Needy Families (TANF) welfare program, which replaced AFDC, exercised cuts on the length of time that recipients can receive aid and imposed "workfare" stipulations, raising mandatory requirements for recipients to find work or to engage in job training. These stipulations were meant to replace the "dependent outlook" of the welfare recipient with the "self-interested, competitive conduct" that neoliberal happiness represents.[88] The problematic psychologies assumed of the welfare recipient can be observed from the nature of job training programs provided by TANF, which focus on psychological states as opposed to skills and education. As Sanford Schram remarks, "From the moment applicants first walk into a welfare office, the emphasis is on assessing them for personal problems that might prevent them from being 'job-ready.' The goal is to get recipients to change their behavior, change their psychological outlook, reduce their personal problems, make themselves not just more motivated but more attractive to employers. Less emphasis is given to assessing a recipient's need to enhance her employability through education and training."[89]

What appears to be a natural proposition—that unemployment causes unhappiness—can mask the efforts devoted to making a world where the unemployed are *kept* unhappy. We get the sense, in the case of TANF, how far this organization of unhappiness is willing to go. After all, those who fail to meet the requirements of welfare stipulations are not just chastised or warned. Under the pretext of curing their "defeatist" mentality, these subjects are allowed to die through the deprivation of nutrition, shelter, and medical aid.[90] Between 1990 and 2008, after the implementation of TANF, life expectancy for America's poorest people experienced one of its largest drops in history.[91] These examples reflect the work that apathy does: it can substantiate the rationale to let people die, to make the space of unemployment threatening to the point that it kills. Thus, thinking of unemployment as an alternative becomes increasingly hard. Given the very real threat to life, it is a lot to ask of people to experiment with alternatives, to carve out different spaces where the normative principles of work can be opposed.

Passion and Resilience

Theorizing from the threatening background of unemployment lends a different perspective to the role that passion plays in the employment process. It is well established that success in the American context of job hunting heavily depends on an interpersonal fit between the job applicant and the hiring manager.[92] But positioned within the cultural construction of unemployment, positivity becomes essential for distancing as much as for connection. If the unemployed are expected to be unhappy, then the performance of positivity is necessary to suggest a mental state free from the stains of unemployment. As the career columnist of the *Guardian* remarks, "being positive" while being "weighed down by the burden of unemployment" can be difficult, but it is "a vital pre-condition for your job search": "If you feel negative or unenthusiastic, it could come across when you meet people, and they won't buy you."[93] This statement highlights the paradox of unemployment. The more that unemployment is made to cause unhappiness to spur reemployment, the more effort the unemployed must put in to distance themselves from the unhappiness assumed of them.

In the following sections of this chapter, I examine a variety of career guides to show how the cultural rise of passion is connected to hiring processes.[94] In conveying the impression of an unassailable energeticity, the passionate job hunter also comes to embody a dauntless working subject who can rapidly shake off the damage of serialized unemployment and continue with productive activity without pause. This narrative creates distance from the damaged, despised model of personhood, a requirement that grows more important as unemployment becomes more damaging. Therefore, contrary to the critique that passion is fanciful and unrealistic, I highlight a cultural logic that reveals passion as absolutely pragmatic in its romanticism, an affect that promises transcendence of the vagaries of the unpredictable labor market.

Career guides are cultural artifacts well positioned to guide this inquiry. Typically written by career counselors and coaches, they are designed to school readers about the protocols of the job-hunting process.[95] They impart what is also known as "employability skills training," improving on the skills used to communicate one's worth to a prospective employer.[96] These involve competencies in the use of buzzwords, strategized responses to commonly asked questions, and a skilled presentation of positivity and enthusiasm. In other words, career guides allow us to see how subjects are made to contort themselves with the language that is expected by the job market and present themselves as holders of valuable labor power.[97]

We can begin with *What Color Is Your Parachute?*, considered one of the most influential career guides and an urtext of passion. First published in 1972, this text has been republished every year since with changes to its content. The author, Richard Nelson Bolles, was involved in annual revisions of the book until his death in 2017. After that, the annual revisions continued to be published under his name until the 2021 version, when career coach Katharine Brooks helped with editing and refreshing its content.

Elsewhere, I have explained how the different editions of the text have developed on the project of passionate self-discovery.[98] Throughout close to five decades of revisions, author Bolles refined one of the most elaborate instruments of the self-discovery of passion, which requires weeks, if not months, to contemplate and complete. Bolles assures us, however, that the time spent will be well invested. Upon completion, readers are promised knowledge of their "dream job," which will personally match the reader's unique interest in seven aspects—namely, their favorite transferable skills, forms of knowledge, working conditions, coworkers, salary range, place to live, and mission in life.[99]

What Color Is Your Parachute? was in the vanguard of this cultural trend in the genre when it was initially released.[100] At the time of its first publication, most guides were still focused on matching workers to jobs based on skills. It was Bolles who proselytized a more comprehensive approach, incorporating inner desires as a guide for careers.[101] In a 1983 preface, Bolles explained that passion provided an advantage by developing enthusiasm in the job seeker, cultivating the disposition that would enable one to leave the strongest impression on potential employers: "We know for a fact that the enthusiastic job-hunter is infinitely more likely to be the one who finds a job than the matter-of-fact job-hunter . . . particularly when jobs are scarce."[102] The "flower exercise"—an instrument he initially hesitated to put in the core of the text due to its length and hefty time requirement—would eventually be shifted from the appendix to the main text in 1987.[103] And by the 2000s, finding one's passion would be invoked as a literal job-hunting technique that netted at least an "86% success rate" of finding a job, far more effective than recommendations from friends (33 percent), the use of a job agency (5 to 28 percent), cold calls to small employers (47 percent), and answering job listings on the internet (4 percent).[104]

By 2013, however, Bolles expressed a different purpose for passion. The heavy drain of job hunting, he noted, had come to require a new degree of human tenaciousness that, in turn, demanded more "hope" from job hunters: "I learned that I can teach the most clever, unorthodox, and effective techniques, but a job-hunter can undo it all if they have the wrong attitude." A person "smoldering with anger" and "gloomy about his future" will find it hard to find a job, no matter how much he knows about job hunting.[105] So the task of a career guide is to convince readers in their hearts. *What Color Is Your Parachute?* is, ultimately, "a Book of Hope, masquerading as a job-finding manual," Bolles writes, and hope is best cultivated through the knowledge of passions, the fervent desire providing the inner fortitude to endure the challenges of job hunting: "Before your job-hunt may have felt more like a duty than anything else. Now, with your vision, you are dying to find *that*. So, you redouble your efforts, your dedication, and your determination when otherwise you might tire and give up. Persistence becomes your middle name, for a prize worth fighting for."[106]

This line of thought is, of course, not limited to Bolles's text. For example, in *Finding Your Career Path without Losing Your Mind*, Michal Fisher makes a similar point, explaining that passion can cultivate the "tenacity and determination" required to ensure that job hunters stay motivated through the job-hunting process. "Hidden dreams," she writes, are important in enabling subjects to "get up in the morning and continue to insist, to fight for yourself . . . in the face of setbacks, disappointments, and crises."[107] "The effort it takes to run a good job search is often much more intense than work itself," adds Jean Baur, the author of *Eliminated! Now What?*; only passion can ensure that job hunters will be affectively prepared for the onslaught of disappointment that will inevitably come with the rejections of job hunting.[108] The more daunting the hiring process is—with abusive hiring managers, capricious promises, and an interminable wait process—the more immediate the need for passionate resilience.[109]

We need to consider this agentic dimension of passion—how its energetic drive surfaces as a means to help job hunters endure the challenges of job hunting. In *The Vehement Passions*, Philip Fisher tells us that affects may be strategically deployed as blockages to preemptively intervene in events with emotional outcomes. Preemption implies an awareness of a pathway to affects, a logical sequencing that is tweaked beforehand, so that a different affective outcome emerges as a result. One example is "spiritedness," an affect that Philip Fisher counterposes with the "low spirits" of "grief, dejection, anxiety, despair."[110] We can see how this would apply to the rhetoric employed by Bolles. Instead of being depressed and depleted by rejections, job seekers can find excitement in passion, becoming enthusiastic hunters who can brush off failures and seize the chance to chart a new path to their careers.

Regardless of what passion actually does, it enables a new story to be told about the possibilities of unemployment. The word stirs the *imagining of a subject* who can have a diametrically different attitude about how unemployment "naturally" unfolds. Philip Fisher hints at this in his definition of spiritedness: "Within the term 'spirited' we *have to* imagine the combination of high energy, youthful freshness, capacity for delight, cheerfulness, confidence . . . as opposed to walking or standing motionless."[111] The words *have to* bring out certain imaginings and tendencies. In this case, the energetic nature of passion is imagined as filling a subject with the unbridled hope that can interrupt the immobilizing weight of unemployment.

Certainly, the romanticization of passionate resilience is a ruse of neoliberal culture. It emphasizes individual agency in economic hardship, placing the burden on the individual to adapt and flourish in an unsustainable labor market.[112] But even as a ruse, resilience does something uncanny to the brutality of neoliberal competitiveness: it makes damage disappear to encode an ability to inflict more. In *The New Way of the World*, Pierre Dardot and Christian Laval write that while capitalism historically has been designed to transform workers into commodities, this violence takes an intensified form in neoliberalism, where "individuals are rendered more capable of tolerating the new conditions created for them."Tolerance becomes a technology of reproduction, where the ability of individuals to endure produces a "chain reaction" of people competing more intensely, which produces an ever harsher environment.[113] Ahmed makes a similar point in *Living a Feminist Life*, noting that "resilience is the requirement to take more pressure; such that the pressure can be gradually increased."[114] The more one can bear, the more hardship one will ordinarily be expected to bear as a "natural" course of events. The role of career guides is to build this capacity for endurance, to teach job hunters "how to get up off the floor when they're knocked down by job loss," so that they can make invisible the damage of serialized unemployment.[115]

The heroism of self-reliance and grit constitutes one of the main tropes of such resilience building. In *Do Over*, for instance, Jon Acuff tackles the difficulty of job loss head-on by arguing that people are often misled into thinking that they need only to be resourceful and motivated when they apply for their first job. However, when jobs are a small part of a longer career trajectory, the "fear" that accompanies unemployment changes to become "not a dragon to be slain once" but "an ocean to be swum daily."[116] Career guides like these, including Martha Finney's *Rebound* and Dan Schawbel's *Promote Yourself*, normalize fears by flattering those who embrace and act on them.[117] Job hunters are named survivors and celebrated for their relentless persistence, capacities of self-reliance, and purposeful grit—terms that play into what Jennifer Silva calls the "mood economy," a neoliberal context which prizes narratives of self-transformation and emotional strength.[118] Consider the following description of *grit*: "Grit makes you feel like throwing up. Grit feels like crying. A lot. Grit feels like losing sleep. It's hard. Next time you feel like a coward because you're about to make a difficult decision and you feel like throwing up, don't beat yourself up. Next time you cry those tears that feel so stupid because you think brave people wouldn't, stop listening to that lie. Look at grit the right way. Grit never feels like bravery because it's not a feeling, it's a choice."[119]

This image of grit transforms the hardship of unemployment into a masculine narrative of overcoming, where abject somatic symptoms—crying, vomiting, and sleeplessness—become evidence of laudable perseverance rather than reactions to anxiety and despair. Such depictions of grit resonate with an endemic culture of overwork, which also tends to twist images of teeth-clenching hardship into celebrated accounts of human tenacity. Almost all career guides remind readers of the necessity of such inner strength: supply of labor has outstripped demand, and so the chances of landing a job depend on the extent to which job hunters are willing to show their enthusiasm and resilience.

This should remind us of Dardot and Laval's suggestion that resilience can endorse a toxic culture of competitiveness.[120] The popular career guide *Guerrilla Marketing for Job Hunters 3.0*, written by Jay Levinson and David Perry, shows us how far the metaphor of the hustle can go. In their view, the effort placed into job hunting needs to extend beyond the traditional work of self-discovery. Hunters need to adopt a "can-do attitude" and a "penchant for action" that are showcased through grueling "commando tactics" of job hunting, with strategies that include walking straight into offices unannounced, asking to speak to managers, sending résumés in a box with a coffee cup and then calling the manager persistently to ask for a coffee date, and, crucially, never accepting an answer of "no" to meetups so as to constantly find ways to get a face-to-face connection.[121] Teetering between desperation and harassment, these accounts demonstrate how extreme forms of enthusiasm also make one vulnerable to humiliation. The requirement to persistently knock on doors and intrusively speak to strangers necessitates a subject who is willing to risk being dismissed, shamed, and demeaned, all for a chance to look "passionate" to employers. With a burgeoning reserve army of the unemployed, however, such displays of awkwardness are deemed compulsory—a necessity for the desperate who need to outshine the many other competitors for a job.

Competitive Passion

This relentless drive to compare and trump others sets the tone for a neoliberal culture of competitiveness. In *Self-Help, Inc.*, Micki McGee explains that a survivalist narrative crept into self-improvement literature in the 1970s as the recession made metaphors of surviving especially culturally relevant.[122] Readers were taught to see life as a battle in which they are contestants, and the objective is to win by beating others to the prize. This trend continues in career guides today, with passion substantiating this narrative by affirming that winning is ultimately possible and that there will be a job out there despite economic circumstances: all it takes is the cultivation of exuberance, resilience, and determination to beat others to the position.

In this section, I look to the role that digital technologies play in sustaining this imaginary by examining another long-standing job-hunting series, *Knock 'em Dead,* a best seller that has been written and revised yearly by Martin Yate since 1985. Unlike *What Color Is Your Parachute?*, which emphasizes passionate self-discovery, *Knock 'em Dead* focuses on the traditional components of the job hunt: strategies for résumés, interviews, job selection, and so on. *Knock 'em Dead* is not necessarily the most innovative or comprehensive "digital" job guide—a contemporary niche that has been populated with titles such as *The Power Formula for LinkedIn Success, Maximum Success with LinkedIn*, and *The 2-Hour Job Search*—but its many yearly revisions provide material to understand how technologies have changed the discourse on job hunting.

The instrumentality of technology to job hunting is seen in the earliest (1985) version of the text, when Yate instructs readers to leverage library books as they apply for jobs. Most job hunters, he laments, believe that looking for a job simply involves responding to a newspaper advertisement, but this approach is ineffective because "there are always well-qualified people looking for the best jobs."[123] To clinch the position, job hunters need to demonstrate self-initiative, to present themselves as the "best prepared" candidate by going through reference books in libraries to learn all about the company's services and products.[124] Yate makes clear that job hunting is fundamentally a competitive endeavor. Mastery in the skills of self-presentation is crucial, because there are always qualified applicants around and the chances of landing a job hinge on the marginal advantage that can set one apart.

Thus, it is not surprising that the internet was originally perceived through this lens, as a tool to empower job hunters to get an advantage over rival candidates. In the 1994 edition of *Knock 'em Dead*, Yate enthusiastically introduces the "electronic job hunt" as the "new weapon in your arsenal" and provides several optimistic suggestions for how the technology can be of significant help.[125] For instance, he is excited about the potential of electronic classifieds, not only because they constitute a large job database but also because the electronic format affords a more comprehensive description of job requirements. Job hunters can thus "customize paperwork and focus [their] expertise in the appropriate direction" and gain a "substantial edge" over applicants who respond to traditional newspaper ads.[126]

His greatest enthusiasm is reserved for database services that can consolidate massive information about a company on short notice. He offers the example of calling a database service before an interview with the 3M megacorporation. With just a quick query over the phone, a "truly remarkable" amount of information can be faxed to the applicant, including "over fifteen pages of data providing a complete overview of 3M from its inception to the present day." All this additional data would give the job candidate a substantive edge. It would be made "blindingly obvious at the interview," Yate offers, "that you were twice as sharp as any other applicant." He adds, "In a tightly run job race, being able to ace the 'What do you know about us?' question could make all the differences [sic]. On-line services can often yield more detailed information about a specific company than you'd ever imagined impossible."[127]

Yet the edge that the internet provided initially would diminish in subsequent years as personal computers became widely available. In fact, by 2000, Yate had significantly curbed his enthusiasm for the technology, leaving only a short section on electronic job hunting in the main text. He even cautioned job hunters about being too dependent on the internet. "Use this amazing new tool to stack the odds in your favor," he writes, "yet despite all its allure and promise do not rely on the Internet exclusively." Yate is responding here to the technological capabilities that allow applicants to "send [their] resume to thousands of employers and headhunters in thirty minutes."[128] Ironically, the efficiency of online job hunting has made electronic applications increasingly unreliable for getting a job. As the number of electronic applications has grown, the likelihood that a résumé will be read and considered without some other factor involved has diminished.

However, though Yate appears to become less enthusiastic about the internet, he does not advocate a move away from digital technologies. His ambivalence, I suggest, relates to his recognition that digital culture is starting to structure a different performance of professional identity. Here, it becomes helpful to look beyond Yate. The ease of submitting applications via the internet has made professional networks more important, since a recommendation from someone in the organization becomes more significant as the number of applicants to a job increases. Many contemporary guides recommend the networking platform LinkedIn, offering that it constitutes one of the best ways to network and expand professional contacts. A large network will render job hunters more visible to LinkedIn search algorithms and provide leads, connections to the company that can increase the chance of being hired. LinkedIn guides assist in this process by tapping into the features of the platform—its recommendations, connections, and search engine algorithms—to teach users to transform and boost their professional contacts to at least the high double digits, the magic number that coaches say will make connections useful.[129]

But again, as we see with the early uses of the internet, the normalization of a job-hunting practice steadily erodes its utility. If job hunting is about proving yourself superior to others, then a normalized practice makes you only "average" and no longer provides the edge that success requires. We see this invoked in the recent career guide *Superconnector*, which begins its pitch by proclaiming the death of "networking" and states that "our more-is-more, networking-for-networking's-sake approach to social media, conference attendance, and, yes, even daily human interaction has bastardized this once reliable pillar of business success into a mere mirage."[130] This development is substantiated by business professor Adam Grant, who writes in the popular text *Give and Take* that the term *networking* has taken on a "negative connotation" and communicates a "faker style" method of knowing someone, giving an impression that is more likely to be seen as duplicitous and self-serving than earnest and sincere.[131]

To be sure, networking has never truly been premised on the sincerity of professional relations. As a genre, networking guides both before and after the advent of social media traditionally focused on the perceptual transformation of human relationships, coaching readers to see a much broader definition of who constitutes a "professional contact." Keith Ferrazzi, writer of the best-selling networking text *Never Eat Alone*, has suggested that most untrained readers would visualize their "relationship garden" as "a tiny parcel of cleanly cut grass," filled with immediate friends, coworkers, and business partners. To make networking useful, however, the garden needs to be imagined instead as an "overgrown jungle with an infinite variety of hidden nooks." Acquaintances of friends and of siblings should be considered potential professional networking targets, along with strangers from gyms and churches.[132] The goal is to make readers see a much broader landscape of professional resources that they can tap into.

But the usefulness of these connections would also decline as social networking sites made distant contacts easier to establish and therefore commonplace and less useful for making a claim of competitive difference. To stand out, more must be done. Hence, as Grant explains, distant connections can be effective only if they are invested with affect. In particular, readers would be advised to be "giving," seeking to help others with their passions and to genuinely wish for their success, so that they could set themselves apart from the numerous others who were just selfishly "taking" or using others for their own gain. Books endorsing this approach to connecting offered different anecdotes of altruistic labor: the generous offering of time to give others advice; the willingness to do favors for others, even against one's personal interest; and the readiness to connect someone newly met to another person whom one thinks might help.[133]

Do this enough, Grant promises, and you will realize the potential of the "reciprocity ring," where enough people indebted to you try to improve your situation in some minor way, making it appear as if the world is plotting your success with ambient goodwill.

Many gurus of networking support this view by citing the "strength of weak ties," a phrase popularized by sociologist Mark Granovetter in his landmark 1973 paper, which proposes that most jobs come not from strong ties—friends or relatives—but from weak ones, since they are more numerous and allow for a more efficient gathering of information from diverse sources.[134] This makes sense. The more connections you have, the more likely you are to have a link to a job somewhere, and therefore the more likely it is that an opportunity will land in your lap. But the competitive employment process steadily changed the meaning of *weak tie*. If the term refers to an acquaintance—someone whom you know but have not really interacted with, in an age of social media when acquaintances abound— investing in your weak ties with more passion is necessary to get them to remember *you*. As Grant repeatedly writes, such advice for altruism is not meant to create "pushovers" or "doormats"; it is meant to make you stand out, to help with your own interest so that an opportunity can be passed on to you.[135] To achieve this, weak ties must be made "dormant," in Grant's parlance, having a background of potentialized affect because of the favors that had been provided before.[136]

But there is something else worth noting about weak ties. Developments on this proposition have shown that the strength of weak ties is not uniformly distributed. As Granovetter himself pointed out a decade after the initial paper, the supposition that weak ties are professionally useful is more applicable for the educated than the uneducated.[137] The value of one's initial social position is an important factor in determining the value of weak ties. The higher your standing, the more that weak ties matter. In fact, subsequent research would suggest that relying on weak ties tends to make one worse off the further down the social ladder we go—women, Black people, the poor, and the uneducated either receive lower salaries or find it harder to get employed if they rely on weak ties.[138] This discovery leads Granovetter to conclude that the weak ties principle tends to lead to achievement "only insofar as the weak ties connect the respondent to an individual who is well placed in the occupational structure."[139]

An early draft of Granovetter's landmark article, "The Strength of Weak Ties," begins with the words "Alienation Reconsidered." In line with his sociological background, he initially intended to highlight the possibility of creating a more vibrant civic life by having people of different social statuses interact. He cites early diffusion studies, which highlight the benefits that those of status can receive from associating themselves, even weakly, with those whom Granovetter refers to as the more "marginal" members of society.[140] These marginal members, having less pressure to conform to norms, can begin a trend that eventually gets picked up by those who have stronger professional reputations to protect, the latter being able to reciprocate by providing those marginal members with status.

Quite clearly, the use of weak ties has transformed with business rhetoric, and the emphasis on passion in networking ensures that weak ties are more likely to consist of subjects of similar rather than disparate backgrounds. This point is related to the thin ways that altruism is conceptualized in networking texts. Since the demand to be giving comes with the demand to be efficient—according to Grant's rule book, favors should, ideally, take no more than five minutes—helping others with their passions cannot come with a blank consideration of one's own passions.[141] As Gerber and Paugh note in *Superconnector*, knowing yourself is key. You can help someone with their passions quickly, efficiently, only if they share your own passions to some extent. And so, even with the best intentions, passion becomes a table around which the similar gather; the gathering "coincidentally" gets people of similar statuses and interests together.

But the story of hustle and grit remains. The reminder that weak ties are not all equal is not meant to discourage. Instead, this knowledge is meant to empower us to direct our passions toward finding and knowing people of status. Career guides would help with this by offering "hacks" to game the system of inborn status disadvantage. One guide offers what it calls the X-ray search, a technique using Boolean operators on the Google search engine to crawl for public profiles on LinkedIn that one would otherwise be blocked from.[142] Steve Dalton would go on to suggest that readers be creative in contacting these high-status individuals, searching for recent articles written by them and then disguising the cold call as "fan mail," expressing interest in the article and then asking to have a more personal chat about it.[143] Passions and technological competencies here form the solution to structural impediments. As with the "commando tactics" spoken of earlier, winning is made dependent on passion—the hunger and willingness to do all it takes to establish a connection with a high-status individual whom one is not born to connect with.

When does a method of empowerment become part of compulsory promotional labor? Colin Cremin writes that the power of employability lies in its fantasy of unachievable self-mastery.[144] The injunction to be employable is so speculative and ambiguous that it is fundamentally unachievable; we have some hints as to how one can be employable, but even these are just signs and never a guarantee of an employable self. Still, given how this projected ideal is rooted in doable practices—one is promised to be more employable through a better résumé, a more skillful presentation of the self, and so on—it does drive individuals to constantly prove themselves as employable subjects. Or more simply, the relationship between desire and the impossibility of its fulfillment is one of "productive failure," because it entices subjects to reattach themselves to the fantasy even as they encounter disappointment with its promise.[145]

The continuous attempt to network and brand oneself may demonstrate one's professionalism and convey the valued attributes of passion. However, it also happens in a context where others are demanded to do the same. Thus, if employability is not an absolute standard but a relative one, it is logical to ask: Where does the need for more branding and networking end? The internet obfuscates this need for heightened labor by providing a vision of empowerment. Workers who fail to find a job are given diagnoses in specific terms: a network that is too small or too shallow, carelessness in curating one's image online, lack of understanding of how one might tap into digital networks, and so on. This reasoning strokes the ego, animates the process of "productive failure," and directs attention away from the impossibility of employability. Further, because figures of success are always culturally available, the common condition of precarity is overlaid by a desire for domination; one is more likely to tap into a discourse on deservingness by highlighting one's relative employability than to collectively come into an understanding of how employability is an untenable target.[146]

Buffer Zones

We can take a different tack by considering what resilience screens: the background work and infrastructures that resilience narratives put in place for the damage of serialized unemployment to disappear. In "Selfcare as Warfare," Ahmed reflects on what she calls "buffer zones," the ways that privilege reduces the costs of vulnerability so that failure is cushioned and breakdown cared for. The buffer found in privilege appears in *The Gift of Job Loss*, for example, where readers are exhorted to see layoffs as opportunities to head for a "dream vacation," "learn a new language," or "spend real quality time" with a loved one.[147] Of course, happy activities like these would help recover enthusiasm for the job search, but they uniformly rely on a buffer: to take time away from work is already a privilege, an indication that one has savings that can make up for the loss of immediate income; to make bonding time out of layoffs suggests that social relationships are not taxed by the absence of income.

Still, the absence of privilege is not exempt from expectations of endurance. Even where privilege is lacking, one is still expected to "properly" assimilate damage without outward signs of harm. This requirement is observed from the very scenes of layoffs where readers are reminded to avoid making impulsive decisions that could harm prospects of future employment. As *Rebound* warns, "Lashing out in a personally insulting or an out-of-control way will make enemies of the very people you will want to have in your corner as you move forward in your career."[148] Resilience here implies an outward display of what another text calls "dignity," leaving the workplace undisturbed as the laid-off take the burden of resolving negative emotions privately.[149]

But how do people manage to maintain a calm facade? This question is especially applicable to those who lack privilege, whose layoffs are not simply a chance for a job change or a break but are also a major financial crisis that will put their families and themselves in jeopardy. We can track the damage of serialized unemployment by considering the practices used to modulate such damage. Readers of *Rebound*, for instance, are advised to "find one short word or a quick phrase that you can focus on, such as 'my family comes first' or 'I'm okay,'" and to repeat it, "preferably silently," as they are escorted to their desk. "By the time you take your seat," author Finney assures, "you may not be okay, but at least you'll be calm."[150] For those who have mortgages to service or children to feed, the reassuring hum of "I'm okay" may be the only buffer holding things together. These techniques can stitch a performance of normalcy, even when someone is *not* okay.

It may come as no surprise, therefore, that YouTube hosts a large archive of layoff confessional videos shot in the interiors of cars and homes, which are the first private zones people come to immediately after being laid off. There, the facade of calm collapses, and we witness the raw costs of serialized unemployment. The footage typically shows intimate scenes of people speaking, ranting, and weeping as they decry the unfairness of the situation and voice their desperation and fears for the future. And yet, even as public performances, this minor genre remains largely private. Often receiving only a handful of views each, the unedited videos are meant as backstage performances. Strategically working against the algorithms of searches and categories, they are designed to observe the norm of how the negativity of unemployment ought to be assimilated: privately, away from public address that allows any traces back to their personal identity.

In this sense, layoff vlogs show not only how resilience can mask a common condition of damage; they also suggest the very thin buffers that some people have. For those without privilege, the anonymous social media crowds of YouTube may be one of the few sites to offer a listening ear. We see a similar buffer enacted in *The Panic Free Job Search*, where readers are warned about the "energy-sapping emotions" that come with job loss. To transform negativity to confidence, author Paul Hill teaches readers a technique of visualization: they are to recall a successful moment and "anchor" it "by making a physical move . . . as well as screaming out a word that feels powerful." This action is to be repeated over and over, revving up in momentum until readers get into a "peak state," where the "speed and exuberance" of the action can be carried over into daily routines of the job hunt.[151]

This technique, though extreme, is not atypical of the general arc of advice found in career guides. *The Job Search Solution* advises readers to get rid of "garbage emotions" by visualizing scenes of their frustration, disappointment, and shock "up close and in color," playing them over and over in their mind until the emotions are "neutralized."[152] Other advice includes taking Prozac for anxiety, mindfully breathing fears away, using the gym for baths and television when electric bills go unpaid, and surrounding oneself with inspirational messages to prevent doubt from creeping in.[153] We can see why these suggestions might be useful: anxiety-ridden states can be temporarily covered and replaced by stronger affects that can conform to the normative schemes of endurance expected of job hunters.

Discursively, the focus on the unemployed subject appears to locate emotional labor solely in the job-hunting individual. Yet, a careful read of career guides shows that this is rarely the case: the infrastructure that buffers unemployment extends into the larger society, recruiting family, friends, relatives, and strangers, even as resilience is typically made a matter of personal overcoming. *Keeping Your Head after Losing Your Job*, for instance, includes sections where author Robert Leahy directly addresses the reader's family, outlining strategies they can use to help the recovery of the laid-off. Those close to the unemployed are advised to be more patient, to offer a listening ear, and to leave notes of encouragement: "Catch your partner being good. . . . Write it down, put it on a piece of paper on the fridge door, and tell them how happy you are to see them doing these things."[154] For Leahy, as for other authors, overcoming unemployment is a matter of "shared responsibilities."[155] Reemployment is a process where everyone should chip in to offer support.

Implicit in this background is the expectation of a supportive network of family and friends, people who are nonjudgmental and who can cheer the job hunter on. This role comes as a normative expectation. *New York Times* career columnist Rob Walker explains that it is not uncommon for spouses to hire career coaches for their laid-off partners, so that they can still appear supportive and not sound like they are "nagging" them to get a job.[156] Family and friends must withhold words that can harm the recuperation of those who are laid off. "The nagging theory of motivation . . . will simply create more problems," Leahy writes, going on to explain the futility of grousing about the hardship that the family comes under when someone gets laid off. "Certainly you have a right to complain," he writes, and to chasten the unsupportive partner, "but will it really help anything? . . . Will your partner get a better job because you are complaining?"[157]

Construing the social as a buffer, therefore, involves transforming the social. Not only are family members and friends taught how to offer support; job hunters themselves are told to treat their social circles as resources, to approach them for help, and to distance themselves from those who would spoil a positive mentality. For instance, *The Proximity Principle* instructs readers to disregard the negative opinions that their family members may have about their passions. Families are meant to support individuals in their passionate decisions, the book suggests, not hinder them from reaching for those dreams.[158] *Getting Unstuck* goes further by instructing readers to visualize their family members and reject the criticisms that they have of the readers' passions. Cautions about pursuing a passion are seen as an impediment to self-actualization, a problem that readers must systematically erase from their psyche because too many people, author Timothy Butler writes, subconsciously try to finish the "unfinished business" of family members rather than seek their own "authentic voice."[159] And so, part of the work involved in becoming passionate means transforming families to be channels of support rather than of fear and discouragement.

This logic also applies to circles of friends. *Do Over* warns readers to distance themselves from discouraging friends who are "actively working against your dream," while another guide recommends avoiding those who inspire a "fear of desire" and a hesitation about going for one's passion.[160] *Guerrilla Marketing for Job Hunters 3.0* tells us to evaluate friends based on the kinds of support they provide. Friends who are too "eager to commiserate" with the hardship of unemployment might hinder the development of the "tough mindset," since too much sympathy can "sap away your energy and self-esteem."[161] A tough approach to such friends is advised: speak to them honestly about their negative impact, and if they agree to change, "spend at least two weeks apart to . . . diminish psychological dependency" and have a "trial period" which "consists of pass-or-fail criteria."[162]

The infrastructures that lend themselves to a buffer come from a broad array of objects. They thread through privilege but also combine everyday techniques and the social sphere to ensure that passionate resilience is maintained in a condition of attrition and ordinary exclusion. This point reveals what can go missing under the broader framework of neoliberal employability, a concept that focuses on the entrepreneurial efforts of the worker. Modern notions of employability, Chertkovskaya and colleagues write, position governments and organizations as "enablers" that provide the backdrop for workers to make their own choices about the best ways to be employable.[163] But organizations and governments are not the only agents of this backdrop—the entire society is recruited into this process. Family, friends, and even strangers are cajoled, advised, incentivized, and disciplined into becoming sources of support. The colonization of the social reveals precisely how fragile resilience is. Structural damage cannot just disappear through willpower alone. It requires a collaborative effort to keep passionate resilience a viable performance.

The Paradox of Passion

In *The Problem with Work*, Kathi Weeks describes work as an ideology, a means by which people become assimilated into economic, political, and familial systems. Through this process, work becomes not just waged labor but a "requirement," a "system," and, indeed, "a way of life."[164] In this chapter, I have focused on how the desiring subject constitutes a component of this system. Apathy is seen as dangerous precisely because it troubles the proper functioning of this system. It challenges a normative productivist order, creating subjects that resist purposing by capital. Read then as morally hazardous and threatening to the happiness of society, apathy permits the increased hardship of unemployment. In this scheme, the withdrawal of welfare no longer represents an act of cruelty; instead, it is merely a technique to rehabilitate workers back into conventions of the healthy will, a will for reentry into the labor market.

If apathy is pathologized as a maladapted adaptive process of unemployment, then passionate resilience constitutes its opposite, becoming a way in which workers are adapted to precisely what refuses bodily adaptation. Through resilience, cold sweat, nausea, migraines, and panic attacks are seen as ordinary accounts of working life—symptoms that subjects and their social networks ought to help assimilate and endure, so that they appear no more than something to be brushed off or used for the narrative of grit and overcoming. Passionate resilience, in other words, makes normal the symptoms of damage by conjuring impressions of a subject that can endlessly be purposed for capital and contorted to whichever productive regime is considered dominant and in need of her labor.[165]

Are all career guides devoid of skepticism about passion? We can find several that are not. Cal Newport's *So Good They Can't Ignore You* warns against the kinds of frivolous passions that encourage people to leave their jobs just because they are unhappy. Acuff's *Quitter* and Kerry Hannon's *Love Your Job* teach readers to like their jobs—to see that passion is sometimes impossible to achieve and can be compromised with jobs good enough to be liked. Timothy Ferriss takes a different tack in *The Four-Hour Workweek* by telling readers to ensure passionate conditions for life rather than work. By undertaking strategies to free up time, workers can enjoy their lives without necessarily working the hours expected of a devoted career.

Career guides that criticize passion yet lead readers back to work as a site of optimism showcase the deep ambivalence that lies at the heart of even antipassion discourses. Since passion includes complex degrees of meaning, career guides can afford to distrust it while maintaining some proximity to it. The poverty in counterdiscourses of passion shows how it acts as an affective structure. We may believe in passion without physically experiencing it; we may also seek it while being cynical about it. Passion cycles through a variety of possibilities, promising that wrong desires can be made good by being attached to better, more authentic ones. In this way, passion accepts a variety of positions without requiring a fundamental change in the structural inequalities that constitute our everyday lives.

We can see why passion functions as a problematic affective structure that has come to normalize employment and legitimate an increasingly punishing culture of both hiring and firing. Passion has rendered a space where damage becomes serialized and intensified, where the burden of handling its recovery is outsourced to the social, and where damage is forced to disappear. As damage is made invisible, protests for change slacken and are diverted into self-reliance instead. These are systemic efforts at maintaining an unsustainable environment of ever-increasing self-mastery, in which resilience is encoded as the capacity to take on more pressure and where alternatives are removed from view.

Still, we need not assume that this has to be the way things are. Just as Peter Fleming finds hope in the levels of disengagement reflected in Gallup polls, I see optimism in apathy.[166] The pathologization of apathy and the effort of economists to make unemployment painful show how fragile the norm of employment is. Adaptation to unemployment is so natural that it actually takes significant effort for it to be made unnatural through financial disincentives and cultural norms. What this shows, however, are the stakes of passionate work as a politics. Passionate work is not simply centered on the extraction of labor power; it is also a crucial process in inhibiting certain forms of life. Apathy, or the unhappy adaptation to a life without work, is this kernel of possibility that we need to reclaim.

3

The Compassionate Imagination

Poor fellow! thought I, he means no mischief; it is plain he intends no insolence; his aspect sufficiently evinces that his eccentricities are involuntary. He is useful to me. I can get along with him. If I turn him away, the chances are he will fall in with some less indulgent employer, and then he will be rudely treated, and perhaps driven forth miserably to starve.... But this mood was not invariable with me. The passiveness of Bartleby sometimes irritated me. I felt strangely goaded on to encounter him in new opposition, to elicit some angry spark from him answerable to my own.

Herman Melville, *Bartleby, the Scrivener* (1853)

The absence of passion may be cause for compassion if it forecloses possibilities to the good life. Authors Byron Reeves and J. Leighton Read conjure a sympathetic scenario in their gamification text, *Total Engagement,* with the tale of Jennifer, a call center worker who holds a "tough but typical information job."[1] Jennifer comes into the company optimistic and driven, ready to perform well to get a promotion. Yet, over the next couple of months, she becomes steadily demoralized by the poor working conditions. Readers are presented with a familiar litany of corporate indignities: Jennifer's supervisors leave her unprotected from the abuse of irate callers and monitor her lunch hour down to the minute. Her work is stressful and her colleagues too demoralized to offer support. As the story unfolds, it becomes apparent that Jennifer is not meant to succeed. The company sees her as being of low value and dispensable, and it has no interest in investing in her future.

For Reeves and Read, these unhappy clichés relate to a long-standing structural injustice, where dehumanizing conditions inhibit workers from reaching their potential. At the heart of the story rests an ethical imperative: Doesn't everyone deserve an environment that lets them do well? For this *Total Engagement* presents a different possibility. In the new scenario, Jennifer begins her workday by logging into a gamified system where she is greeted by a personal avatar, assigned a team, and shown the game setting for the week: a pirate ship. The software converts her job performance into points in real time, which adjust the speed with which the pirate ship moves. Jennifer is excited because she knows that the faster she moves up to the next levels, the sooner she will be promoted to her "dream job," as an agent soliciting proposals for her company's charitable foundation.[2] Motivated, she reaches out to an underperforming team member and coaches him to do better, hoping to land a better team score. And when the ship is first to arrive on an island, she is told that she has won a real-life reward for her hard work: a vacation fully paid for by the company. In this new scenario, Jennifer is not hindered by the nature or value of her work. With the help of game design, she is able to experience passion in her job and earn the tangible rewards of it.[3]

The corporate drama depicts the utopian implementation of what industry practitioners have called "gamification," a trend defined by the use of game mechanics to effect behavioral change.[4] By tracking and translating performance into points, awarding badges for small tasks, providing levels as feedback, encouraging competitiveness through leaderboards, and incentivizing tasks through rewards, gamified interfaces purport to be able to increase the motivation of their users in a variety of settings, ranging from fitness to education and from employee engagement to brand engagement.[5]

While there are multiple threads to the beginnings of gamification, the crucial factors in its ascent took place in February 2010, when Jesse Schell spoke at the Design, Innovate, Communicate, Entertain (DICE) conference, describing a future where games are incorporated into everyday smart gadgets.[6] As illustration, he used a gamified toothbrush, an ordinary household item that had been outfitted to calibrate points based on the habits of oral hygiene. While Schell spoke, an image of a toothbrush was projected behind him, flashing as points were chalked up—the strange combination hinting at the possibility of things that could be made game-like. The same month, Jane McGonigal's TED talk, "Gaming Can Make a Better World," reinforced this vision.[7] McGonigal, the director of game research and development at the Institute for the Future, spoke to thunderous applause about how games could bring about "the best version of ourselves." In a book published in 2011, McGonigal argued that "reality is broken," because "reality doesn't motivate us as effectively"; it is neither "engineered to maximize our potential" nor "designed from the bottom up to make us happy."[8]

Arguing against Johan Huizinga, who emphasizes frivolity and innocence in play, McGonigal sees the potential in games to produce real-world consequences, to achieve goals and outcomes.[9] Thus, the link between games and passion is made explicit: games can engineer zeal for overcoming challenges, whether for self-gain or for the improvement of community and society. "In our real lives, hard work is too often something we do because we have to do it," McGonigal relates, but if hard work could be structured to be as satisfying as games, then such work would no longer feel hard: "What a boost to global net happiness it would be if we could positively activate the minds and bodies of hundreds of millions of people by offering them better hard work."[10] This trend would be normalized in the years to come, producing conferences, a module on Coursera that would attract tens of thousands of students each enrollment, and a multibillion-dollar technology and consulting industry with effects registered in companies such as Uber, Lyft, and TaskRabbit.[11]

Game Thinking and the Human Will

In this chapter, I examine the relationship between compassion and passion and the politics involved in recovering the good life—for those traditionally excluded from its boundaries—through gamification. To be clear, I am not implying that gamification is intended for benevolence. The valuation of the gamification industry—more than $5 billion in 2018—is largely driven by what Shoshana Zuboff has called "surveillance capitalism," the potential of technologies to fluidly monitor and modify human behavior for oversight and profits.[12] Gamified systems are valued for their capacities of soft control—their ability to nudge consumers, workers, and citizens toward voluntary behaviors desired by companies and governments. For example, gig drivers may be encouraged by milestones, quests, and dynamic surge pricing features to drive longer, to hit a certain mileage, or to drive within specific spatial parameters.[13] A responsive interface that provides timely prompts to guide workers to the next task—a gamified feature of Amazon Mechanical Turk—can also instigate workers toward repeated acts of piecemeal labor.[14] Far from being compassionate, gamification is often read as an instrument that leverages exploitable human tendencies, as a "mind hack" that interferes with critical faculties, and as a distortion that robs games of meaning and promotes norms of corporate and governmental order against open possibility and resistance.[15]

From this perspective, it is tempting to dismiss gamification as yet another duplicitous corporate initiative—and that would not be entirely mistaken. The reformative fantasy of play has a long history, one that Hannah Arendt traces back to F. Nitti's thesis in 1895, which expressed that the pain of labor "is a psychological rather than a physiological fact."[16] Still, I offer that gamification remains important because it illustrates how passion can function as a means of transposition, allowing a privileged community to imagine a condition of rescue for workers trapped in hopeless, unhappy circumstances. More than self-serving rhetoric, compassionate narratives of gamification reveal the bargain involved in transformative passion— the politics that constitutes the affective structure of passion, especially when privileged communities imagine a condition of affective rescue.

I begin my assessment of gamification in those terms, thinking of its benevolence as an instrument of governance, a means to help those left out of the circumstances of the will necessary to the good life. The human will, Sara Ahmed offers, is an object of experienced intention and desire: "To will is to put one's energy into becoming accomplished in this way or that. This sense of the will as *energetic*, as getting the body 'behind' an action is important."[17] The previous chapter discusses how management texts struggle over rights to voice the true wants of workers, tying wrong wants to weak and wrong wills. An apathetic worker, who is uninterested in finding passion in his work, is presented as a worker with a defective will: one oriented wrongly toward the optimistic possibilities of the good life. However, what happens in situations where "right" intentions exist, where workers will "correctly," intending to do well in their jobs and to achieve the good life through their efforts, but institutional configurations are at odds with the realization of these intentions? Here, the problem is not so much about a right or wrong will; instead, the situation of work itself is too trying for the energetic dimension of the will to be sustained.

The example of Jennifer raised in *Total Engagement* is unexceptional in that regard. The desperate subjects of bad work whom gamification promises to help include Target cashiers, assembly line workers, McDonald's servers, and Starbucks counter employees.[18] In these situations, gamification is praised for its ability to transform the experience of banal, mind-numbing work. For instance, in her article for *Fast Company*, Lydia Dishman uses provocative terms to describe the work of traditional call center employees, referring to them as "digital slaves" performing "soul-sucking" work for a "minimum wage."[19] But gamification, she suggests, can help "call center employees not hate their job" and even radically make these unhappy jobs enjoyable. Gabe Zichermann and Joselin Linder explain how a simple game can inject fun into the repetitive work of Target cashiers. The Target Checkout Game, as it is colloquially known, flashes G or R on the checkout screen, depending on the amount of time that passes between each item scan. Such game mechanics, Zichermann and Linder continue, give "people doing a repetitive job a sense of control," allowing them to recover their sense of "agency . . . the belief you are in control of your destiny."[20]

Certainly, there are many problems with these accounts, but the compassionate terms of the narrative are generative. To take one example: in a blog post, Andrzej Marczewski criticizes detractors who describe gamification as being "manipulative." While he admits that gamification influences behavior, he insists that its manipulation is of the "benign" variety. He writes, "If we are honest, very few jobs are meaningful," but gamification creates "more efficiency, better work environments, better systems, more engagement, higher levels of motivation." Marczewski makes clear that gamification is not meant to correct problems such as low pay and unfair treatment. But if these issues are absent, then "why not make happy employees happier?"[21] Marczewski's rant may be read as an instance of compassionate anger, of righteous indignation against those who are delaying him from the urgent work of alleviating suffering. He rages at detractors to "stop being part of the problem . . . and let the rest of us get on with what we are trying to do."[22] The ethical urgency that comes from compassion can protect gamification from criticism and make skeptics the objects of critique instead.

Marczewski's argument is supported by the historical realities of mundane, unvalued jobs. Many of the jobs described in gamification texts arrive from a long lineage of unhappy work situations, usually jobs too unappreciated, repetitive, and banal to be profitably transformed. These occupations, industrial reformers bemoan, highlight the limits of enlightened management, since there are "large segments of our society to which these prescriptions [of work reform] cannot possibly apply."[23] No matter how benevolent the reformer, there remains mundane, repetitive work that will resist efforts to be made intrinsically meaningful.

Hence, attempts at motivation typically follow what Kevin Werbach and Dan Hunter describe as the antiquated method of "carrots and sticks": "Cashiers at McDonald's are probably not asking 'Do you want fries with that?' because it's fun. Salespeople work longer and harder because their end-of-year bonus is dependent on sales. Employees know if they get a bad performance review, they don't get promoted."[24] For Werbach and Hunter, not only are such methods ineffective, but motivation through discipline is fundamentally unethical, because it stirs unhappiness and keeps workers in their place, removing the possibility of social mobility. It is not difficult to imagine the unhappiness of servers at McDonald's, who are unappreciated and deprived of the motivation to improve their lot. The reductive ease by which we can imagine these bad jobs is telling and gestures toward the conventional limits of sustaining an ideology of meritocracy.

The compassionate imagination ensues from gamification's capacity to transform the conditions hostile to the materialization of the energetic will. Werbach and Hunter explain that the will is most effective when you do something that "you really, really want to do," when intention merges effortlessly with affect—in short, when you work on something you are passionate about. Gamification expresses the hope that feelings of passion can be fairly distributed; it can alter the sense of "a stultifying job" by transferring some of the feelings typical of good careers to "jobs that are just that: jobs."[25] Points, leaderboards, game aesthetics, mechanics, and code are looked to as the instruments of redistribution, allowing those who work "in the context of tasks that are often repetitive and dull" to reserve hope for "a sense of purpose and aspiration" in their work.[26]

Compassion for the Passionless

Through what agencies does such compassion coalesce, and if the impulse is to recover a chance at the good life for hopeless working subjects, then what exactly are the shape and form of this good life? The Latin root of the words *compassion* and *passion*—*pati*—provides a basis by which we can consider the relationship between the affects of passion and compassion. *Pati* has traditionally implied a passive state of suffering, a condition of being beset by an emotion imposed externally that needs endurance by the victim.[27] The addition of the prefix *com* (together) makes *compati* (compassion), which communicates a condition of empathic suffering, where one experiences the pain of another that drives the impulse for the correction of injustice.[28] Such synergies in feeling make compassion an especially laudable variant of the moral sentiments. While regret, mercy, and remorse typically bind the bearer as the cause of the misfortune encountered by another, compassion comes with a "built-in clean-hands clause."[29] "The compassionate person," Candace Vogler writes, "sympathizes with misfortunes that she did not cause and that would not otherwise touch her life."[30] Compassion comes from pure benevolence; it is stirred without being culpable for the suffering it observes.

Previously, I discussed how the change in the meanings of the word *passion* might be understood as a shift from a passive to an active conception of desire. We can read *compassion* through the lens of this transition, bringing workers from states of passivity, "reactions to invasions from something external to the self," to states of activity, "the very activities of the mind, its own motions."[31] In gamification, suffering is diagnosed as disengagement, a lacuna of passion that interrupts the achievement of the good life. The feelings that result—apathy, loneliness, unhappiness—are all passive emotions, not only because they sap energy leading the body to inertia but also because they can thwart the will, affecting us even when we wish them not to. During such states, our bodies are felt as hindrance: the lethargic body, the clouded mind, and the persistent failure to be positive fail to align with the affective states that best enable the achievement of our wants.

Engagement, on the other hand, describes a frictionless relationship between wills and bodies. William Kahn, widely recognized as the pioneer of engagement in management theory, defines it as the task-based expenditure of energy aligned to one's concept of a "preferred self," a role identity that people "prefer to use and express in the course of role performance."[32] Like passion, engagement emerges through a meeting of desire and action. In this state, the will disappears as a sensed source of struggle.[33] Wants are fluidly expressed through what McGonigal calls a "right frame of mind," a mental state where "all kinds of positive emotions and experiences" are generated. Engaged bodies and minds are attuned to desire: "all our neurological and physiological systems that underlie happiness—our attention systems, our reward center, our motivation systems, our emotion and memory centers—are fully activated."[34] Unlike those who are unengaged and who routinely experience the challenge of forcing themselves to do something that they have no interest in, engaged individuals—to return to Zichermann and Linder's problematic but telling definition—have a feeling of "agency" or "belief you are in control of your destiny."[35]

But however benevolent, the compassionate terms of rescue imagined by gamification do not lack class distinction. Marjorie Garber offers that unlike emotions of sympathy and empathy, which imply a concordance of sentiments between subjects of equal standing, compassion is often built on grounds of disparity.[36] The exerciser of compassion is commonly understood to be superior to the one in distress. We see this inequality enacted in gamification when we are told that the workers suffering from disengagement are *they*—the call center workers, cashiers, and servers who are remote from our personal professional experience. On the other hand, the model of the engaged worker that gamification holds as ideal is built after *us* and our own experiences and beliefs about our careers. Adam Penenberg makes this imbalance clear when he distinguishes between a job and a career, noting that while "*anyone who has held a stultifying job* can attest to how slowly the day passes," the experience is "a completely different story for *most of us with careers*."[37] This statement captures how the passive-active shift is symbolic of classed feeling; an affective public that is higher in corporate hierarchy extends aid toward those who are trapped in the unvalued job positions they seek to transform.

And if compassion comes about from members of different social standing, then to feel the suffering of another is necessarily also a reflection of our own imagination of what suffering is. In *The Theory of Moral Sentiments*, Adam Smith notes that the imagination is central to compassion, because the human senses are incapable of properly experiencing someone else's pain. Senses can never "carry us beyond our own person," he writes; "it is by the imagination only that we can form any conception of what are his sensations."[38] Smith understands that the accuracy of this imaginative sensation will always be in doubt, but he holds faith that the sentiments will yield sufficient similarities to drive altruistic action. Though the imagined suffering "can never be exactly the same with original sorrow," the feelings will have "a correspondence with one another . . . [and] though they will never be unisons, they may be concords."[39] Smith positions the state of imaginative feelings—not necessarily their form or intensity—as a barometer for action. It matters less whether our imagined feeling of suffering is accurate; the very act of imagining suffering is capable of driving altruistic action that can alleviate the pain of others.

Compassion, however, does not lie outside emotional ideologies.[40] Judgments about who deserves compassion, how it should be offered, and the appropriateness and extent of its expression are bound up within the consideration of the compassionate act. Such a normative dimension of judgment to compassion is critical. For in being driven to deliver someone from suffering, we also have to imagine the suffering the subjects are in and the ways by which their suffering can be relieved.[41] For suffering to be recognizable as suffering, it must violate a sense of moral rightness. Sufferers must fit into the model of injustice, and the suffering needs to conform to models of pain that are socially recognizable for compassion to be made possible.[42]

The unhappiness found in the lack of passion requires minimal justification precisely because it is a normative kind of suffering that resonates within the public sphere, whether through self-help texts, medical advice, Gallup surveys, or the ideology of the American Dream. And it is this normative quality that allows the imagined suffering to slide from imagined to real subjects, from the particular to the general. In gamification, the bodies of call center workers, cashiers, and servers become representative of the generalized others whose labor suffers the same fate of being unmotivated and devalued. The drive to alleviate the scene of suffering is influenced by the same normative beliefs about what an experience without suffering is. The ideological synergy of feelings lies at the heart of the compassionate imagination: the desire to feel right through the compassionate act hinges on ideas about how the suffering subjects will feel right if we help them in the ways we think are right. The "right" feelings, wills, and experiences suggested by gamification advocates are the socially accepted ways in which these unhappy situations are to be transformed. As with Jennifer, whose story ends with a better position and a vacation overseas, gamification promises the hopeful resuscitation of the good life and thereby "fixes" a lapse that was previously present.

This vision has attracted no small critique. One prominent voice of opposition comes from game designer and professor Ian Bogost, who argues that gamification corporatizes the art form of games for business gain. Gamification, he contends, is "bullshit," because it has no real interest in changing the lives of those whom it cites. It seeks only to leverage the rhetorical power of games, their "mysterious, magical, powerful" aura, to offer a transformation of everyday experience.[43] But in being narrowly interested in what games do instead of what games are, gamification does violence to its object of inspiration. It scrapes games of their narratives, aesthetics, and playful logic and leaves behind their raw states—points, badges, and leaderboards—which are repeatedly made commodifiable. This critique is echoed by other game designers, such as John Ferrara and Margaret Robertson, who describe gamification as a "lie" and a "con" that ignore the most meaningful dimensions of what games constitute.[44]

While I sympathize with the critique of corporate appropriation and denigration, Bogost's account inadvertently sets up a problematic separation between earnest and dubious intentions, a binarization that misses the overlaps between the utopias assumed by playful frivolity and gameful instrumentality. Huizinga's and McGonigal's visions—one animated by childlike play, the other distilling play into real-life consequence—both embed an urge to preserve an aspect of the creative human spirit. Thomas Henricks notes that Huizinga wrote *Homo Ludens* in the shadow of the Fascist ascendancy of the Second World War; he associates the capacity to play—"to hold the world lightly and creatively"—with his wish for play to suspend prejudices and clear ground for plotting "a common future."[45] This notion also emerges in McGonigal's work on ubiquitous games. In her dissertation, McGonigal argues that gamification can produce responsive environments that transcend our individual self-interest and enable interaction and collaboration between strangers.[46] The magic circle, for both, represents an idealized cleansing sphere of reconciliation, a hope for a life lived in common.

Similarities in these social visions reflect the relevance of the compassionate imagination to gamification, a logic that also became more important as gamification was normalized and naturalized. By 2015, the initial luster of gamification had significantly declined. Technology entrepreneur Sergio Nouvel, for instance, notes that while gamification used to be the "darling of business talk," the term today "sounds a bit outdated and tired."[47] He and others attribute this development to the sullied brand of gamification and to critiques that raised public skepticism about the manipulative intent of the trend. McGonigal distanced herself from gamification on such grounds, saying, "I don't do gamification. . . . I don't think anybody should make games to try to motivate somebody to do something they don't want to do."[48] Stack Overflow insisted that its success depended on its users' own desire to "help other people" and "learn something new," rather than the gamified system of reputation built into the site: "At best the points, and the gamification, and the focused structure of the site did little more than encourage people to keep doing what they were already doing."[49] Rajat Paharia, the creator of the gamification platform Bunchball, also described the decline with nonchalance: "Whether or not the term sticks around, I don't know and I don't care. At the end of the day, my definition of gamification is about motivating people through data."[50] These individuals strategically disassociated themselves from gamification on the grounds that it is either too simplistic or manipulative. Then, under different terms or emphases, such as *big data* or *motivational science*, or with the absence of the term *gamification* itself, the existing relationship between games, passion, and the good life continued to be promulgated.

Returning to Bogost, I offer that his characterization of gamification as "bullshit" might be examined in a different direction. Here, the question is not whether gamification is well intentioned or well designed; rather, we need to examine how the productivist discourse of play reveals something about utopia in contexts of historical exclusion. Harry Frankfurt, whom Bogost draws from, explains that *bullshit* is a creative act directed toward invention rather than falsehood: "A person who undertakes to bullshit his way through has much more freedom. . . . It is more expansive and independent, with more spacious opportunities for improvisation, color, and imaginative play."[51] Bullshit is an exercise of the imagination, a thought experiment in the potential of games. Although the experiments expressed in gamification may repulse even those who see games as an art form, it is precisely this nonchalance with the nature of games that allows consultants, entrepreneurs, and futurists to imagine how play can ameliorate the problems of humankind. Freed from rules of how games should be, gamification practitioners have greater room to imagine its transformative possibilities. And so, though problematic and solutionist, this discourse gives us a glimpse into the kinds of utopias that capital constructs in the present, especially with regard to the long-standing limit of management's transformative impulse that sees repetitive work as having no redemptive value for restructuring.

Flow and Compassionate Agency

I trace the politics of this imaginary beginning with a study of flow, a popular psychological theory of concentration developed in the 1970s by psychologist Mihály Csíkszentmihályi, which is often raised in gamification. The appeal of flow in gamification likely stems from the theory's intuitive argument about the link between skills and challenge. An experiential quality of concentration, the theory offers, hinges on a match between the difficulty of the challenge and the person's ability.[52] The more skillful the person is, the more challenging the task must become to elicit a concentrative state of flow. This explanation lends itself easily to the adjustable difficulty settings of game systems, providing also a convenient rationale for why gamification "works."

The context for flow theory can be found in the opening of Csík-szentmihályi's early monograph, *Beyond Boredom and Anxiety*, published in 1975. It begins with a story, recorded by the historian Herodotus, about how the ancient Lydians survived a famine of eighteen years by absorbing themselves in play. In this famous tale, the Lydians coped by alternating between games and food; one day, they would eat, and the next they would play with knucklebones, dice, and balls to ward off their hunger pangs. This practice presumably allowed the Lydians to stretch their meager supplies for eighteen years. The story constitutes a very minor part of history that Herodotus recorded,[53] but to Csíkszentmihályi, it captures the powerful potential of play. "People do get immersed in games so deeply as to forget hunger and other problems," he wrote. "What power does play have that men relinquish basic needs for its sake?"[54]

The story has a seductive appeal: the very simplicity by which famine was gamed implies that it is possible for hardship to be experienced in ways that are nontraumatic. Suffering is not only effectively absolved; its means of absolution is painless as well. This tale resurfaced as inspiration more than three decades later when McGonigal referred to it in the introduction and conclusion of *Reality Is Broken*. But whereas Csíkszentmihályi acknowledges questions about the anecdote's historical accuracy, McGonigal amasses evidence to support its veracity. Elaborating on several recent findings that back the plausibility of the anecdote, she argues that what had commonly been thought of as a legend now offers the "astonishing claim" that "we may owe much of Western civilization as we know it to the Lydians' ability to come together and play a good game."[55]

The transposition of the story across historical time—from an ancient Greek narrative to the modern writings of Csíkszentmihályi and McGonigal—reflects the inherited quality of a utopia of play. As Csíkszentmihályi makes clear, a principal purpose of *Beyond Boredom and Anxiety* is to bring out the potential of play and to illustrate how play is a psychological orientation, an interpretation of an act rather than an act itself. The pleasure derived from play does not lie within the game but arises through its factors: where goals are clearly stated, feedback is constantly given, and skills are properly matched with the challenge of the task. "Almost any object or any experience is potentially enjoyable," Csíkszentmihályi insists; all it requires is a change of the psychological orientation toward the object or experience.[56] Thus, Csíkszentmihályi forwards a curious list of playful figures: the adherents of the Protestant work ethic, businessmen in pursuit of wealth, English master weavers, and indigenous farmers and hunters. These odd choices demonstrate his attempt to universalize the potential of play outside culture, history, and circumstance, particularly where it comes to the area of productive activity.[57]

Play in this mode hinges on what Csíkszentmihályi calls "flow," an optimal experience of human freedom that is absent boredom and anxiety. Those in flow experience a state of deep concentration, where distractions and feelings of uncertainty are eliminated and replaced with a strong sense of control (see figure 3.1). Self-consciousness vanishes. Awareness of the body slides away, crowded out by an intense focus on the task; negative bodily and psychic feelings such as discomfort, pain, fear, unhappiness, and fatigue disappear. The experience of time is also transformed. When in flow, time flies by without the person's realization, and though one does not necessarily feel happy during flow, since feelings are not consciously reflected upon, retrospectively these sensations are described as enjoyable. Hence, flow is known to be autotelic, an intrinsically rewarding experience that drives people to seek it out for its own sake.[58]

Today, flow is often described as a phenomenological expression of passion. Wellness organizations such as the Flow Genome Project and the Flow Consciousness Institute regularly advertise workshops that claim to help participants find their flow so that they can live more passionately.[59] Self-help resources also instruct participants to find their flow to know their passions. The link between passion and flow is not off the mark, since flow was initially modeled after the work ethic of artists, an exemplary model of the self-sacrificial, passionate, neoliberal cultural laborer. In his early work as a graduate student, Csíkszentmihályi was particularly curious about the absorption that artists demonstrate. Artists are "almost fanatically devoted to their work," he writes; "yet as soon as they finished a painting or a sculpture, they seemed to lose all interest in it."[60] Csíkszentmihályi speculated that there is a playful pleasure in the act of creative self-expression that cannot be wholly attributed to the creative product.

This observation would turn into a lifelong study of the human experience. By the 1970s, Csíkszentmihályi was involved in larger scholarly discussions about the crisis of sentiment in work, and his attempt to address the problem led him to a choice number of industrial workers who were able to take a psychological orientation of flow toward their labor. One exemplar he frequently cites is Rico Medellin, a worker tasked with a set of "ostensibly boring" operations on the production line: "Most people would grow tired of such work very soon. But Rico has been at this job for over five

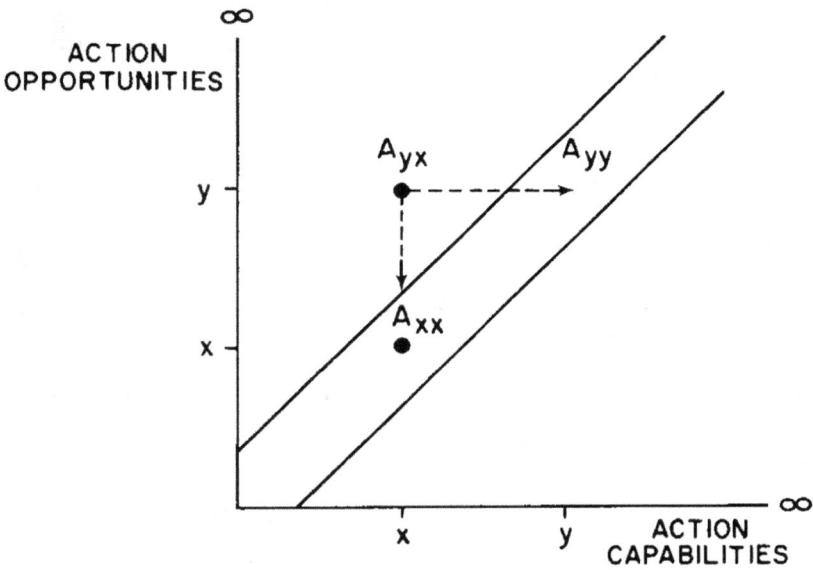

Through the axes on this chart, Mihály Csíkszentmihályi elaborates on how someone can enter flow. "People in a state of worry can return to flow through an almost infinite combination of two basic vector processes: decreasing challenges or increasing skills." From Csíkszentmihályi, "Play and Intrinsic Rewards," 60.

3.1

years, and he enjoys it."[61] Rico's enjoyment stems from his ability to make a game out of hard labor: "Like the runner who trains for years to shave a few seconds off . . . Rico has trained himself to better his time on the assembly line. . . . He has worked out a private routine for how to use his tools, how to do his moves. After five years, his best average for a day has been twenty-eight seconds per unit."[62]

Rico showcases the control that people can have over their work experience. While many find assembly lines dull and alienating, Rico "loved the exhilaration of using his skills fully," Csíkszentmihályi declares.[63] This switch of mentality, which Jesse Schell describes as a turn from obligation to volition, shows how play can be cast in the form of everyday action.[64] From that perspective, anything can be made engaging—all it takes is a flexible change in how the activity is approached. As Rico is quoted as saying, work on the line is "better than anything else—a whole lot better than watching TV."[65] A mastery of flow can make the dreariest labor a mode of entertainment.[66]

War and the Compassionate Solution

At first glance, Csíkszentmihályi's thesis seems no different from what management has long sought to deliver: a productive workforce that labors in harmony with industry leadership. But where management is driven by the bottom line, flow is inspired by a larger purpose. In a chapter titled "Happiness Revisited," Csíkszentmihályi writes about the limited control we have in how lives unfold: "There is not much that we as individuals can do to change the way the universe runs. In our lifetime we exert little influence over the forces that interfere with our well-being. It is important to do as much as we can to prevent nuclear war, to abolish social injustice, to eradicate hunger and disease. But it is prudent not to expect that efforts to change external conditions will immediately improve the quality of our lives."[67] Conditions that make for unbearable life may not always be avoidable or alterable, and psychological mastery stands as the only certain source of defense against the whims of fate.

Csíkszentmihályi's skepticism about structural change is rooted in his experiences during the Second World War. In 1944, at the age of ten, Hungarian-born Csíkszentmihályi was brought to Italy, where his father worked as a diplomat under the Hungarian Nazi regime.[68] The war was drawing to a close, and in less than a year, the Allies would enter Bellagio and raid the hotel where his family was staying. It was during that period that Csíkszentmihályi learned about the power of play. In an interview with *Omni*, he explains that chess was his escape from the death and incarceration of relatives and friends: "I discovered chess was a miraculous way of entering into a different world where all those things didn't matter. For hours I'd just focus within a reality that had clear rules and goals. If you knew what to do, you could survive there."[69]

This experience prompted a long-standing interest in psychology. In a TED talk, Csíkszentmihályi relates how he was inspired to understand the human psyche when he saw "how few of the grown-ups . . . were able to withstand the tragedies that the war visited on them, how few of them could even resemble a normal, contented, satisfied, happy life, once their job, their home, their security was destroyed by the war."[70] War schooled Csíkszentmihályi in the limits of structural optimism: structural change cannot be guaranteed, and even if circumstances improve, change often happens too slowly to prevent harm.[71]

I do not raise this example to make a reductive relationship between Csíkszentmihályi's past, the theory of flow, and the notion of survival. Nor am I suggesting that the theory of flow is entirely built on the experience of war. However, to appreciate the cultural and psychic complexity of flow, it is necessary to understand the ground from which it emerges. In an introductory article about the field of positive psychology, Csíkszentmihályi clarifies that his intention has never been to construe a "value-free" psychological theory of the "average" human being. In fact, he is primarily intrigued not by the suffering of those affected by war but by the "few who kept their integrity and purpose despite the surrounding chaos." He explains, "They were not necessarily the most respected, better educated, or more skilled individuals," but they "kept their decency during the onslaught of World War II." These people, he insists, "held the key to what humans could be like at their best" and represent models of the idealized psychological theory he wishes to build.[72]

The theory of flow thus aspires to realize a resilient human psyche modeled after survivors of war. Prisoners of war cited in his books are admired for their ability to survive without being traumatized. They include Christopher Burney, an operative who endured solitary confinement by learning ways to make ordinary objects interesting; Eva Zeisel, a ceramics designer who played chess in her mind; Albert Speer, Hitler's architect who devised for himself a walking game at the prison yard and used it to "travel" to far-off places; and György Faludy, a poet who passed his time by recruiting other prisoners to help retain the memory of an elegy made for his wife.[73] In *Flow*, Csíkszentmihályi writes that "even the most degrading situation can be transformed into a flow experience." He quotes Aleksandr Solzhenitsyn, who used poetry to help manage the oppressive conditions of the Gulag camps: "'Sometimes, when standing in a column of dejected prisoners, amidst the shouts of guards with machine guns, I felt such a rush of rhymes and images that I seemed to be wafted overhead. . . . At such moments I was both free and happy. . . . Some prisoners tried to escape by smashing through the barbed wire. For me there was no barbed wire. The head count of prisoners remained unchanged but I was actually away on a distant flight.'"[74]

As contrast, we may turn to Giorgio Agamben in *Remnants of Auschwitz*, who quotes Primo Levi about a soccer match played between the ss and the representatives of the Sonderkommando, the Jews assigned to the disposal of gas chamber victims. The match seemed to function as a brief interlude to reality. "Other men of the ss and the rest of the squad were present at the game; they take sides, bet, applaud, urge the players on," Levi writes, "as if, rather than at the gates of hell, the game were taking place on the village green."[75] But where "this match might strike someone as a brief pause of humanity in the middle of an infinite horror," Agamben himself considers it "the true horror of the camp," because it demonstrates how casually evil can be hidden behind a facade of banality: "hence . . . the shame of those who did not know the camps and yet, without knowing how, are spectators of that match, which repeats itself in every match in our stadiums, in every television broadcast, in the normalcy of everyday life."[76]

While Csíkszentmihályi celebrates the heroism of endurance and survival, Agamben's account cautions us about what these narratives might screen. Indeed, universalization—and, therefore, the irrelevance of the initial context—is the very goal of Csíkszentmihályi's psychological theory. In response to Gonzalo Bacigalupe's argument that the field of positive psychology embeds racial values because it is primarily conceived by a white scholarly community, Csíkszentmihályi expressed his belief that "our common humanity is strong enough to suggest psychological goals to strive for that cut across social and cultural divides."[77] His prioritization of abstraction and circulation is evident: where something stems from is less important than how it might be made applicable more generally.

This standpoint can be read as an effect of compassion. The desire to absolve the pain of another may drive one to be strategic in the imagination of a solution; abstraction and circulation are pragmatic decisions aimed to make a solution more universal and useful to those who are suffering.[78]

This desire to feel right and do right, Lauren Berlant offers, constitutes the agentic impulse that lies at the heart of compassion. However, the pragmatic approach may also incorporate a misrecognition of suffering and the conception of the solution.[79] If compassion involves the compulsion to aid another whose circumstances are radically different, a theory that legitimates universal psychological sameness will be useful in producing a path forward. But such a compassionate solution also carries the consequence of repressing difference, and the eagerness to offer an uncomplicated, wholesome panacea to pain can gloss over deeper issues that are harder to address.[80]

The result can be unintended consequences, a key one being individualized blame. As Ghassan Hage suggests, the celebration of the universal human spirit to endure carries a disciplinary opposite: if survival is possible, and some have endured and survived, then the inability to survive can be attributed to the psychological deficiency of the individual in question, rather than the conditions that produced this hardship in the first place.[81] Thus, Csíkszentmihályi tells the story of assembly line worker Julio Martinez, who is unable to concentrate on his work because he notices that one of his car tires is getting flat and his paycheck will not arrive until the end of the following week. The realization that the tire would be unfixable until then fills Julio with great anxiety, affecting his mood through the workday. He is irritable and unproductive; his mind is preoccupied with worries about whether he can return home with a flat tire and come to work the next day.[82]

Wages, wealth, and unions are not raised as issues in Julio's case. Instead, Csíkszentmihályi chides Julio for failing to interpret the flat tire positively. "The outside event appears in consciousness purely as information," he explains; "it is the self that interprets that raw information in the context of its own interests, and determines whether it is harmful or not."[83] Julio's problem is attributed to a lack of knowledge about credit, his poor networks, and his low self-confidence. Flow here slides from being an idealized to a normative theory of survival. What started as a means to help the survival of individuals has changed to a scheme of privatized blame; the focus on individual psychological change has made people responsible for their own feelings.

Trajectories of Suspension

But this leads to another question: Is the experience of flow *always* healthy and empowering? We might turn to Natasha Schüll's study of gambling machines to understand different qualities of the flow experience.

In *Addiction by Design*, Schüll observes that while addicts of gambling machines are deeply engrossed in play, such concentration is not characterized by the "exhilarating, expansive, enabling experience of which Csíkszentmihályi wrote."[84] Instead, she finds these addictive gaming experiences to be liquidating and annihilating; addicts go so deep into concentration that they become chained to their machines, unable to leave until their bodies and pockets are depleted.

In his criticism of McGonigal's book *SuperBetter*, Nathan Heller argues that McGonigal misrepresents the positive phenomenological qualities of digital games.[85] McGonigal writes that games can help us lead happier and healthier lives by liberating us from the unhappiness of "ordinary negative events."[86] Drawing from a medical study, she suggests that concentration games such as Tetris can crowd out unhappy thoughts by absorbing the entirety of a person's mental processing resources. Players are less likely to recall negative events while playing Tetris, and after playing, they are also capable of recalling raw images without the corresponding traumatic consequence. Heller, however, questions if this study would warrant a straightforward interpretation of the therapeutic quality of games. If Tetris does block out trauma, he offers, it would do so by numbing rather than curing. Games produce an evasion of trauma only by distracting us from reality: "The immersive world of video games . . . numbs us to our own."[87]

The same argument is mounted by Schüll: she offers that players are often addicted to slot machines because machines provide a sense of safety. The odds of gambling machines may be weighted against the player, but these machines are predictable; their familiar operations and the foreseeable losses give people a sense of control in a world where they would otherwise be overwhelmed with worry and anxiety. Although "interactive consumer devices are typically associated with new choices, connections, and forms of self-expression," Schüll observes, "they can also function to narrow choices, disconnect, and gain exit from the self."[88] Games offer this space of compromised respite; they allow for what Scott Richmond calls a sense of "vulgar boredom," "an ambivalent retreat from desire" that distracts from the unhappy present through a suspended state of the machine zone. Through play, the individual experiences an erasure of himself. He becomes "relieved of wanting, waiting, or acting," which suspends the pressures of everyday life.[89]

Much research on the theory of flow has focused on one side of the equation: the aspect of intense concentration that characterizes the autotelic feeling of pleasure. But concentration also entails distraction and self-erasure. Jonathan Crary writes in his historical study of attention that "attention and distraction were not two essentially different states but existed on a single continuum."[90] We also see this continuum in the theory of flow: "The loss of self-consciousness in flow marks the fading of Mead's 'me' from awareness," Csíkszentmihályi writes, and it happens "as attention is taken up entirely by the challenges of being engaged."[91] Concentration and suspension are inversely joined: the concentration necessary for flow crowds away extraneous stimuli, leaving one inattentive to everything but the task at hand.

The stories that Csíkszentmihályi cites, whether of the Lydians or the prisoners of war, are typically described through the perspective of concentration, but what is key to the evasion of trauma is the muting of self-consciousness that comes with deep focus. The two facets of this experience—concentration and suspension—can bear different degrees of relevance for workers, depending on their circumstances. For creative workers, concentration can better describe the pleasure of creative expression. However, for those whose work is mundane and tedious, it is the numbing sensation of suspension that makes flow relevant. The "negation of perception" that constitutes suspension can provide a bulwark against routine attrition, where the numbing quality of game elements opens a horizon of endurance for subjects who are denied the good life.[92]

Suspension would initially seem to contradict the self-realizing pleasures assumed of passion. Suspension gestures toward the mechanical and the automatic, qualities that Lorraine Daston describes as having traditionally been contrasted against the human, the former signifying the repetitive, rigid, and stupid, while the latter represent the creative, flexible, and intelligent.[93] This Cartesian separation is connected to a history of racism, usually tying the automatic to the racialized Other, depicted also as diminutive, servile, and less than human.[94] But can suspension come to take on a different purpose? When raised in gamification, suspension is often attached to this antihumanist, mechanical problematic. Miguel Sicart and Tae Wan Kim, for instance, propose that the main ethical problem of gamification is that it offers ready-made packages of the good life, which prevent people from reflecting on the moral worth of the objectives implemented.[95] As Sicart emphasizes, "The good life is *not only* the practice of activities, it is *also* the capacity to reflect about the role of those activities in one's life and sense of well-being."[96] This perspective resonates with Graeme Kirkpatrick's argument that gamification narrows lines of possibility and directs them toward preordained routes that privilege normative systems. If play has traditionally implied a creative act that broadens potential in the radical imaginary, then gamification appropriates this potentiality and "channels it towards the requirements of the system," which renders these radical possibilities unthinkable.[97]

I am sympathetic to these critiques, but it remains important to differentiate between the demands that come from subjects. Radical reflection may not be of equal relevance to those historically excluded from the good life, and the inclusion into normality may be felt as liberation rather than conformity for those worn down by everyday indignities of exclusion. As Berlant points out, the yearning to be "nearly normal" is not simply a want for the similar or familiar; rather, the wish for normalcy comes from a desire "to be in proximity to a feeling of something that is strangely both enigmatic and simplifying."[98] Offered here is a reminder of the politics of the quotidian: normality can be simplifying in ways that dial down the complexity of life's demands, bringing the subject into a reassuring zone of sensed possibility. Sometimes liberation may come as a wish to think less, to feel that the world can be navigated with less hesitation and consideration, to feel that the ordinary can be a site for being at peace, to possess an optimism for the betterment of one's life.

Recall again that Reynold Lawrie defines passion as an affect characterized by pursuit, a wanting for something that magnetizes action by the subject.[99] To pursue means to follow; to be in pursuit entails moving in a trajectory of following after something, a movement that is not characterized by aimlessness but by a sense of a "proper" direction, a direction that feels as if someone is doing what she is meant to do in order to advance.[100] The opposite of pursuit may come as a sensation of "stuckedness"—a feeling of being trapped and bereft of options worth pursuing.[101] Stuckedness can arrive as a sense of exclusion, an affective zone of social displacement, where the world becomes steadily devoid of worthwhile attachments.[102] Or, drawing from Mark Kingwell and Ramus Johnsen, feeling stuck can feel like "a stall," a condition where the world fails to open up its potential, where desire is turned back on itself because the subject lacks the "know-how to interact with the demand or anticipated fulfillment that the situation or phenomenon requires of her."[103]

Opportunities for pursuit will be more vague for those excluded from the conventional trajectories of career development. But as options blur, one also becomes more willing to accept alternate terms for entry into an affective zone of possibility. In *The Problem of Distraction*, Paul North uses the analogy of a hunt to highlight the relations between three objects: "the non-deviating horse, the still-inclining heart, and the emptyheaded fool."[104] North focuses on the heart and head, signifying the will and agency, to explain how distraction can sometimes advance one's will while being devoid of intentionality. We can take this analogy in a different direction. In the case of gamification, it is the "non-deviating horse"—the setting—that appears to be the most relevant. It matters less how agentic one is; it is more important that the designed mechanism can direct the subject's actions, to follow a trajectory regardless of what the player does. Suspension can be used as a pathway *into* normality, folding the subject into a conventional sense of possibility about the present and future, a zone of expectation that is easily mistaken as an ordinary way of being for the general population.

In *What's the Use?*, Ahmed notes that pathways prescribe not just the direction of travel but also its ease of movement: "The more people travel on a path, the flatter and smoother the surface becomes. When something is smoother, it is clearer; the more a path is followed, the easier it is to follow."[105] Ahmed talks about the normalization of use and the ease that repeated use incites, but pathways can be seen as doing more. Good pathways propel. They can build momentum, driving the subject forward in a trajectory that lessens the burden on *their will* to walk and progress. Thus, in the same way that economists can premise nudges for subjects too worn to make "right" decisions for themselves, exclusion and wearing out can coalesce to outline an unhappy population that could benefit most from this scheme: those who are overwhelmed through no fault of their own, or workers who want to do rightly but are hindered by the nature of the work.[106]

In some ways, however, the compassionate imagination of gamification goes further than any of these suggestions. Gamification's trajectory involves the supersession of agency; it means trusting the software to become the key agentic actor to lead the player along. While Csíkszentmihályi would still require subjects to change their interpretation of the situation to enter flow, as in the example of Rico, gamification burdens subjects with no such transformation. Found here is an ethic that Peter Sloterdijk calls "voluntarily sought passivity," a practice where the subject cedes agency to fulfill her will. Sloterdijk writes, "The statement 'I took myself in hand' is now replaced by a more complex formulation: 'I put myself in other hands so that, after completed treatment, I would once more be able to take myself in hand.'"[107] In this way, gamification brings flow to its utopian end: if flow is limited by the human inability to freely interpret the context, gamification removes this challenge by absorbing workers into gamified cybernetic systems. The excessive liveliness of the mind and body—a body that recognizes no boredom and fatigue—and receptiveness to being amended by digital forces open an imagination into a different possibility of the good life.

Hopeful Suspension

In the last sections of this chapter, I turn to several enactments of gamification to exemplify visions of what I call "hopeful suspension."[108] Suspension here is incited by the compassionate imagination: the wish that a subject encountering a difficult situation can psychologically overcome it by acting without avid self-awareness. Suspension does not always have to be hopeful. It can come simply as a means to numb oneself from the unhappiness of life. However, suspension becomes hopeful when it attaches that numbness to desire, where workers are precisely best equipped with what they want when they are passive and willing to cede themselves into the algorithmic flow of the machine. In this, suspension pivots from survival to flourishing, becoming invested with the compassionate hope that workers in repetitive, often devalued jobs will be reincluded into the affective structure of passion.

The Open Badges project designed by Mozilla can help elaborate this formulation. Launched in 2013 along with the 10 Million Better Futures initiative supported by former US president Bill Clinton, the Open Badges project was envisioned as an educational technology that could supplement formal educational institutions, providing digital badges to recognize the informal learning processes that people undertake in their everyday lives. But from the early days of the project, it was clear that digital badges could also be used to democratize and equalize the gain of human capital. While the developer of Open Badges, Erin Knight, has primarily conceived of badges for superperforming students who were ahead of their peers, Clinton, when introducing the badging movement, stressed its usefulness for returning veterans who were unable to get jobs because of an *unfair* lack of certification.[109] "I got interested in this because of my concern that the unemployment rate among returning military veterans persisted after the financial crisis," he explains, "and veterans were repeatedly required to go back to college to get degrees in subjects where the study involved far less scope of responsibility that they had already shouldered as members of the military."[110] The proper certification of skill sets is thereby presented as a moral responsibility: digital badges allow for a *fairer* capture of skill sets, allowing veterans to demonstrate skills for jobs they would otherwise be disqualified from doing and to become reemployed after their service.[111]

Clinton's appeal relates to the concept of "human capital" most famously advanced by economist Gary Becker in the 1960s.[112] In its basic form, human capital imagines human subjects as sites of speculative investment: it considers, as Michelle Murphy argues, the "embodied capacities of a person that can produce future economic benefits for that person, her employer, and even her national economy."[113] Human capital describes the horizon of someone's anticipated value as commodity labor power. The more human capital people have, the more employable they will be as they continue down the path of expected potential. But to allow for the fair computation of human capital, a larger range of everyday practices needs to be classified as investable skills and assets and included in the consideration of this potential.

This trend has led to an expansion of what is meant by the term *skills*. As Ilana Gershon observes, "While skill used to refer to manual or mechanical knowledge (perhaps sewing or plumbing), now almost anything that can be tested or ranked can be considered a skill."[114] Serialized unemployment has added pressure for individuals to present themselves as holders of value, and *skills* is deployed as an intuitive term that can explain one's potential for labor. The more skills one has, the more valuable the worker is assumed to be. Of course, this is not always true: skills are not always transferable. Knowledge gained in one domain may not move well into another, and a worker with more skills is not necessarily a faster learner. But making the claim of human capital requires such heuristics, and so workers are tasked to leverage this rhetoric, to abstract and universalize their knowledge, and to make the point that "skills" represent, above all, the human potential to adapt, learn, and creatively develop.

It is in this regard that technologies of assessment are judged to be inaccurate and biased. This argument was taken up by former US secretary of education Arne Duncan with regard to childhood education, where it is suggested that inequality can obstruct the proper calculation of human capital, especially among the poor. "Talent is much more evenly distributed than opportunity," he explains, but schools in poor neighborhoods with few resources are often unable to properly differentiate between the talented and the talentless because they are unable to capture the complex skill sets gained by a child beyond the usual assessments.[115] The child's ability to solve problems, learn, and pick up skill sets independently is a talents that will be missed if they are left unassessed and unrecorded. The same point is easily transposed to working adults. In a webinar, "Sal" was introduced as a prototype of a worker who is unable to find a new job after his retrenchment because he is incapable of demonstrating the skills that he has gained through his long career.[116] As in the case of veterans, the webinar's point is that current modes of assessments do not give enough credit to the human capital of a particular group—often workers in jobs that are assumed to be low-skilled—which would not only disqualify them from jobs but also render them uninvestable for better jobs that can see greater growth.

It thus becomes a matter of ethical responsibility that technologies capture the "larger networks of learning" to account for the complex competencies of individuals.[117] During a talk, badging advocate Doug Belshaw introduces this idea by using two jars of rocks. The first holds only large stones, which leave space for numerous gaps in between; the second contains not only big rocks but small pebbles, which fill the gaps. Belshaw offers that the aim is not to do away with traditional educational institutions (large stones) but to "round out the holistic version of who you are . . . by putting in the little pebbles around it, to fill up the jar." Digital badges, he offers, can be those little pebbles. They can reveal the hitherto uncredentialed skill sets that constitute the complex knowledges of the working subject.[118]

The Open Badges project thus emphasizes the ambient growth of human capital, especially with skills that are not easily captured in formal certification processes. Promotional videos often portray digital badges as currencies that can be earned amid everyday activity. In a video produced by the MacArthur Foundation, we see a child accumulating points toward a "Nature Explorer" badge while she strolls in a reserve; other scenes show a young worker learning from a mentor and accumulating points that will land him a badge in the process; yet another shows workers engaging in a meeting contributing toward badges that will reflect teamwork and social skills (see figure 3.2).[119] Digital badges propagate an imaginary of human capital that accrues ambiently, that captures skills of all kinds, and that can be stored and "stacked" for life, meaning that it can be "leveled up" to highlight the increasingly complex competencies that are acquirable. In this imaginary, all experiences are attached to potential value; gaining human capital centers less on the "right" schools to attend or organizations to join and more on the motivation of subjects to learn, work hard, and continuoually seek forms of self-improvement.

Still from a video explaining digital badges that recognize ambient **3.2**
skill sets. From MacArthur Foundation, "What Is a Badge?"

The animating fantasy of badges is significant not only because it addresses a long-standing structural problem of credentialing. The technicality of the solution is also a factor of this optimism. Badges are undergirded by the Open Badges v2.0 technical protocol that serves as the standard for determining, verifying, and evaluating the worth of the informatic human capital embedded within.[120] Every badge produced through the Open Badges v2.0 program must be standardized with coded metadata that includes reference to the owner of the badge, the institution that issued it, the type of badge issued, and so on. With standardized metadata, badges can be collected in one location and be moved through platforms for verification and evidence of achievement. To be put into protocol, Alexander Galloway writes, is to be placed into "voluntary regulation within a contingent environment."[121] Protocols serve as a mode of recognition. Something put within protocol is officially registered in larger networks meant to subjectivize an individual, whether as worker, citizen, student, or patient. Recognition, of course, entails surveillance. Much of Galloway's argument on protocols features the Deleuzian logic of surveillance, where informatic individuals are parsed as biopolitical forms of management. But recognition can also fuel a fantasy of access. Open Badges can count as the grammatical structure that provides excluded subjects with an official language for their justification of worth and potential. As with the returning veterans that Clinton cites, badges are poised to provide an alternative system that values the human capital traditionally excluded from formal credentialing systems.

This vision is extended into the "connected ecosystem" used to promote the Open Badges infrastructure. The badge is a currency that promises to open a networked pipeline of other technical procedures that can assess and bolster employability. Each badge earned goes into a person's "badge backpack," which is portable across platforms. Badges earned from an educational institution, for instance, can be stored with badges from the workplace, ensuring longevity and uniformity to this language of human capital and allowing badge earners to accumulate badges as a form of lifelong skill acquisition.[122] This ecosystem is also integrated into social media platforms such as LinkedIn and Facebook, so that users' achievements can easily be presented as self-brands. An education technologist offers that badges can be thought of as a "tapestry of skills and achievements," materials with which to craft a professional story.[123] Badge earners are encouraged to see themes emerging through the badges they have accumulated and from there to craft their professional story by looking out for complementary badges to develop the rounded, passionate narratives that they wish to tell.

In being funneled into a protocological logic of human capital, then, digital badges appear to fulfill a fantasy of habitual empowered action. Ordinary things that people do now have a chance of sparking a chain of events that push them up the career ladder. The badge-issuing platform Credly illustrates this fantasy in several images. In one, a graphic time chart shows how a badge earned for speaking at conference opens a range of new opportunities, first with a bigger speaking engagement, then with the personal motivation to take a course to earn more badges, and finally with a promotion because of the number of badges the speaker has earned (see figure 3.3).[124] Here, capital breeds capital, but what is required first is the protocological form of recognition that can take the soft skill of public speaking into account. It requires an ambient system of accountancy that can recognize the learning that takes place even in the most routine of contexts. From there, things drive themselves forward, propelling the subject into passionate pursuit of career advancement.

We might now observe how the optimism of badges can coincide with a state of suspension. In *Office Arcade*, Jason Suriano shows how two models of gamification ethics can work in conjunction: a behaviorist model that emphasizes the goals of the designer and a liberal, paternalistic model that emphasizes giving what the user "wants." Like many other designers, Suriano believes that gamification needs to be designed around a "trajectory," with intermittent steps carefully planned to achieve the goal that the designer wishes. Points and badges are to be used as dopamine hits, mental rewards that can get the user to perform in the way that the system wishes. At the same time, those points and badges are channeled into a process of "deep scoring"—a system that allows these gains to become something more substantive outside the gamification program itself.[125] In this ideal world, objectives of the corporation and of the worker would coincide. The pursuit of points and badges accrues toward the productive outputs of the company, and those same points and badges help showcase the worker's competence.

We see this scenario put into action in a demo produced by Badgeville, where a telemarketer is rewarded for every action he takes on the interface.[126] When he enters a sales opportunity into the software, the interface immediately responds with a notification that he has received six points. Twenty points are offered when he schedules a contact with the lead, and fifteen points for doing it faster than normal. The immediacy of this feedback—and the way it is structured so that one action leads to another with progressively greater rewards—indicates a behaviorist system that is engineered to have telemarketers work in a particular way. But Badgeville does not leave badges and points as rewards confined to the interface. Instead, points and badges can accumulate toward what Badgeville calls the "Future of Work" (see figure 3.4). In the visual, every badge earned is made translatable into the accretion of economic personhood.[127] The image shows an employee with various trophies: a level-three "western region expert," "big thinker," and a "voice of change," among others. The awards suggest not just how competent the worker is but also how the worker can use them as currency for a future position. Suspension, with the dopamine hits, may thus be seen as adding to, rather than impeding, the desire of the subject. By following the trail of points, one becomes a good worker and is rewarded with tokens that mark the possibility of advancement of human capital.

In gamification, suspension feels hopeful. Every small accomplishment is automatically collected and parsed as points, badges, and rewards that remind users that they are "advancing," moving forward in a trajectory. While Csíkszentmihályi has conceptualized suspension primarily as a hollowing out of time to survive a particularly difficult period, the new programs of gamification have designed suspension into their very programs of progress. As one acts, distracted by points, badges, and leaderboards, one also gains the credentials that mark one's steady gain of human capital. Points accumulate toward badges, and badges accumulate in the badge backpack that could eventually become the ticket to career progression for the worker. In this scenario, suspension is not simply numbing; it is full of empowered possibility—it presents a chance to be promoted, to get a better job, to be recognized for performing well. Human automaticity gains utility, even moral luminosity, as it numbs the sensations of fatigue and tedium and allows workers to enact the work ethic of their own desire.

Though far from being passionate in the usual sense, suspension remains empowering for its capacity to yield a trajectory for those excluded from the good life. Substituting revolutionary hope for realistic expectations, gamification gestures toward a good life that aspires not to the exceptional but to the quotidian affects of possibility that resuscitate hopefulness for minor forms of inclusion. This also constitutes what I call a compromised good life, one that accommodates precarious, excluded subjects by working within, rather than outside, their circumstance. Technologies that optimize the human zeal are envisioned here as tools of reform, allowing even those trapped in low-paying or exploitative jobs to

DESIGN. LAUNCH. SUCCESS.

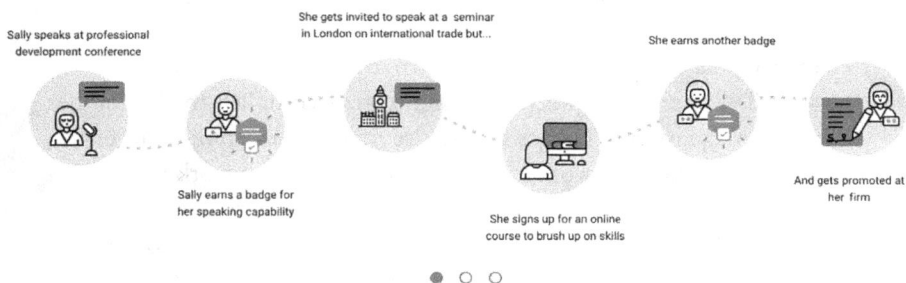

Still from a video explaining digital badges that recognize ambient   **3.3**
skill sets. From MacArthur Foundation, "What Is a Badge?"

This graphic from the Badgeville website purports to show   **3.4**
"the future of work," where employees can earn badges
and points toward career advancement. From Badgeville,
"Visualize the Future of Work."

catalyze a conventionality that makes, as Berlant offers, "possible imagining living the *proper* life that capitalism offers as the route to the *good* life."[128]

Intolerable Hopefulness

None of this, of course, makes gamification any less a con. Alexander Galloway reminds us that games are "action-based media"; they are interactive media that require the subject's participation to function.[129] And the gamified interface is precisely designed to accomplish that. Whether it be the image of gray badges or the rise of scores of competing teams, everything reminds the worker to put in more effort, to work harder and not fall behind. Games elicit labor, and the seductiveness of gamification comes from how it can direct more of the worker's capacities toward the object of work without improving the structural conditions of labor.

Further, gamification deepens the surveillance that constitutes such work. In a promotional video produced by gamification company Bunchball, a supervisor notices that a customer service representative has exhibited abrasive behavior. But instead of chastising him directly, the supervisor heads to the gamification application programming interface (API) to give him a personal mission on "etiquette training"—a standardized educational program built into the system.[130] The scene is meant to evoke the beauty of gamification, as both the supervisor and worker are freed from the discomfort that a confrontation might produce. At the same time, this seemingly ideal treatment of the worker normalizes a standardized protocol of management that is both distant and depersonalized. By relying on the system, the manager remains oblivious to the personal reasons for the worker's behavior. In this way, reprimand, demotions, and dismissals are likely to be centered on the pure efficiency of metrics: the numbers and charts that the gamified system captures through the routine work of employees.

These are legitimate concerns that I do not wish to downplay. Yet, I offer that hopeful suspension must be understood as one of the more troubling developments of this trend. One immediate problem lies in gamification's normalization. For their part, gamification advocates have often sought to assure concerned readers of the earnestness of their motivations by pointing to the possibility of "opting out" of any gamification implementation. The argument is that gamification should not be forced on workers and that workers should be given an option not to play if they so choose. This equates volunteerism with freedom, but if happiness and productivity are not value-neutral notions, then opting in and opting out are not neutral options either. When the route to happiness is offered as a possibility, its rejection can make one look ungrateful, uncooperative, unmotivated, and unwilling to get with the flow. If gamification is a good thing, then its rejection signifies problems in other areas: workers might be too skeptical of management's intent or, worse, too unmotivated to seek a better life. Volunteerism can thus become a means whereby individuals are blamed for failing to will properly.[131]

But the technical possibility of opting out is also more complicated than what gamification advocates appear to claim. As the Open Badges initiative points to, gamification is designed to be implemented as a system rather than as a contained software procedure—its goal is one of "deep scoring" rather than just a behaviorist box.[132] And to accomplish the ontology of the "deep score," it is necessary to implement gamification as a protocol, a process that renders the vocabularies of points and badges critical for articulating the skills, achievements, and abilities of workers. Once locked into protocols used to evaluate, promote, and fire employees, gamification no longer is a choice. Playing by the rules of the game may be the only way that the demonstration of aptitude, competence, and skills can proceed. Opting out of gamification would be equivalent to opting out of a process of employability itself, the choice likely to intensify the precariousness of life for the worker already deemed replaceable to begin with. Passionate work can rationalize techniques of biopolitics; the willingness to accept gamification may determine the rights to employment, wages, and survival when it becomes a part of the protocol.

This explains my concerns with the compassionate imagination. I do not believe that the disgust with the disingenuity of gamification will fully disappear: the critiques of gamification and the ways that workers seek to game gamification and cry foul when it fails to be fair reflect ambivalence about this vision.[133] McKenzie Wark has described games as "allegorithms"; games are meant to be perfected allegories of the real world, with fairness built into their algorithms.[134] And so, when games actually *become* the real world, their imperfections easily incite resentment and skepticism. Our tolerance for a faulty system decreases when perfection seems achievable with an adjustment of code, when the games that we play show that hard work and skill can indeed give us a better score and an epic win. The magic circle resists instrumentalization.

Yet, the risks of hopeful suspension extend beyond the call for fairness. Protocols establish the grammar of a system; they do best in determining the terms by which a problem is to be approached. The dangers of "passivity competence" that Sloterdijk writes about lie not just in their capacity to numb and remove critical judgment. Protocols can also determine the routes by which thoughtfulness is to be channeled.[135] As more becomes dependent on algorithmic fairness, I am concerned that it will come to stand in for structural fairness, and the former will ultimately determine the terms by which the good life can be envisioned. What Robert Pfaller calls "interpassivity" and what Jodi Dean considers "communicative capitalism" are deeply entrenched in our technological systems and passions; we are used to having things be active in our stead. Gamification plays on this desire, reducing the range of objects we can attach hopes to, even as attachment itself becomes ever easier: a badge, a score, an item purchased, an algorithm.[136] Certain kinds of hope are worth keeping intolerable, and the effort directed toward making suspension hopeful deserves opposing at every turn.

4

Urban
Preserves

In December 2014, Googleplex designer Clive Wilkinson presented the "Endless Workplace," an ambitious architectural proposal that layers a large suspended open office over the roofs of buildings in the city of London.[1] Conceptual schematics depict a glistening, glass-covered, sun-lit structure meandering across the skyline, punctuated by floating circular courtyards that reveal the sights below (see figures 4.1 and 4.2). This design, according to Wilkinson, is meant to address a "technologically liberated future," where work has become untethered from a fixed site. By having the workplace float over apartment buildings accessible by an elevator ride, workers can avoid the tiresome London commute and enjoy a comfortable, temperature-regulated ecosystem meant to foster creative and intelligent work. The vast open floor plan of the suspended structure, he elaborates, would encourage collaboration between "coworkers from different disciplines," relieve them from "numbing isolation of working at home," and foster "village-like communities," where professional relationships can be made personal.[2]

This hip architectural vision shows how urban infrastructure can condense the longing for utopia within information work, where work takes on the aesthetic embodiment of cool, and where life is made convenient and stimulating. Clearly, the structure was not designed with everyone in mind: it is directed toward the entrepreneurial, creative class, the workers emblematic of the New Economy. But exclusivity, architectural critic Antara Jha offers, understates the problem of the Endless Workplace.[3] The realization of the utopian vision rests upon the creation

4.1   The Endless Workplace addresses London's congested road
and train systems by imagining a new infrastructure for work. Built
as a connected platform over the city's rooftops, the Endless
Workplace also functions as a giant coworking space that residents
can reach from the elevators of their residences. Artist's
rendering of Clive Wilkinson's proposed "Endless Workplace."
Clive Wilkinson Architects, Los Angeles.

Artist's rendering of Clive Wilkinson's proposed "Endless   **4.2**
Workplace." Clive Wilkinson Architects, Los Angeles.

of a dystopia—the world underneath the workplace—which would be blanketed in shadow by the floating structure. Only the "scenographic beauty of London," its monuments, and its landscaped parks would receive sunlight provided through cutouts in the Endless Workplace.[4] The rest of London would be covered by the towering workplace, leading to a dank, gloomy city for the inhabitants beneath. For this reason, the Endless Workplace does not simply blur or prioritize the world of work: it goes further to divide the sensory encounter of London along the hierarchies of labor.

Such accounts of splintered urbanism—its implied access to protection from the damaged developments of the urban city—is central to Wilkinson's imagined utopia.[5] To drop out from the Endless Workplace means being denied mechanisms that support life; it entails being forced to navigate the dark, damp, and congested streets of London below without the protections that the workplace offers.

I open this chapter with the Endless Workplace to highlight a relationship between material infrastructure, passion, and precarity. In previous chapters, I have considered how passionate work might enable horizons of survivability for disenfranchised subjects. But how does this manifest itself for the declining fortunes of the middle class, who face an uncertain future? Wilkinson's fantasy gestures toward the binaries of aspiration and fear, of the good life and the bad life. In his concept, embodying the ethos of passion does not just create access to the amenities, prestige, and community of the Endless Workplace. Those who fail to inhabit its ethic would lose their classed privileges and the life-supporting technologies tied to it.

This attempt to model the workplace after a preserve is not limited to Wilkinson's imagination. Consider the statements of Rex Miller and his colleagues, consultants on office space, who advise corporations that they have to provide "a safe place for employees . . . marked by relief, hope, focus, and achievement."[6] They describe the world outside the workplace as an "external jungle" filled with stressors too numerous to count: "People around you seriously struggle with special-needs kids, long commutes, economic pressure, teenager and marriage problems, health challenges, single parenthood. aging and infirm parents." Given the hostile conditions of urban life, they argue, it is necessary to have offices as therapeutic refuges if corporations wish to cultivate "engaged and inspired" workers.[7]

These discourses highlight a different aspect of the perceived function of the workplace. Here, amenities are not primarily aimed at igniting the aspiration or productivity of workers. Instead, the infrastructure is designed to resist the anxieties of social and economic dislocation. My understanding of urban infrastructure as an affective response to the economy draws from Berlant's theorization of the affective conditions of the middle class when "the promise of the good life can no longer mask the living precarity of this historical present."[8] Berlant is especially skeptical of the claim that a shared condition of precarity can unite workers across geography and class and give rise to the political sensibility of the global precariat. Berlant highlights that precarity is a profoundly affective condition, and subjects conditioned to class privilege might even hold on more firmly to structures that propagate inequality out of fear of dislocation. The fear of slipping, in other words, may encourage a tightened grip over one's class privilege and its implied fields of social survivability.

This chapter gives an account of the ambivalence involved as urban infrastructure functions like a tightening grip. Using the coworking movement as context, I highlight the collaboration of human and nonhuman actors in maintaining a structure of coherence for middle-class subjects, whose notions of the good life have come under threat. To be clear, I am not suggesting that coworking necessarily aims to propagate inequality or that the fear of dislocation is strictly phenomenological. However, coworking does address and shift middle-class values to recuperate a vision of the possible good life through one's labor. And in being focused on the act of improving work, coworking also propagates the ethos of a passionate laboring subjectivity.[9]

"A Happiness Business"

As the term suggests, "coworking" involves having people of different professional affiliations work together in one space, rented from a coworking space operator. These coworking businesses include a variety of brand names. Some, such as WeWork, NextSpace, and the Hub, are larger and span multiple cities, while the majority are smaller businesses catering to specific communities. The users of coworking are equally varied, ranging from freelancers and small business owners to entrepreneurs and start-up teams, who specialize in fields such as programming, accounting, writing, consulting, marketing, and legal advice. Though some coworking spaces exercise exclusive memberships or admit solely workers of a particular industry, most offer no restrictions, and coworkers usually are similar only in being a burgeoning category of information workers untethered to a fixed worksite and unaffiliated with a specific corporation.

The kinds of workers inhabiting the space suggest how coworking is aligned with the contemporary organization of labor. Adam Neumann, the founder of WeWork, one of the largest coworking space operators, highlights the cultural currency of the trend by describing the recession as a boon for the coworking business. He explains that contrary to prevailing opinion, his coworking business actually experienced a surge in demand during the 2008 Great Recession: "Some people are gonna get laid off; they're gonna start new businesses; some companies are gonna wanna downsize."[10] Similarly, in a virtual conference, Jerome Chang from BLANKSPACES argued that the coworking trend would probably accelerate with the coronavirus pandemic because the number of freelancers was likely to grow with layoffs. Businesses with their leases expiring are also likely to choose cheaper and more flexible office sites now that people are more accustomed to remote work. Whether this is true for coworking businesses in general, these statements indicate how coworking is a response to changes in the labor market—an infrastructure designed to accommodate changes to work as traditional employment is being dismantled, where livelihoods are turning toward forms that are more contingent and precarious.[11]

The actual number of contingent workers is difficult to ascertain due to the many different definitions by which temporary work can be defined.[12] Estimates of the size of the US gig economy, for instance, vary from 0.1 to 34 percent of the full-time employed.[13] Regardless of the variability in numbers, however, there is a general sense that contingent workers constitute a growing portion of the workforce with the rise of the gig economy. A survey commissioned in 2019 by Upwork, a major digital freelancing platform, indicates that 35 percent of workers have done freelance work in the past year and that 28 percent of this group would consider themselves full-time freelancers.[14] Some of these contingent workers might have the status of what Jody Miller and Matt Miller call "supertemps," or "top managers and professionals . . . who've been trained at top schools and companies and choose to pursue project-based careers independent of any major firm."[15] The majority, however, grapple with issues related to an unstable salary, low wages, the absence of insurance, and the stressful need to be constantly reskilled and adept at self-branding.[16] Seventy-nine percent of those surveyed by the Freelancers Union, for example, reported having insufficient freelance work in 2010, and many in this group had to dip into savings or run up credit card debt.[17] More recently, in a 2019 survey by Upwork, 59 percent of respondents said they live from paycheck to paycheck; only 43 percent described themselves as having the finances to go for two weeks without pay.[18]

The conditions of contingent work may explain why most coworking businesses refuse to describe themselves as space rental businesses and elect instead to position themselves through more affective propositions of value. Alex Hillman, the founder of Indyhall and one of the most prominent leaders of the movement, states simply, "I am definitely not in the desk rental business, I am in the happiness business."[19] This is not just sales talk: proponents of coworking often make this distinction by distancing themselves from Regus, a global giant that sells office rental space. Indeed, Brad Neuberg, widely regarded as the pioneer of the coworking movement, describes Regus as the antithesis of coworking. Interviewed by *Deskmag*, a digital magazine dedicated to reporting on coworking, Neuberg explains that Regus was only interested in providing "shared utilities" to save costs; it was unconcerned about the well-being of its customers. He refers to his time at Regus as "utterly non-social," adding that it "had a very corporate drone feel to it."[20] John Battelle also makes this point when he compares images of Regus and WeWork. While the corporate photos of the former show empty, sterile, white-gray rooms, the latter's show groups of people mixing and working together in trendy settings. The contrast, he offers, indicates how Regus, by lacking the inspiring "culture" present at WeWork, makes its service feel like "corporate bullshit."[21]

Similarly, in a discussion via a coworking Facebook group, space operators overwhelmingly leaned toward describing coworking in affective terms: as a "hospitality," "connecting," and "happiness" business, as opposed to a "space" or "real estate" one. Liz Elam, the founder of Link Coworking and the organizer of coworking conferences, even deliberately omits the word *space* from her sales pitch, stressing instead that she sells "work-life balance, happiness, inspiration . . . [and] human contact."[22] This was also my personal experience in coworking spaces. Though the hosts I encountered detailed the different options of space available, they often sold their spaces by telling me about their "community," the coworkers using the space, and the networking sessions that could help connect me to the workers within. Hillman told me in an email conversation that "space is the red herring in the larger motif of coworking": "Most of the people in coworking spaces don't need space. They could work from anywhere, often for free or close to it. Yet they choose to pay. This is the biggest clue that coworking has very little to do with space (in the long-term), and more to do with the verb of 'coworking', which I define as the intentional choice to work around other people instead of alone."[23]

Coworking thus represents a cultural attempt to transform the experience of work: to make it more authentic, intimate, and exhilarating. Toward this end, coworking spaces highlight a number of different aspects of their service, including their tasteful interiors, the community and serendipitous connections that workers can cultivate within, the reliable flow of good coffee and networked connectivity, and the prestige of being located in an exclusive, branded space. These aspects, the coworking community believes, address the needs of the contemporary worker, who is no longer interested in simply finding a place to work. Instead, the space itself must offer something of additional value; it needs to encourage workers to work at their "creative, innovative, and productive best."[24] And such a quality of coworking, the community asserts, does not just result in increased productivity; as a survey by *Deskmag* tells us, 72 percent of coworkers are "happier at work."[25] And so the answer to "Why coworking?" appears self-explanatory: because, as the video suggests, "coworking makes you happy."[26]

Neoliberalism and the Origins of Coworking

This ideology is embedded in the historical narrative of coworking, which frames the roots of the movement as a story of self-transformation and discovery. The origin story is typically told through Brad Neuberg, a figure referred to as the pioneer of the term *coworking*. Neuberg is an attractive candidate for this heroic tale, possessing the qualities that embody the ideal post-Fordist subject: he is risk taking, creative, entrepreneurial, adverse toward bureaucracy, and genuinely committed to finding passion in his career.[27]

Neuberg begins his story in 2001 after he left a job at Google, frustrated with the traditional routines of a corporate job. Like other young, white, countercultural youths of the late twentieth century, Neuberg believed that he would be able to find his passion by living "outside the system." Over the next few years, he experimented with alternative living communities in California, Thailand, and Vietnam, hoping to find the fulfillment that had been lacking in his corporate job. But when happiness remained elusive, Neuberg was left confused and disappointed. The travels were meaningful, but his lifestyle was lonely and costly to maintain. The divergent routes to happiness, the traditional notion of a stable job, and a counter-cultural bohemian lifestyle were all found to be unsatisfactory in his case. The answer eventually came to him in 2005 through what is supposed to have been the first coworking space, an arrangement that combined "freedom and independence" with the "structure and community of a job." This finally provided Neuberg with the satisfaction that he desired and formed the narrativized bedrock of the coworking movement.[28]

Neuberg is resolute in his belief in passionate work and relentless in his pursuit of it. The experimentation along the way and the resulting narrative, from dissatisfaction to satisfaction, describe passion as a constant possibility, even when previous routes to happiness fail. This outcome, however, is made contingent on a flexible subject willing to take risks to revise her circumstances and find the happiness desired. Notably, Neuberg never references economic or social issues in his interviews and talks. Rather, his story makes passion a matter of dogged pursuit. Thus, even as coworking aims to build an infrastructure for passion, it also lays the burden of reinstating the fantasy of the good life on the individual subject and reframes the disappointment in structural conditions as a personal issue that the subject needs to overcome.

The transposition of the structural to the personal opens the question of whose unhappiness counts and whose solution to unhappiness is deemed to be legitimate. As Sara Ahmed points out, even fantasies of happiness are unequal in their social availability.[29] Neuberg's family resources, his freedom of relational ties, and his Ivy League education allowed him to make the self-discovery and self-transformation needed for happiness. Others may have different journeys for happiness, but not all might be valued similarly.

Laura Johnson's account of a coworking initiative organized by the Toronto government to meet the needs of women teleworkers in 2003 highlights how the movement's history could have had a longer, more diverse origin story.[30] This project predated Neuberg's first effort by two years, and many qualities of coworking in the present can also be found in Johnson's account. Yet this early initiative is never mentioned as part of the movement's history. The omission of Johnson's account as an origin story, I suggest, highlights the political economy of happiness. The women in Toronto were seeking a place to balance their work with childcare—they were not passionate entrepreneurs trying to restructure their lives, but people looking for ways to deal with the dual responsibilities of home and the workplace. The subjects of this history did not have the same relationship to notions of labor and the good life. They were not working in glamorous professions, nor did they have a high expectation about how work should be fulfilling. Making ends meet was their key concern.

If coworking is indeed a "happiness business," then whose happiness is it concerned with, and what shape does that happiness take? The choice of narrative to situate coworking's history, I argue, is nontrivial, because it illustrates the movement's ideology. While the women teleworkers in Johnson's story used coworking to find balance in their commitments, Neuberg's inspiration for coworking is placed within the context of a higher purpose. His question "How do I create happiness for myself?" is situated in relation to the aspiration for passionate work—that is, "How do I make work work for me?" And that thirst for passionate work is spun around a neoliberal ethos, focused on the entrepreneurial efforts to create conditions for happiness rather than using the infrastructure built by the state—as was the case with the Toronto initiative.

In this sense, Neuberg's contribution to coworking is not just historical. Instead, by proclaiming what coworking has "originally" sought to fulfill, he has legitimized and set the direction of the core values of the business while limiting alternatives of what coworking can become. Over time, this narrative then becomes a naturalized history of passion for a business whose "heart" involves connecting "people with meaningful work and a life they love."[31] Consider, for instance, the continuity of this history in WeWork's origin story, which Neumann likens to a religious conversion. He recalls that he was once attached only to lucre, but his wife started to question his focus, asking him, "What's your intention? What's your meaning behind what you do?"[32] These questions gradually led him to a new philosophy of entrepreneurship: that every business requires a deeper goal behind it. As he sagely offers, "When there is actual meaning behind your work, and when you truly love it, success will follow, money will follow, and happiness will be a part of it."[33]

Such ideals are unexceptional in the coworking movement. Collective Agency is one of the many spaces that aspire to be a cozy place to work "alongside people doing work they're passionate about and committed to."[34] While applying for membership at Impact Hub, a coworking space that caters to "socially conscious entrepreneurs," I was presented with a sign-up page that required me to write down my passions, so that the hosts could help with my venture. And interviews of coworkers by Gretchen Spreitzer and her colleagues led them to write in the *Harvard*

Business Review that people "thrive" in coworking spaces because those "who use coworking spaces see their work as meaningful."[35]

These beliefs are held to such an extent that space operators can feel frustrated when people hold differing views about what work is meant to fulfill. In a coworking Google Group, when space operators were discussing how they might articulate their "higher purpose" to their members, Susan Dorsch of Office Nomads complained, "Words can only do so much when faced with people's own desires & expectations when they walk in the door. . . . Sometimes you can explain yourself and your community until you're blue in the face and you are still met with 'OK well I'm still just going to pay you to use your meeting room. If I have to become a "member" or whatever to do that then fine' [facepalm]."[36]

This frustration reflects the centrality of passion in our work culture: people should strive to make their work meaningful rather than just treat it as something that they have to do. An attempt to treat coworking as a purely infrastructural resource (a "meeting room") is met with annoyance— an indication that the member does not understand how fulfilling work can be. This is one of the reasons why there has been much contention among space operators about the hyphen in the term *co-working*. In a highly discussed post in a Google Group, space operators maintained that though the term *co-working* is true to the Associated Press style guide, it invokes the idea of a "co-worker," a person who is simply working next to you, as opposed to the deep collaborative relationships that coworking prides itself on.[37] Central to this debate is an attempt to clarify what the brand of coworking stands for: a passionate workplace as opposed to one that simply affords the sharing of space.

Not all space operators will likely be equally committed to the ethos of passionate work, and not all members will yearn for this ideal, but the evangelical efforts of the community's outspoken members have enabled the movement to coalesce around passion as a shared mission—an act that furthers the ideological vision of work as a route to the good life. As a manifesto for a coworking conference in Los Angeles proclaims, coworking aims to help people "better connect their work with their passions": "Maybe in this century, we will have the opportunity to shift our relationships with work from one which is viewed as a necessary drudgery done for someone else to an exciting opportunity to realize one's potential. . . . The nature of the work that faces us is a race in the decades ahead [and] is going to require more than just showing up. It is going to require our complete creative faculties and our hearts and our souls. Coworking is providing a path to a way of approaching work that supports that."[38]

Tony Bacigalupo, the founder of New Work Cities and the writer of the manifesto, presents this revolution with conviction. However, since coworking mainly attracts contingent workers, this push for passion happens at the same moment when the outlook for work is getting increasingly dismal. Therefore, if passion is the goal, how does coworking foster passionate work for this historic bloc, whose beliefs about the good life have come under threat? We might seek to understand this by first situating coworking in two broad discourses: the "crisis" of loneliness and the newfound values of the creative class. Both discourses acknowledge the precarity of the present but locate coworking as a solution, thereby retaining work as a placeholder for the good life even as its traditional objects of optimism fade.

Freelance Loneliness

The freedom afforded by freelancing is often presented as a qualified perk, accompanied by the threat of isolation that freelancers must learn to manage. The media are replete with articles on the subject: the *Guardian*, for instance, calls freelancing a "lonely business," resources are readily available online to help make freelancing "feel less lonely," and *Quartz* even explains why freelance loneliness can "make us physically ill."[39] To be sure, this warning about freelance loneliness is not new: early telecommuting literature in the 1980s had already provided warnings about loneliness as workers left the structure of the workplace.[40] Its cultural salience, however, has increased significantly in the recent years with claims about the "loneliness epidemic," the allusion to loneliness as a "public health" crisis, and, in the United Kingdom, the creation of the position of "minister of loneliness" specifically to tackle this persistent problem.[41]

One prominent speaker on loneliness is US surgeon general Vivek Murthy. In *Together*, he explains how loneliness has appeared over and over as the binding theme in common ailments. Though it "wasn't a front-line complaint," he writes, "loneliness ran like a dark thread through many of the more common issues that people brought to my attention, like addiction, violence, anxiety, and depression."[42] What follows is a business proposition. In a booklet published by the *Harvard Business Review*, Murthy suggests that corporations should lead the battle against loneliness because workplaces are "where people spend the bulk of their time."[43]

Loneliness affects everyone, he argues, ranging from chief executive officers to factory workers, doctors, small business owners, and teachers. Addressing loneliness should form the basis for us to be "healing one another," as we use work relationships as a way of strengthening our health and well-being.[44] Overwork has ironically created occasion for the deeper insertion of work into our social lives as a means of curing our disappointment in social relations.

This push for a corporate cure is especially perverse if we consider the historical nature of loneliness. Cultural historian Fay Bound Alberti explains that the word was used in the sixteenth and seventieth centuries to describe a physical rather than psychological experience.[45] *Loneliness* then referenced aloneness, a state of being by oneself not necessarily accompanied by emotional distress. It was only with industrial capitalism and urbanization in the early nineteenth century that loneliness began to take on its modern form: the psychological quality accelerating and increasingly tied to the material demands of modern life, the weakening of communal bonds, and the individuation of lifestyles. But even so, none of these aspects can adequately account for the recent interest in loneliness. Lars Svendsen notes that "it is difficult to find any other 'loneliness epidemic' than the one present in the mass media itself, in which use of the term 'loneliness' has been significantly rising for years."[46] The intensified attention to loneliness relates to something beyond its frequency as a mental state. I agree with Jill Lepore that *loneliness* is a term that serves as "a cover for all sorts of things most people would rather not name and have no idea how to fix."[47] Loneliness is a diagnostic to a problem that denies a quick fix, but its ambiguous character has allowed for its appropriation for business use.

Our discussion can begin with a consideration of the role that coworking plays in the loneliness epidemic. As a business centered on community building, coworking easily fits into what *Vox* has called the "big business of loneliness."[48] In a 2019 conference presentation on community cultivation, Bacigalupo tells the audience that community is important "not just because it is good business . . . but because what we are doing is really important in a context of a much larger thing" called the "loneliness epidemic."[49] The search for community was especially relevant during the period of the coronavirus quarantines, when many space operators took this mission to heart and busied themselves creating online events for their members, seeking to help them combat isolation. Such efforts support Steve King's assertion that 89 percent of coworking survey respondents reported feeling less lonely after joining a coworking space. King explains that he had not anticipated this finding, but the social aspect actually showed up as the "most valuable" one for his respondents, reinforcing the value of the sociality that coworking can provide.[50]

This claim can prompt skepticism. But when Patrick Clark wrote in *Bloomberg* that coworking is "an expensive cure for loneliness," the co-working community showed remarkable solidarity, banding together not only to refute the article's claim of profitability in the coworking business but also to insist on the authenticity of relationships cultivated in the space.[51] Detractors of coworking too often criticize at a distance, space operator Oren Saloman suggests, and in doing so they fail to grasp the emotional reality of coworking. "Until you've experienced the sense of belonging in a coworking community," he writes, even a "one Euro a month" membership fee will feel exorbitant. On the other hand, someone who has encountered true community will find the membership to be "well worth every penny paid."[52]

This view is strongly held within the coworking community. As Hillman writes in a blog, one should never set out to "convince" people to try coworking, since that tactic is likely to find the wrong kind of member for the community.[53] Suitable members are those who see value in connection and belonging, those who want to be a part of the tribe. And these people are already likely to need coworking—they just have not seriously considered it yet. Thus, Hillman explains, his pitch simply consists of describing his own experience of loneliness: "the feelings that I had when I was all alone and working from coffee shops. And when you describe those feelings, anybody who has had those same feelings instantly 'gets it.'"[54]

But what exactly do people "get" in Hillman's story of loneliness? After all, loneliness is described by Hannah Arendt as "one of the fundamental experiences of every human life."[55] Our want for connection will not always be met, and loneliness is a banal condition that will affect us at different points in our lives. For Hillman, however, loneliness represents an affliction prevalent among the professional class of freelance workers. His story consists of frustrating interactions in cafés when he was surrounded by "bodies" but not "people": "If you turned to the stranger sitting next to you in a cafe and asked for help with a project you're working on . . . or to celebrate a small win . . . or to share in frustrations . . . you'd most likely be met with a raised eyebrow."[56] In one aspect, this narrative reveals a longing for what Ray Oldenburg calls a "third place," a space that supports an informal sociality among the familiar and the strange.[57] At the same time, implied in Hillman's account is a warning about the professional need for sociality, for networks where one may receive advice or help.[58]

Sara Horowitz and Toni Sciarra Poynter note that success in freelancing especially "depends on connecting with people" to build a reputation.[59] Since freelancers do not have colleagues, these professional exchanges are important in displaying one's "knowledge, reliability, and commitment to high standards," which improve one's occupational reputation and prospects for referrals of future work.[60] Furthermore, the "most important source of value" in post-Fordist informational capitalism, Adam Arvidsson argues, comes from "the ability to appropriate an externality"—that is, to draw on inspiration, knowledge, and resources from one's social networks and environments.[61] Freelancers deemed to be most competent usually do not have expertise in only one field; they also know whom to turn to if they need help for more complicated projects.[62]

Key to this discourse on loneliness is a perceived absence of emotional support. Space operators I interviewed echo Hillman in telling me that freelancers can easily feel lonely, as such work lacks the guarantees typical of employed work. They cite a long list of potential problems: without support, freelancers can easily become anxious when gigs are slow in coming, or they burn themselves out when they take on too much. They can be overwhelmed or distracted by household tasks and be unproductive. They can have nobody to vent to when they feel frustrated, to share ideas with when they are inspired, or even to be encouraged by when those ideas are realized.

The traditional corporation, with its compulsory sociality and nine-to-five circadian rhythm, may seem distasteful, but at least its regular paychecks, appraisals, and promotional schemes ensure that middle-class workers feel in sync with the conventional rhythms of capitalism. And without a support structure, freelancers may find it easier to lose their focus, develop unhealthy sleep patterns, and be less confident in their work.[63] These states highlight how loneliness is a feeling and a symptom; in addition to being unpleasant, loneliness can damage freelancers' professional interests, leading them to be unproductive, uncreative, stressed, outdated, and, ultimately, a failure in their career.

These warnings about loneliness show how the psychological need for connection is entangled with one's economic status. As Thomas Dumm notes, the word *alone* is a compound of two words, *all* and *one*—a composition that "condemns us to being no more than a weed in the wall at the same time as it allows us to be the most powerful of sovereigns."[64] The human condition, pregnant with self-regard, and the neoliberal injunction to use connections as a measure of commodified self-worth cannot be easily distinguished, because both are founded on the existental anxiety that the self will fail to be recognized and meaningfully joined with others.

We can return to Arendt to understand loneliness in those terms. A person experiences loneliness, she writes, "if he is no longer recognized as *homo faber* but treated as an *animal laborans* whose necessary 'metabolism with nature' is of concern to no one." Loneliness differs from the experience of solitude, because the latter is characterized by a distance from others while the former comes about "only when the most elementary form of human creativity, which is the capacity to add something of one's own to the common world, is destroyed."[65] Although Arendt's understanding of loneliness has an important historical context—she was writing at the close of the Second World War and was concerned with loneliness being a precursor to totalitarianism—her theorization leads us to see an important relationship between loneliness and labor. For Arendt, loneliness involves a sense of displacement from the sensual world because of the perceived worthlessness of one's labor. Loneliness is suggestive here of impotence: a gap between the realness of the self and the external world that the subject is unable to affect, where ideas, opinions, and abilities are made pointless and irrelevant to the world. Therefore, Arendt explains, a person is truly lonely not when they are isolated but when they feel "superfluous."[66]

What form can superfluousness take? Citing Marx, Nick Dyer-Witheford describes superfluousness as the very quality of the proletariat, an individual who, "economically speaking," is "nothing other than a 'wage laborer,' the man who produces and valorizes 'capital,' and is thrown out onto the street as soon as he is superfluous to the need for valorization."[67] Notably, superfluousness arises here as a condition rather than an event. The worker is not superfluous because she is retrenched and unemployed. Rather, it is the state of the worker's disposability, the minimalist definition of someone's worth that is demonstrated only by productive output, that makes one superfluous to begin with. Superfluousness marks a replaceable life, a life whose worth is made dependent on its instrumental definition of a wage and which cannot be valued in other terms, since it must always be made potentially replaceable by yet another life that can produce the same for less.

As common as it may be, superfluousness is subject to different experiential valences. The more that one's life is seen as valuable, as worthy of being protected, the more its disposability can become temporarily screened.[68] And the screening of disposability, Jill Stauffer writes in *Ethical Loneliness*, is key toward bracketing the forces that allow for the expression of energeticness: "When I am happy, full of energy, or simply up to the task at hand, existence does not strike me as a problem, does not strike me at all."[69] Those protected from vulnerability can engage energetically with the world with more ease; the world can appear as a canvas for actualization and as a display of talents, worth, and uniqueness: "Here we find the subject who is so confident that conditions will offer her a space of intelligibility that she does not even know that this belief requires confidence, or belief. She merely thinks that is what the world is."[70]

Stauffer reveals how the experience of loneliness works against the expression of passion. In her view, loneliness functions as an *interruption* to confidence, a state of abandonment that forces an encounter with the weight of existence. Loneliness accentuates the risk of action; it creates doubt in judgment that leads to uncertainty in action that can show up as a "lag," a misalignment with productive time where acting is delayed, where one is unable to act exactly as one wills with no hesitation.[71] The lonely might become depressed or sapped of energy, or she can doubt, as Thomas Dumm offers, her "sensual experience" that makes it hard to draw from social worlds to maintain and produce value.[72] One can find and express passion on one's own, but for it to achieve economic meaning, to have guaranteed worth as a commodity of labor power, one needs to find an exteriorized form of affirmation. Returning to Hillman's description of loneliness, the lonely subject is unable to find an objective vantage point outside herself to understand the strength, value, and meaning of her work and the ways to improve it. The lonely person is disconnected from the regime of value, thrown out of a trajectory where the world's potential fails to open and illuminate.[73]

Taken in these terms, loneliness might be understood as a spectral threat of the damage involved in precarious existence. Looming at the edges of consciousness, loneliness reminds us of the slippery work involved in maintaining one's position within a system of value and the ease with which one may lose one's footing and fall out of normative middle-class worth. It is not that loneliness makes one superfluous, but its affective quality reminds us of how close to superfluousness we are. The lonely, we are told, are less productive; less inspired; unable to grow their business contacts, which can improve their earnings; and more likely to have their start-ups fail.[74] In a moment of compulsory social capital, the lonely are vulnerable to free-fall in failure, uncushioned by others who can volunteer help and unable to increase the value of their labor, to appropriate the social to the value propositions that they offer.

Certainly, economic reason alone cannot fully account for the complex experience of loneliness. The feeling is relational, political, and social and needs careful situational consideration. But I focus on its economic thread because loneliness is increasingly parsed in that direction, as an outcome of the loneliness epidemic that reverberates through economic precariousness. Angel Kwiatkowski of Cohere, for instance, struck a chord when she posted a notice of a coworker's suicide in a coworking Google Group. Offering that the member's battle with depression was known by only two individuals, she urges space operators to build stronger, more supportive communities so that such tragedies may be avoided in the future. Though she acknowledges that causes of suicide may be complicated, her remedy remains centered on strengthening ties to beat back loneliness. "Weave a tight web among yourselves that is unbreakable even by the worst depression," she writes, continuing to offer how other people have come to share their struggles with depression since the tragedy, which matters because "we can tighten the net for them" by providing them with more care.[75]

Efforts like these have led Janet Merkel to describe coworking as an "emancipatory practice challenging the current neoliberal politics of individualisation."[76] Space operators, she writes, create "new work-related and social experiences in the city" by assembling and arranging human and nonhuman actors to foster the values of sharing, collaboration, and care—values that encourage socialities that oppose the formation of self-absorbed, individualistic subjects.[77] Kwiatkowski and Beth Buczynski, for instance, tell us that people who work alone are absent their tribe: "You didn't know it at the time, but you NEED people around you. Coworking fills that need."[78] And in seeking to fill that need, coworking adopts a more sustainable philosophy of the laboring self, where workers are treated as "renewable resources" rather than "another input in the business process, something to be managed, maximized, and often discarded when the process was complete."[79]

While I recognize the value in the initiatives proposed by Kwiatkowski, it is nonetheless crucial to note the normative structures involved in the care that is expressed. In particular, loneliness is presented in coworking as a problem of bad relating that necessitates middle-class values of care and wellness. The dependencies developed in coworking spaces, which Merkel describes as "challenging the current neoliberal politics of individualisation," are still built on the goal of restoring an independent, functioning subject. Loneliness is framed as a condition to be rehabilitated from; a lonely person is a misfit who needs therapy to veer back to a "healthy" individuality. The stigma attached to loneliness means that subjects are told to be emotionally reflexive, to monitor themselves for feelings of loneliness, so that it may be arrested through corrective forms of neoliberal sociality that stress productive, instrumental relations.[80]

Indeed, one of the selling points of coworking is that people can find like-minded individuals to propel them forward.[81] Freelance subjects are not told to relate to *everybody*, only to those who share a similar professional ethic within coworking support groups. Coworkers I interviewed often talked about their want for sociality in instrumental terms. Nick explained recently about leaving a coworking space because "nobody there was from my industry," and networking did not make professional sense. Grace opined that it is important to consider the "quality" of people in coworking spaces: "Can they help your business? Are they useful as networks?" And when I asked about the importance of building relationships to fight loneliness, Nick replied that this rationale might be "important for some people, but most people I know are there to work, not to hear sad stories about your life." He added that people do make "small talk" or "joke around"—standard forms of sociality—but he thought that it would be "weird if someone opened up to me" in a more intimate way. In fact, "most people already have their own group of close friends. . . . Coworkers are good for a chat if you need to take a break," but it is unrealistic to expect "something deep."

I do not intend to demean the community and sociality that coworking offers. Given the variety of coworking spaces and social relationships, it is not possible to generalize about all coworking relationships from these responses. And loneliness can occur for reasons other than economic ones. But coworking is ultimately built for economic relations, and vulnerable self-disclosure is often at odds with the impression of a professional self.[82] Thus, by necessity, most disclosures must remain bounded within the confines of lightweight sociality. At times, in fact, sociality for coworkers may not go further than a "vibe." At a conference, Bacigalupo explains that creating a feeling of community typically requires no more than ten dedicated members. These ten, he offers, will often produce a "halo effect" that will attract other members to feel a sense of belonging, simply because they are tangentially connected to one of them. The use of social atmosphere to fight loneliness shows how coworking can reduce loneliness while at the same time fail to create the conditions for people to come to relate to others more deeply.

Hence we can see how this coworking sociality can involve another kind of politics. In June 2015, there was a protest by WeWork janitorial staff in New York branches. At that time, WeWork janitors were paid an average of eleven dollars an hour, less than half the average wage of unionized New York janitorial staff. When the WeWork staff tried to unionize, it was reported that the company threatened to have them fired.[83] Demanding higher pay, benefits, and vacation time, the signs held up at this protest—with slogans such as "wework here too"—raise an issue about the shape that coworking sociality takes and the costs that accompany its manifestation. As Brendan O'Connor points out, though Neumann refers to people in WeWork as the "We Generation," not all within its space are a part of this circle, and not all kinds of socialities are encouraged. Janitors who wish to unionize—a type of professional social relation—are prevented from doing so.[84]

But even those who fit within the definition of the "We Generation" may be exploited, as in the case of Tara Zoumer, an associate community manager of WeWork, who was fired after she refused to sign a new arbitration agreement with the company. Zoumer told the *New York Times* that her salary was too low for the cost of living in Berkeley, California, where she worked, and the long hours that should have warranted overtime pay were dismissed by WeWork as part of her job as a "brand ambassador."[85] Emotional labor, as the author of *The Coworking Handbook* informs us, is crucial toward ensuring the "right atmosphere in the community." Hosts of the space have "to be always 'on'" to put tenants at ease and to develop the connections they have with each other.[86] But emotional labor is not just hard. As the case of Zoumer highlights, emotional labor may also serve as grounds for the legitimation of the borderless nature of work and the denial of overtime pay.

Who loses out in this care for loneliness, and what connections are we told to build to stem our feelings of isolation? Melissa Carroll writes that loneliness presents an opportunity for us to recognize our shared condition of precarity and the deep interdependence of the social: "It is in fact because of loneliness's sheer indifference to bodies, boundaries, and borders that being lonely is potentially the most ethical way to relate to one another."[87] There is a degree of disempowerment common to the janitor, the community associate, and the lonely tenant of WeWork, but when loneliness is presented as an absence of productive, instrumental relationships, the chance to forge political and affective consciousness is curtailed. Instead, coworkers are more likely to see individuals in terms of their labor value: the janitor ensures the cleanliness of the setting, the community associate makes the tenant feel good, and the tenant is encouraged to build collaborative relations that can facilitate middle-class advancement. These socially ordered relations might be reassuring, but they leave loneliness unpoliticized and afford the continued exploitation of people across different professional classes.

Reorienting the Good Life

While coworking is often discursively marketed as a service to restore workers to healthy sociality, it also aspires to present an idealized impression of work. How does coworking manifest this ideal? In *Architecture and Utopia*, Manfredo Tafuri describes architecture as "symbols of the American longing for something other than itself, terms of reference for a society continually terrified by the processes it has itself set in motion and indeed considers irreversible."[88] The iconography of architectural marvels, he remarks, can bring about "a sublimation of real phenomena" and redeem "the misery and impoverishment" of city life with an image of liberation.[89]

This idea has a historical basis in corporate architecture. In the 1950s, large American businesses envisioned what Louise Mozingo called a "pastoral" corporate landscape, constructing office parks and corporate campuses in suburbia to avoid the deteriorating living conditions of the inner city.[90] This trend is replaced in the present by what Alexandra Lange calls "Silicon Valley urbanism," where companies such as Google, Amazon, and AT&T have relocated their campuses back into the city while remaining insulated from its streets with spaces large enough to include their "own restaurant, [their] own artworks, [their] own store, [their] own bowling alley, and [their] own clubs."[91] This heterotopia comes with a cost. Deploying culture in service of productivity, these developments appropriate ideas of the urban—its grit, vibrancy, and authenticity—while detaching themselves from the ethics of occupied space, which usually results in gentrification, securitization, and the expulsion of economically vulnerable minorities.[92]

There are a number of similarities between coworking spaces and the workplaces of these valued businesses, partly because technology companies such as Google have been used as a role model for the coworking experience.[93] Neuburg, for instance, explains that coworking should aspire to produce the "benefit of working for Google without having to work for Google."[94] Miguel McKelvey, the cofounder and chief creative officer of WeWork, sees this as a right: "Having a nice office is not just something for cool tech companies like Google."[95] The Google model is manifested in the aesthetics and the trendy values that coworking promotes—community, sharing, and accelerated serendipity—which reflect a similar impulse to construct a material utopia detached from the conditions of the city.

Yet, few coworkers are Google employees, and many fall short of the status of this group of esteemed workers. In this sense, the aspiration to experience the amenities of Google reveals the gap between desire and reality, utopia and precarity. To understand the politics of the gap, we first need to situate coworking within a discourse on austerity propagated by ideas about the "creative" and "sharing" economy. Alessandro Gandini partially gets at this point when he describes how coworking is similar in "vibe" to Richard Florida's thesis on the creative class.[96] I agree that co-working needs to be read in relation to the neoliberal urban development of cities that prioritize creativity, entrepreneurialism, and a carefully curated image.[97] But while Gandini, following critics such as Jamie Peck and Andy Pratt, takes aim at Florida for his glossed simplification of the quality of creative jobs and the unsustainable urban development that the cult of urban creativity has propagated, I am more interested in how Florida describes a reorientation of happiness as necessary to the happiness of the creative class.[98]

This might sound like a familiar argument. After all, Florida premises his argument for creative cities on the supposed new desires of the creative class. In *The Rise of the Creative Class*, he states that his "interview subjects recounted their desire and *need* to live in places that offer stimulating, creative environments.... People not only want to live near their workplace, they want to *like* living there."[99] The words *want, desire,* and *need* locate the argument for creative cities in the natural desires of creatives themselves, as if such preferences are founded in the social and biological inclination for a creative, stimulating lifestyle.

But in *The Great Reset*, the lesser-known book that follows his more widely read *Rise of the Creative Class*, Florida positions the reorientation of happiness not only as a demand but also as a necessary austere measure that responds to the economy. He makes the argument by borrowing David Harvey's concept of the "spatial fix."[100] Yet while Harvey deploys the concept toward criticism of capitalism—namely, how capitalism tends to overaccumulate in regions only to eventually destroy them to make "openings for fresh accumulation in new spaces and territories"—Florida presents spatial fixes as economic destiny, as evolutions that work on boom-and-bust cycles.[101] The Great Recession, he explains, has triggered a need for spatial fixes that force cities to remodel their urban programs to create "a new economic landscape that is more closely in sync with the improved productive capabilities of the underlying economy." This change would represent a "reset" that would usher in "a whole new economic landscape" and "a whole new way of life."[102]

The distinction between natural and pragmatic desire is less clearly defined in this instance. For example, when Florida speaks against an "ownership society," where people seek to possess houses and cars as signs of upward mobility, he grounds his argument not in terms of what people want but in terms of what is most economically sensible: "Owning your own home made sense when people could hope to hold a job for most or all of their lives. But in an economy that revolves around mobility and flexibility, a house that can't be sold becomes an economic trap, preventing people from moving freely to economic opportunity."[103]

This "new way of life" that refuses the purchase of expensive fixed items such as houses and cars—as well as air conditioners, dryers, and microwaves—is born out of a pragmatic need for subjects to be mobile, "to move more quickly" to cities with opportunities so that they might survive and shrink "the time it takes to move from crisis to enduring recovery."[104] Even the experiential goods that Florida describes the creatives as enjoying are now framed, at least partially, as the necessary objects that help craft a more employable self. He believes that the funds not spent on houses and cars should be directed toward "new forms of personal development and new experiences," so that creative workers will always be up to date. And while workers may brew their own beer and start vegetable gardens as a method of self-expression, they may also do so "to adopt a more sufficient do-it-yourself ethic." Whether or not it is truly pragmatic, the "creative lifestyle" recommended by Florida is undergirded by a different instrumental purpose: to survive a period of economic uncertainty and hardship.[105]

Florida asserts that the route to true happiness is found in these austere measures: subjects who practice them "recognize what psychologists of happiness have shown: it's not money per se that makes you happy but rather doing exciting work and having fulfilling personal relationships."[106] What does it mean when a measure designed for your survival becomes something that you instead desire, because it lies closer to what "true" happiness is? Florida endorses a different politics of proximity, offering that we may be happier and even more passionate about our work despite worsening structural conditions because the survival of hardship will draw us near to the "true" objects of happiness, which lie in fulfillment within work and community. Hardship equates to happiness in this scheme, because it forces us to adapt to a more minimalist definition of life that comes closer to our authentic passions.

This line of thought is substantiated in Rachel Botsman and Roo Rogers's book on the sharing economy, *What's Mine Is Yours*. They write that "economic necessity has made people more open to new ways of accessing what they need and how to go about getting it."[107] At the same time, this need to share has made it opportune to recover "old virtues" such as "meaning and community in our lives."[108] Since sharing can optimally function only when people build "anchors of commonality," the excuse to share can actually provide permission for people to know each other better and form new social bonds.[109] Similarly, Horowitz and Poynter of *The Freelancer's Bible* write that "profit and community" are becoming indistinct because people have realized that new economic conditions require collaboration. This development has prompted the values of what they call "New Mutualism," where people practice sharing and exchanging to make ends meet. "New Mutualism isn't just a feel-good thing. It's a survival thing," they explain, adding that a loving community is the best defense against hardship: "How else can freelancers hold the line against downward mobility through lower and lower pay" unless they learn to give, share, and collaborate, to strengthen each other as a community?[110]

The discourse on survival, built into the ideas of sharing, collaboration, and community, highlights a process of reorientation, where the previous objects that structure the good life are rescinded in favor of more pragmatic ones that provide newfound pleasures. Stephane Kasriel, the former chief executive officer of Upwork, tells us that the priorities of workers will change because the traditional elements of the good life are no longer a tenable prospect for many. "Professional growth," he explains, is getting harder for the middle class: "Their salaries aren't growing as much, and they aren't getting as many promotions." He continues, "And when economic payoffs are less than desirable, they start optimizing around other factors, such as how much they can learn, whether they have better work-life balance, or whether they can live somewhere more pleasant for less."[111]

The grounds for happiness in work are always prone to shifts because of the fundamental challenge of expecting happiness from a capitalist system. When the "traditional conception of the American Dream" grows more distant as a possibility, new means will be invented to reconcile the wish for satisfaction at work.[112] The hope invested in the new trends, of course, does not mean an end to the aspiration for upward mobility, but it does endorse a different perspective on the fulfillment that work can offer. Deteriorating structural conditions are offset by the promise of stronger communities, deeper intimacies, a trendier lifestyle, and a life more happily and ethically lived.

Collaborative Freedom

But how is the compromised vision of the good life manifested? In considering the reorientation of happiness, we have to examine the various technologies involved in making this cultural bargain plausible and attractive. In this section, I turn to my fieldwork observations to explain how coworking has transformed the key rhetoric of freelancing—freedom—into a material and experiential consumable object. In the first instance, the coworking product is itself packaged as consumer choice, something that the worker can voluntarily select. "Unlike a traditional worker, who has to go to the office the company dictates, you have to choose your coworking spot," space operator Randy tells me, adding that "our space is not for everybody, and I encourage people to try different spaces to find out what they like."

The experimentation of coworking spaces maps the pleasures of consumption onto the freedom that workers have in adopting nontraditional arrangements of labor. Most coworkers I have spoken to are tenants of more than one coworking space. Jessie, who was based at WeWork, explained that the monthly membership had allowed her to relocate easily: "I didn't like how isolated I felt at WeWork, and having been there, I had a better idea of what I wanted." After trying different arrangements, Jessie finally made her choice to situate herself in the current space: "This place is much closer to my home and has a friendlier community." When I asked if she had ever felt pressured to stay at a location, she expressed that she had never had a negative experience leaving, and "perhaps if I do, then it's a good sign I should go." These statements highlight how coworking is structured to have workers experience work as consumers: by reducing the challenges involved in the "freedom" to experiment, and by emphasizing personal fit, workers are taught to evaluate their working space like a purchase—a reminder of how they, as freelancers, have a choice about where they want to work based on the space's appearance, location, amenities, and people within.

The notion of freedom is also ideologically built into the layout of the space. Almost all coworking spaces I visited share the same approximate layout, with divisions between the lounging and working areas. In Coloft, a Santa Monica, California, coworking site, a lounge area is decorated with a beautiful, homey set of red and gray couches, resting on a geometric-patterned carpet (see figure 4.3). Steps away is the work area with standard brown desks, Herman Miller Aeron chairs, and neutral beige flooring. Places such as BLANKSPACES include alternate sitting and standing arrangements, with such features as bar-top counters with stools instead of chairs and hanging tables built for workers who prefer to stand. Others have leisure areas, with arcade machines or a miniature golf set. These different demarcations of space, space operator Janet told me, serve the instrumental purpose of giving coworkers "freedom to move around and to be at where it is most suitable for them at that point in time. If they want to socialize they can go to the couch, or they can go all the way to the back of the room if they do not want to be disturbed."

While I had thought of her statement more as a sales pitch when I first heard it (people can and do talk at desks and lounges, and the soft lighting makes for excellent photos to market spaces), I gradually noticed that the different allocations of space communicate something more important: that coworkers are encouraged to move around, which reinstates the experience of freedom characteristic of freelancing. Unlike a library or a café, where people are hesitant to move because seats are limited and they are surrounded by strangers, coworking spaces create an atmosphere where people feel free to move, stretch, get coffee, or head to the restroom. One coworker described this as a nontrivial benefit, citing an absence of "distractibility": "When I was at the café . . . I was always distracted. . . . There were people buying things, but also those moments where you need to go to the restroom, and there is no restroom in the place, or you have to pack everything up [to go to the restroom], or if it's really crowded and you feel bad taking up a seat. . . . It occupies your mind, and it is hard to concentrate. Here you can just leave. I leave my things on the desk and I know it's safe."

These minor disturbances reveal how the freedom of "work" is a collaborative construction. The idea that work is a productive sphere, where people can professionally clock in and clock out and be left to focus during that time, relies on a background of preparation and outsourced labor—care work that entails the washing of clothes, the caring for children, the availability

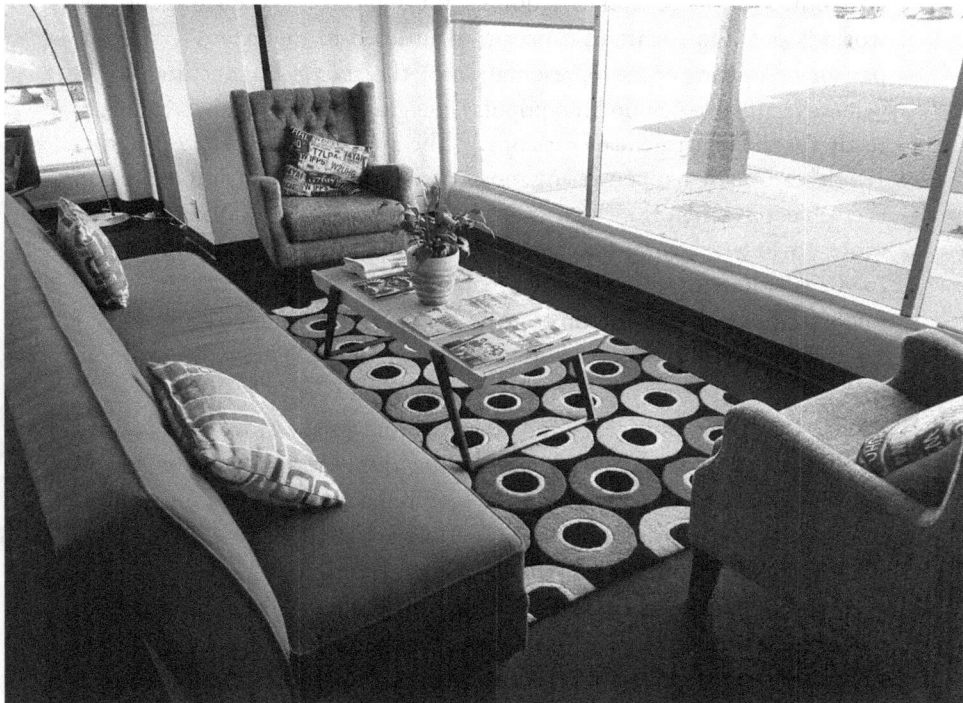

Lounge area in the coworking space Coloft in
Santa Monica, California. Photo by author.

of an undisturbed space, the provision of food already made.[113] Reinhold Martin writes that corporate offices have largely maintained this fantasy through an "organizational complex," architectural spaces where work is created to be insulated from the world outside.[114] When the workplace is gone, however, this illusion easily encounters cracks—even a table, as we can see with the cafés, cannot be guaranteed for use.

Let us return to Stauffer's argument on the provisional nature of our sovereignty. In her view, the energetic capacity to act is predicated on existential confidence, a certain assurance about how the world is meant to accommodate the sovereign action of the subject. For the energetic, the world is put into a state of expectation, attuned to the expression of our passions. Popular media representation of the always-on, hustling, high-value executive relies on this popular imaginary, a world that is always ready for the enactment of passions.[115] The fantasy suggested here is that "work" can easily happen at any moment, as and when inspiration strikes the subject or when the client calls. As Stauffer explains. "What could be more obvious than my freedom to interact or not interact with objects in my surroundings? If I want to eat the apple sitting in a bowl in my kitchen, I'll reach out and do so. And if I don't, I won't, and so perhaps I am sovereign with regard to apples in my kitchen. Objects leave us room to reach toward them but also to withdraw from them."[116]

Manipulating an object simply because one wishes to, unconstrained by uncertainty, is an expectation conditioned by the setting. If having an apple requires you to get up from the seat to buy it, which can mean a loss of the seat, then getting an apple is no longer a straightforward decision. Or if this is not your kitchen, then getting an apple may not be so simple, even if the apple is within reach. This is why Stauffer calls such confidence a kind of "wishful thinking." The belief that the world is out there for you to act upon is structured by an affirmation of the context. Paddy Scannell explains that the "care-structure" of technologies is built into things and concealed "in order to 'let us be.'" Caring technologies, from this perspective, are those that provide permission for us to act as sovereigns, fully in charge of the freedom that we are purportedly given.[117] We see here how the freedom promised by freelancing is a collaborative construct. When the world seems to help you along, it can become easier to act optimistically, boldly, and spontaneously—to hustle.

For this reason, coworking might be said to be an urban preserve, providing for a structure of coherence that maintains the value of work through a curated space. As most interviewees explained to me, coworking is never a need, in the sense that workers can often choose to do their work elsewhere. But having a coworking space that one returns to maintains the valuation of the object of work or, as coworker Kathy explained, "so it doesn't look like I'm doing odd jobs like a gig worker." The contradiction would not be lost on Kathy, who is freelancing as a marketer. What she distances herself from is the idea of "gig" as a temporary job, a nonprogressing career. Though her clients may change, her career is progressive, she insists; her income is tied not to hours but to her skills and reputation. The more sophisticated her skills and the stronger her connections, the larger the fee that she can charge her clients.

Like the idea of trajectory described in the previous chapter, coworking provides and supports this sense of the "normal" in middle-class labor: a career with steady progression, developing in worth as the subject gains more experience and reputation. We can see how coworking supports this belief with its emphasis on community talks on "leveling up" skills, master classes, and the argument that serendipitous encounters in coworking spaces may eventually lead to profitable start-up ventures. This belief also explains the context of the optimism that Kathy offers: coworking provides coherence to the core middle-class imaginary of an investable future of work, a fantasy that remains even as the conditions of labor turn recognizably precarious.

Of course, being in a coworking space does not guarantee that all encounters with work will be pleasant. In my time coworking, I observed different instances where coworkers left their seats in frustration after a particularly difficult phone call or email. On one occasion, I saw a coworker angrily slam down her phone after a call with PayPal and complain to someone else that the company had frozen her account and left her unable to pay her bills. In another situation, a coworker left his laptop in a huff, heading down to a café to rant to someone about how a company had asked for extensive information and a breakdown of a quoted price, only to use it as leverage to hire someone cheaper. In both instances, the coworkers were able to leave their spaces without hesitation. Closing the lids of their laptops, they could leave for cafés, take walks on the street, or go to the gym to relieve the tension.

This may sound like a minor point, but to move in the world without extraneous care is a privilege of the middle class. Leaving without fear that the laptop will be stolen or the seat taken is a privilege offered by a securitized workplace that gives the worker the right to be. Being located near gyms, yoga studios, hip eateries, coffee joints, parks, and condominium complexes is also a deliberate decision made by coworking space operators to ensure a heterotopic work experience for their members. By making a world where "work" is a tightly bound concern, coworking helps in excluding other fears and enhances one's agency to be, and even to recover. It tightens the gap between panic and relief, pulling these temporal transitions together to cover up the concussive superfluousness that so saturates the unmediated precariousness of work culture. This point also explains the coherence that coworking can bring. Coworking provides a feeling of being cared for, a sense that attenuates the precarious reality of their labor.

This aspect of freedom extends to the realm of sociality. As Peter Bacevice writes in *Money* magazine, most coworking spaces aim to build "just right" communities—"that is, just right in that they involve newcomers as much or as little as they want, without any pressure."[118] Similarly, space operators informed me that coworking provides a "no-pressure" or "no-strings-attached" socialization, meaning that "you can be as social as you want, when you want it," and the design of the interiors encourages this dynamic (see figure 4.4). Having a desk nearby, coworker Amita said, means that "you always have an excuse to return to your table" by saying that you have a "deadline to rush or a call you need to make." She told me that this makes people feel in control of the sociality that occurs; if they wish to talk, they can work nearer to the pantry or in the lounge, but if they do not want to be disturbed, they can put their headphones on.

This flexibility reflects what Steven Miles refers to as "complicit communality," which he defines as "a sense of communality that is deemed by the individual to be communal *enough*." Miles uses this concept to explicate the overlap between individuality and collectivity in commodified spaces. The public atmosphere promoted in these commodified spaces, he writes, facilitates "an alternative form of communal, one in which you retain your individuality, whilst exploring communal alternative through physical opportunities that consumption provides."[119] Such sociality is designed—for example, in coworking spaces—to be unthreatening and therapeutic. The norms of the space—the use of headphones and shared desks—allow coworkers to realize their need for sociality while respecting their comfort level with social interaction.

Perhaps this aspect of sociality is made clearest with the rise of the "work sprint" initiatives in coworking space. Work sprints describe a social agreement where workers gather for a certain period of time to work on their projects, with the tacit agreement to focus and avoid distraction. The gathering—usually supported by productivity time-management

Bar area in the Berkeley, California, branch of WeWork. **4.4**
Photo by author.

techniques and, in the pandemic situation, a teleconferencing program such as Zoom—encourages everyone to come together to keep "social accountability." We see how sociality is presented here as atmosphere and instrumentalized into a technique of productivity for workers to drive each other. Along with other trending events, such as sessions for meditation and yoga and morning/lunch dance parties, these sprints form the new creed of productivity-based social gatherings that keep sociality to a comfortable boundary and create a community without its messes.

And so, it comes as no surprise that the most common complaint about coworking spaces is also its most intrusively social: noise. As *Deskmag* reports, one in four coworkers is uncomfortable with the noise level in these spaces.[120] "Some people appeared to show off their important phone conversations by speaking as loudly as possible," a coworker named Campbell complained to the *New York Times*. "Even those who thought they were sharing an idea with their small teams managed to broadcast across the whole room."[121] Indeed, most space operators told me that it is difficult to ensure the comfort of all members given that the tolerance for sound is "subjective." Still, they have tried to cater to all tenants by building soundproof phone booths and separations so that unwanted noise in the space may be reduced.

Miles does not assume that complicit communality is necessarily detrimental. The logic of consumption may manifest as a means for individuals to feel empowered, as if they are taking "possession of the neoliberal city rather than being possessed by it."[122] Similarly, coworking spaces offer a means to relieve some of the anxieties involved in crafting neoliberal personhoods. They provide the potential for making light professional connections while minimizing stress in the encounter. The paid membership also legitimizes—at least to a point—the view that customers should have a right to a comfortable workplace and can make demands when the sociality of the place crosses their degree of comfort.

Right Spaces, Right Feelings

The feeling of being cared for is bound up in the positive aesthetics of coworking spaces. WeWork, one of the more highly designed spaces that I have visited, makes a conscientious effort to engage in what Neumann calls "floor psychology."[123] Framed slogans and multimedia motivational messages are found everywhere in a WeWork space. At the Berkeley, California, branch, I was greeted at the entrance by a flat screen monitor displaying a quote from Thomas Edison. Inside, on a pillar next to a foosball table, were framed slogans: "Just keep making," "Good work takes hard work," and "Never settle ever." On the side of a pantry wall were stacks of black mugs embossed with the injunction "Do what you love."

Although few of the other coworking spaces I visited are as elaborate in their design, most take the effort to produce a similar positive atmosphere. Many are crammed with slogans and wall art. Some, including NextSpace, have boards displaying photos of members and notices of their recent achievements. Others, such as Impact Hub, have chalkboard walls or Post-it notes where members write positive messages about why they like coworking. Sometimes there are also little gadgets or fixtures that make the space distinctive. For instance, a place in Los Angeles has soft toys littered everywhere and a miniature sand garden placed on a high table next to a window.

Besides aiming to personalize the space, such attention to design highlights how brands and architecture are increasingly focused on the sensate quality of spaces.[124] At the 2016 Los Angeles coworking conference, several keynote speakers talked about the science of the senses and why they matter to the coworking business. Melissa March, the founder of PLASTARC, an architecture firm that merges "social data" with "design," told attendees to be sensitive to "multisensory design"—namely, how sight, sound, touch, taste, and smell can improve the productivity of workers and make them "happier." Central to the senses is a feeling of "delight," she explained, and providing it can help coworkers have a better work experience. For instance, operators could "intrigue" coworkers' sense of smell by supplying coffee, flowers, candles, and air fresheners. To appeal to the sense of taste, she told operators to consider infused waters or to mix up a variety of flavors such as mint or vibrant fruitiness. Color, textures, and music were discussed to address the senses of sight, touch, and sound.[125]

The attention to the relationship between design and the sensate qualities of the body reflects how coworking prescribes more than an ideated notion of the good life. During my time at coworking spaces, I was treated to mouthwash dispensers in restrooms, bamboo plants on tables, carpets that mimic grass in "nap rooms," infused water, and flavors of branded coffee and tea. As Alan Liu theorizes, postindustrial capitalism has positioned "leisure *within* work" and shifted objects of the good life away from the large things, such as annual vacations, toward "micro-leisure": "the ergonomic chair that injects small doses of comfort throughout the day; the rounded corners and muted colors of a cubicle evoking something like a transient rest home for the chronically overworked; the advanced photocopy machine that collates and staples automatically so that we may have a brief, vacuous respite staring into space."[126] Liu highlights how technological pleasures have been intertwined with the everyday nature of work and how coolness and hipness have become abstracted into the little things that compensate for fatigue and mental dullness at work. Yet the sensate qualities of coworking function less as instruments of relief and more as objects that remind us of how pleasurable work is or can be. Framed signs reading "Do what you love" or "If you don't build your dreams, someone would build it for you" and mural art that speaks of love and creativity contextualize the sensate environment in a discourse of passion that seeks to ignite a "sense of purpose" in workers.[127]

One way to think about this discourse of passion is to understand it as a feeling of rightness, a sense of being in sync with the rhythms of capitalism. As Nigel Thrift offers, the sensory configurations of time and space may be used to foreground a particular sense of "rightness," "an attempt to capture and work into successful moments, often described as an attunement or a sense of being at ease in a situation."[128] The word *attunement* connotes an adjustment to harmony; it means that one is able to identify and realign a feeling of "wrongness" to one that feels "right." Understanding passion as a desire for rightness means understanding it as an everyday form of diffused affect, where bodies are molded to normative capitalist rhythms, so that pleasures through work might be more easily experienced and negative affects more easily controlled.[129]

When I asked coworkers if they felt more driven in the space, most mentioned to some extent the "energy" involved in having people around them. This energy, Harold told me, is particularly useful when he has to do something he dislikes, such as working on his accounts. Harold explained that the presence of coworkers and the capacity to move around make the banal task more bearable. The sense of freedom presents a means to control and modulate a feeling of boredom; workers find relief from the tedium of work by making quick conversations or by leaving their desks momentarily to take some coffee—while knowing that the sight of others still working will compel them to return quickly. As Dan explained, being surrounded by others who are working keeps him on track when he feels like procrastinating: "When there are people next to you, you have the extra push to continue because you feel bad if you stop. . . . You get the impression that if they can concentrate, so can you." The sight of others working nearby makes concentration normative and encourages everyone to devote the same degree of attention to their work.

The arrangement of human and nonhuman actors in coworking spaces creates an opportunity for this sense of attunement, which is a harmonization with the work rhythms of capital. And this implies more than just productivity. As Jessie told me, there is a sense of rightness that comes with coworking: "I think most people are still not used to working alone, even though it is now getting common. You can feel lonely and lose track of the value in what you are doing." Indeed, I was initially surprised by the low levels of interaction in many of the spaces I visited; most of the time, people were working rather than socializing. However, over time, I recognized that even with minimal interaction, coworking has an ambience that facilitates a particular affective quality to work. Jessie told me that she is not looking for personal validation to know the value of her work, but having people around makes it "more substantial": "It communicates that I am serious about my work and I am confident about it. . . . It makes it more meaningful."

The "meaningfulness" that Jessie relates to stems from a combination of factors: among others, the experience of freedom, the solidarity of working alongside others, the shared values coalesced under a brand, and, of course, the cool furniture, coffee, and strong Wi-Fi. As Charles Taylor points out, the mutual presence of individuals can "help build a common mood or tone that will color everyone's action." Even though people may be acting by themselves or in small groups, "it matters to each of us that others are there, as witnesses of what we are doing and thus as codeterminers of the meaning of our action."[130] Coworking reinforces this feeling with a range of experiments that instill meaning into work. Besides the usual gamut of happy hours, skill shares, game nights, and occasional spa parties, coworking spaces have also introduced ideas such as "fuckup nights," where members celebrate their failures, and variants of the PechaKucha presentation, where members give concise explanations of their projects that everyone tries to celebrate. These presentations concretize the work that coworkers do—they make their expertise seem valuable, worthy of being shared, and included as a part of one's career narrative.

Through these efforts, coworking creates conditions that make work seem meaningful and, possibly, even weighty. As someone relates of the WeWork space, "They have really discovered the secret sauce on how to make this place feel hip, feel new, feel innovative. Having guests come into this environment actually adds a real sense of, hey, we're a larger company than we actually are."[131] It is not surprising, then, that a survey by *Deskmag* found that over 90 percent of those interviewed expressed feeling more "self-confident" after they joined a coworking space.[132] Coworking has created a setting where individuals can feel happy about their new circumstances.

The feeling of rightness created in a coworking space produces a possibility for middle-class happiness even as opportunities for economic advancement recede. Deploying the shared agencies of human and nonhuman actors, coworking replaces and augments the desire for social mobility with an experience of personal contentment. WeWork, for instance, describes itself as a place that redefines "success measured by personal fulfillment, not just the bottom line." Opodz declares that "we want this space to work for you" and that it welcomes suggestions on "seating arrangement to chair types to lighting to coffee brands," anything that can help people "feel motivated and excited to be here every day to work on achieving your goals."[133] These mission statements highlight how passion has become the guiding principle of coworking spaces. Spread across the urban landscape, these infrastructural objects serve as placeholders for the good life, even as traditional objects of optimism fade.

An Opening: Structures of Care

A good coworking space is comfortable and can improve one's capacity for work. But as I visited coworking sites across California, I was struck by the distinction between the coworking interiors and their immediate surroundings. This was clearest at the Hollywood branch of WeWork in Los Angeles, where I had to navigate a long row of hustlers and tourists before I got to the place. The beautiful interiors provided a striking contrast to the chaotic world I just traversed. WeWork had an atmosphere of controlled busyness; the smell of coffee was in the air, most people were plugged into their headphones and staring at their laptops, and the associate at the counter greeted me with a warm smile. At the ground level of WeWork, the scene of Hollywood Boulevard was carefully controlled. Wallpaper was pasted over the transparent glass to block tenants from the distractions of the street and to prevent others from looking in. Working out of this temperature-controlled, hip place with high-speed Wi-Fi, ergonomic furniture, and good coffee, one may forget the hustle of the streets—though coworkers within are hustling too.

The atmospheres of the places we interpret, Ahmed reminds us, are always angled.[134] Or in other words, what we think is a vibe of a place not only represents the atmosphere of something that is external but is mediated through our social expectations and wants. The conditions of the coworking space make optimism material; freelancers may experience less loneliness by being members of a community, and their work may indeed feel more passionate in a space built for the contemplation of meaning. Coworking reminds us that passion is a means of organization—as a structure of feeling, it ensures a form of potentiality within work. In being passionate, coworkers are said to become more entrepreneurial, productive, inspired, socially connected, and, therefore, more financially successful or capable of coping with contemporary insecure labor conditions. Passion lifts work as an object of optimism.

Still, it is necessary to ask: What does coworking forsake in guiding us to feel right? As Thrift points out, affective technologies that harness potential have to divert from the possibilities of another potential: "The necessarily formulaic nature of this technology is bound to mean that certain sensings of potential are diminished or even go missing."[135] In creating a reassuring space of smiles, coworking also must necessarily suppress the existence of unhappy circumstances.

In this chapter, I have shown how coworking supports and permits the neoliberal fantasy: a belief that the decline of the middle-class good life can be stymied through self-transformations afforded by an infrastructural object. A common retort by space operators to questions about precarity is that freelancing or entrepreneurship is less precarious because it is harder to lose all sources of income if you have different gigs to support you. As Debra Osnowitz found through interviews with freelancers, individuals can feel more confident about maintaining employment as freelancers when they see companies shrinking their manpower.[136] But this assumption stands on a configuration of a particular neoliberal subject: one who has perfected the art of the hustle, a subject who has perfect knowledge of untapped markets and who is capable of molding their skills to tap into them. Further, it also assumes a resilient freelance market that is always pregnant with jobs.

Coworking suppresses the reality of those problems, emphasizing that it can accelerate serendipity or the creation of networks that can increase collaboration or the possibility of business prospects. While I do not deny such a possibility, this idea of collaboration also contributes to fantasy: coworking spaces, for instance, advise members to avoid treating each other as competitors so they can create a nurturing environment of collaborators. But this particular instantiation of collaboration suppresses the reality of inequality: that labor markets are fundamentally limited, and so are good gigs. What this process of collaboration does is to narrow good gigs to networks that deny others good jobs; instead of producing the inequality of individuals, it produces the inequality of networks. And whether or not people can get access to those valuable networks, coworking nonetheless perpetuates an internalization of blame; it suggests, as operators told me, that everyone has their own specialties and that they should compete against themselves instead of others, which also places the burden of failure on the self.

In these ways, coworking reproduces the idealisms embodied in early virtual communities: informality, low cost of entry and exit, capacity for building niches, personal intimacies, and relationship to economic gain. But as Mike Crang critiques, these communities have also been insular, prioritizing the interests of their private groups over those of the public and placing personal and group gains over social responsibility.[137] The utopian quality of cyber relations has the tendency to erase troublesome, uncomfortable social relations in the real world.[138] Coworking relations are often not virtual, but their norms—their reliance on a comfortable context, a sociality that is manageable, and their attempt to minimize loneliness— make coworking relations feel virtual at times. And by having those same values, coworking skirts around the broader social responsibilities that it is positioned to address.

This point also explains how coworking perpetuates political and class divisions as it seeks to reinstate the middle-class norms of the good life. By presenting care as a business opportunity, coworking legitimates a neoliberal ideology that absolves the state of welfare responsibilities, favoring the privatization of important life-providing facilities. As a result, people unable or unwilling to pay for coworking are denied entry to the space, even though they might need it.

This is not to say that coworking operators are not earnest in trying to remake the possibilities of work. Cat Johnson, for instance, writes about how she felt when a 2016 coworking conference held in Los Angeles was "hijacked" by people who were more interested in "expanding their business center empires" than "strengthening their community connections or opening a coworking space in a small town." Her discomfort is primarily directed toward Frank Cottle's view toward office spaces. A consultant on business real estate, Cottle expressed in a keynote lecture that coworking spaces are like business centers and that the "community" is a "product" that coworking space operators offer. This sat uneasily with the attendees, including Johnson, and Bacigalupo responded with a spiritual twist as he quipped, "Community is a product like a soul is a body part."[139]

But what does the association of "community" to "soul," and "product" to "body part," achieve in material terms? Despite their best intentions, co-working operators are unable to conceive of a language that allows them to bypass the ideologies of entrepreneurialism and neoliberalism. Not all people are equally prized; not all may be likened to the "soul" or be a part of the community of coworking. Only those who may be converted to a product—potential customers—will be welcome in the coworking community.

As Harvey tells us, limitations in our imaginations of utopia relate to the dearth of the processes mobilized to materialize them.[140] He reminds us that utopia needs to face relations of power at every turn, and it is more productive to find ways in which this can be encouraged and developed. Part of this process, then, requires us to confront the idealisms of work. Instead of trying to deny optimisms in work, however, it may be more productive to build spaces where idealisms may be experimented with, dismantled, and possibly rebuilt. In other words, it may be more productive to construct what Davina Cooper calls "everyday utopias," "places *from* which to think and *about* which to think."[141] These spaces afford not "static perfection" but concrete acts of striving, which are critical, dynamic, and changing in relation to a future that is always in the process of being remade.[142] Survival, then, may take on a more important role: for it speaks no longer to a continuation of middle-class norms but to an actual effort to sustain oneself as those norms are challenged with a better world in mind. Coworking is not without its possibilities, but their affordances—their means of offering a respite—need to be taken more literally as a respite from contemporary capitalism, instead of being shrouded by ideological utopianism. Can we perhaps then think of developing coworking along the lines of Cooper's advice? From there, perhaps, a different means of understanding labor can emerge.

Conclusion

Passion in the Last Instance

In the spring of 2017, an education forum was held in Singapore to discuss the future of work and the role of its universities in light of rapid developments in artificial intelligence. The forum would have been relatively ordinary, charged with the usual recommendation for youths to be adaptable in a world of disruptive change, if not for a curious piece of advice on passion.[1] Speaking to a room of high school students, the president of a local university expressed that the speed of technological developments has made the future uncertain and that using predictions about the market is no longer a reliable way to choose a degree. He advised that instead of pursuing degrees that are in demand, students should instead "follow your passion in what you want to study," because passion is a better guarantor for jobs: "Go for what you like to do, and then . . . look for the interesting jobs perhaps in that new economy."[2]

This fidelity to passion was referenced by another university experiment—Stanford University's *Stanford 2025*—which reimagines a model of higher education based on purpose and passions. Students in this program were asked to declare their missions rather than majors and then to fluidly weave their coursework and real-world experience into a six-year package to realize their stated idealisms.[3] This model of education argues that passions will spark entrepreneurialism and innovation, which will galvanize the best qualities of students and make them more successful, creative, and flexible in their career choices. This proposal is not new, but Stanford's efforts indicate the normalization of the passionate self as the future of the working subject, spreading the subjectivity of what Neff calls "venture labor" deeper into the social, where work is made equivalent not to wages but to the internalization of risk and the pursuit of dreams.[4] Still, there is a notable difference: while venture labor takes risks for passion with an eye toward a payoff, the risky choices of the passionate subject are presented as defense against the riskiness of the market. Playing it safe has not only become an outmoded subjectivity; the safe subject is, ironically, most at risk of being unable to survive the changed economy.

Passion travels, and in traveling it mutates, involving different dynamics of culture and power. What caught my attention initially is how passion is being transposed from Stanford to Singapore schools, from universities to high schools. and how it has transformed from entrepreneurship to resilience and into a vanguard against the uncertainty caused by the onslaught of automation. Passion is invoked in the last instance; the authentic self and one's innermost desires are being galvanized as the final guarantee for a form of improvisational security when projections can no longer guarantee a job, even if one were to astutely follow what is in demand. Refracted through many different strains of culture, an affective structure of passionate work maintains a semblance of reassurance, promising that regardless of conditions, passionate work can still provide one with a compromised space of goodness in life.[5]

When I started my research, my premise was that passionate work was a discourse designed to harness workers' affect, knowledge, and energies. In line with the scholarship on creative work, I was prepared to explore how people from different occupations were led to follow their passions and the compromises they took in doing so.[6] The dominant logic described of this dynamic is that of the trade-off. In following their passions, workers gain pleasure, hope, and autonomy, which are met with exploitative conditions in return: low wages, insecurity, long hours, high stress, individualized burden, and a winner-take-all market. Nonetheless, such work remains attractive, because passions are promised to pay off in the long run. The suggestion is that the present compromise is but an initial step toward launching workers into an ultimately economically comfortable career.[7]

Studying this subject is important, especially considering the pervasiveness of the advice to "do what you love."[8] But this dynamic is only one topic in the larger discursive field of passionate work. Whether or not workers themselves *feel* passionate, the word *passion* nonetheless does things, and one thing it does well is to condense a simplified relationship between work and the good life. The promise is that passion will yield good outcomes, and by holding steady that basic promise, passion can travel from one context to another, moving from tech gamification companies to call center workers, from coworking operators to freelancers. Along the way, passion manifests and accumulates under other signs. The indiscriminate spread of the passion promise is the basis for its ambivalent, even nonchalant, multivalent modulation across cultural sites.

No wonder so many are passionate about passion. To champion for passion means to champion something good. On that basis, it becomes difficult to push back against passion. When I criticize passion, am I advocating that workers be dispassionate? The normativity of passion comes up in the question with the implicit warning of a killjoy, a threat to the happy scene of a room, as Sara Ahmed so beautifully puts it.[9] What does this resistance to a critique of passion indicate, though? Perhaps it is not that people are disbelieving but that the threat to passion makes them feel fragile. Passion is energetic, putting people on trajectories that are loosely cobbled together with vague promises. Challenging passion entails putting the very notion of these trajectories into question: What do I do if passion is not what I should pursue? The unwillingness to question passion does not always come from investment; it can come out of desperation too. Passion arrives at the last instance. We hold on to passion because we wonder what else we can hold on to.

In this sense, dispassion cannot stand as a viable alternative to passion. There is no guarantee that dispassionate jobs will not be exploitative, and even the "good" model of dispassionate work, characterized by the Fordist past of bureaucracy and stable wages, was historically afforded only to the valued population of middle-class white men.[10] More important, though, antipassion discourses are easily subsumed by passion.[11] We have heard these refrains. Passion exploits you, but you cannot be happy without passion, so try to find some measure of passion for recovering your sense of enthusiasm about life. People will try to exploit your passion, but you will not be able to get a job without it, so find your passion to sustain yourself. It is naive to follow your passions, so do what you are good at, because you are likely to grow your passions for what you are praised for. Approached this way, using dispassion against passion provides an occasion for a return to passion as a balm: be skeptical, but not too much.

Suffering and Passion

The indispensability of passion tells us something about our understanding of alienation. In his early manuscripts, Marx relates passion to a distinct form of human consciousness, a motivation for humans to express their existence as a species. Following Hegel, he argues that being sensual and worldly, humans are driven to interact with their environment to survive (to eat and drink, breathe, get shelter) and to express their being by leaving an imprint on the material world: "To say that man is a corporeal, living, real, sensuous, objective being with natural powers means that he has real, sensuous objects as the object of his being and of his vital expression, or that he can only express his life in real, sensuous objects."[12] For Marx, such entanglement results in suffering, because it makes humans vulnerable to the actions of others. To be embroiled in the natural and social world means that one experiences a state of nonsovereignty. Sense perception makes humans cognizant of the effects on them of things outside themselves, which can make existence uncomfortable, if not unbearable.

But the capacity of affectedness also drives humans to affect, to labor and mold objects of life expression that can materially transform the world. Marx writes, "Man as an objective, sentient being is therefore a suffering being, and, since he is a being who feels his suffering, he is a passionate (*leidenschaftliches*) being. Passion is man's faculties energetically striving after their object."[13] There is a keen relationship between suffering and passion in this conception. Suffering is not simply a condition of being affected; it also produces the passion for affecting, for interacting with the world.

The consciousness of suffering is therefore nontrivial: sentience of suffering—not just the feeling, but its cause—is necessary for the direction of passionate intensity. As Ahmed points out, these passages by Marx indicate that alienation involves not only the estrangement of the process of labor but a "feeling-structure, a form of suffering that shapes how the worker inhabits the work."[14] Alienation from "feeling-structure" involves a state of false consciousness, where the interests of the social field are masked. The subject is experientially conscious of suffering "but misrecognizes the cause, such that the misrecognition allows the cause to 'cause' suffering."[15] Consciousness of the cause of suffering does not always lead to revolutionary action, but a misdirected cause closes off possibilities of address. Passion is inhibited when the subject suffers but is unable to properly direct his energies after the cause of suffering.

Two points of this argument should be noted. First, Marx's assertion about passions resonates with the general arc of how passionate work is conventionally critiqued. Central here is the claim that passions are misdirected into work when they should be channeled toward other objects that can yield the transformative change desired. This misdirection can be described as a form of false consciousness, an alienation of the feeling-structure that makes harm unrecognizable. Passion itself is not the problem; the problem lies in what follows, its attachment to "work," the object of cruel optimism. This account is partially right. As I have offered in the first chapter, the politics of passionate work is one of transposition. Its prominence as an affective structure constitutes an ideological project naturalized as a want that workers have demanded for themselves. Resisting the ideology of passion requires us to struggle with the relations of optimism and assess the compromises involved in attachments, such that the social interests of our attachments may be more clearly revealed.

In chapter 2, I wrote about how apathy legitimized intervention into the adaptation of unemployment, which has made unemployment a space that is unadaptable, hostile to the experimentation of lifestyles that can be untethered from the necessity of the wage. Sites of attachment do not appear on a flat plane, impeded only by the imagination. Some have deliberately been *made* unthinkable, unlivable, untenable. From this perspective, passionate work's turn to recuperation represents an intensified attempt at making work a stronger determinant for survival while limiting the futures that can be considered possible outside and beyond work. Demands for difference must turn biopolitical; they must oppose schemes that make oppositional forms of life unlivable.

Second, reading passion as an affective structure should help us see how passion precedes the formation of its subject. Passionate subjects are estranged not at the moment of influence, when they follow their passions, but when they enter into a world where suffering and passion are read a particular way. This is, at one level, keenly obvious. Passion—in the past and present—has remained a reading of some form. From an affliction that clouds the reasoning mind in the *passio* of Aristotelian ethics to an interiorized sentiment of the secularized "emotion" and even to the Romantics' tendency to regard passions as divine sources of inspiration that need protection from cold reason, the reading of passion has played an integral role in determining the scope in which "suffering" is be apprehended and addressed.[16] But our contemporary approach toward passion generally refuses this versatility.

Awareness of differences in the interpretations of passion should lead us to question the normativity of passion today: the idea that we need to be invested in something, to own our passions, and to express them actively. If the meaning of passion is historically inconsistent, we can then proceed to ask: How can its use best shift to accommodate the politics of the present? A critical study of passion gestures toward this possibility: a chance to expand on the repertoire of what it means to be affected and to affect.

Postwork Imaginaries

The narrative of passionate work relates to several crises happening at this historical juncture: serialized unemployment, persistent precarity, inequality, stuckedness, and the anxiety of class slippage—all of which have become highly visible problems that are globally endemic and affectively real. Consequently, passion is no longer just directed toward the production and capture of labor power; it is now regularly spoken of as a means to recuperate the damaged subject of capital. It substitutes for the retreat of social institutions meant to ensure the well-being of their citizens. As a discourse that traverses everyday life, it makes endurance and the ordinary continuation of life possible where conditions of enablement have thinned. The analysis around apathy, suspension, and loneliness captures this shift. In these accounts, we hear of how passion exploits workers of their labor power inasmuch as it produces new zones of recuperation. Healing and capture; enjoyment and exploitation; recuperation, reattachment, and reinsertion into circuits of labor—all are bundled up in the discourses of passionate work and its promises of the compromised good life.[17]

This is insidious, because social reproduction is a site of political possibility. Recuperation offers a way of forging cooperative relations that allow the act of staying alive to hold potential for difference, but passionate work would deploy therapy to redirect potential back toward an ideology of work. Work becomes a space to recuperate only to have the subject work more, to work without showing the signs of its injury. Recall Marx's point that the sentience of suffering is essential for the direction of passionate intensity. Only by recognizing what causes harm can people labor to produce a material world that is more conducive to life. The opportunity for this diagnosis, however, is suppressed when one is demanded to be passionate about what causes harm. Or worse, passionate work can render diagnosis pointless; it can encourage complicity, making us unable to see the terms of resolution even when we recognize the harms they cause. Resisting the affective structure of passionate work would thereby require effort at challenging the schemes that make nonnormative forms of life unlivable and their experimentation difficult.

The pandemic has made clear the violence involved in passionate work. We see it, for instance, in the public messages that thank Amazon warehouse and delivery workers for their continued labor during the pandemic—a necessity as cities are locked down. These messages belie the lengths to which the company resisted maintaining a living wage for its logistical workers lowest down the value chain.[18] Workers in Amazon warehouses have protested the withdrawal of "hazard" or "hero" pay—the hourly supplements for working during the pandemic—at the same time that the company is accused of neglecting their safety while packing more desperate, jobless workers into poorly ventilated warehouses to keep up with the surge in online purchases.[19] In this instance, the pandemic can even be leveraged as a tool of violence: to quash a bid for unionization at a warehouse in Alabama, for instance, Amazon attempted to force in-person voting, hoping to reduce the number of voters showing up.[20]

The hypocrisy found in these contradictory messages of heroic affirmation, of course, is not unique to Amazon; workers in other large corporations struggle with similar battles.[21] Hence, as a structural trend, these events highlight a deeper problematic. We are made to think of the heroic selflessness of workers rather than the conditions that make work a forced choice. Work is made morally luminous even as it becomes brutally existential, when going to work can literally take your life. The systems of a workerist society, including a health insurance system that is made dependent on employment and minimalist policies on paid leave, have perversely shown how joblessness is regarded by many as more painful and risky than catching the coronavirus. That such risk often filters down to the lives that are least valued—the workers deemed "essential" at the same time that they are the most replaceable, the majority embodied by the incarcerated, the working class, and Black and Latinx people—shows primal biopolitics in practice. As the US National Center for Health Statistics notes, in 2020 life expectancies for Black and Hispanic people showed the largest declines in decades. The drop of 2.7 years of life expectancy for Black populations, to an average of seventy-two years, wiped out the improvement seen over almost two decades.[22] And while these numbers were influenced by deaths from the coronavirus, they were also driven by an increase in suicides and drug overdoses in this period—the "deaths of despair" that accompany conditions of structural neglect.[23]

Thus we see how heroism and endurance—the usual symbols of passionate work—can be utterly brutal in their logic, supporting an untenable, inhumane condition of work by making damage a site of patriotism. Work here is gathered as a form of sentimental citizenship, a way of getting everyone to stand "in solidarity" with workers who would be perversely labeled as unpatriotic and undeserving of compassion should they refuse to work or to feel grateful for this outpouring of thanks. Recuperation and violence become entwined in a cycle, and passionate work serves as the affective structure that permits investments in healing to cause even more damage. To this end, passionate work might be understood as an instrument of what James Tyner calls "necrocapitalism," a way of extracting value from the premature death of laboring bodies deemed to be most disposable and replaceable: "Capital values those bodies deemed both productive (e.g., in a position to generate wealth) and responsible, with responsibility conceived of as the ability to participate fully as producers and consumers in the capitalist system while, simultaneously, not incurring a net loss to the system. Those individuals who are deemed nonproductive or redundant, based on an economic bio-arithmetic, are disproportionately vulnerable and increasingly disallowed life to the point of premature death. The differential exposure to death shows how value can be maximally extracted from the most disposable bodies through their willing consent."[24]

The affective structure of passionate work has played a major role in forging this compulsory attachment to labor, making work a necessary presence for survival. In a time of crisis, then, passionate work narrows our options and even rationalizes human life as a site of experimentality. The reckless call for herd immunity, for instance, shows how an attachment to work, lumped with the abstracted appeal to save the "economy," can be used to risk the lives of citizens all around the world, to downplay the risks of the coronavirus so that a seemingly "normal" life of work can be maintained. In this example, the firmly held attachment to work has the consequence of justifying premature death.

Challenging this idea requires experiments in different relations of social reproduction, ones that do not locate survival and recognition within work. Passionate work may be considered one of the most successful projects of the twentieth century (chapter 1), but our commitments to it need not always stay the same. In fact, the shifting attitudes toward work reveal that such attachments are fragile; holding work as a source of hope may in fact require more energy than discarding it. However, given that this attachment has historical materialist grounds, challenging it requires attention to various ways that survival is codified into work through employment processes (see the section on social unemployment insurance in chapter 2).

In his postwork manifesto, Franco Berardi makes a strong point about the need to rethink our processes of social reproduction—the ways in which we can find care, concern, and community and produce conditions of livability and flourishing outside waged labor. "In the days to come, politics and therapy will be one and the same," he writes. "Our cultural task will be to attend to these people and to take care of their trauma showing them the way to pursue the happy adaptation at hand."[25] Berardi points us in the right direction, but therapy, as we see through the book, is a terrain of struggle. Efforts must continue to untether survival from wage and status, in both material and cultural forms; and this push is urgently needed, given the ecological crisis, the erasure of jobs with automation, and the extensive disorder caused by the pandemic.[26] In the workerist present, decentering lives from the normativity of capitalism might be the most innovative and disruptive thing that we can do.

Passio Passions

Such changes require struggle, but our understanding of struggle needs also to accommodate different affective openings. At the heart of passion lies an assumption of necessity—that we need to have passion about things to live meaningfully and happily. From that perspective, the demand to be passionate can grow stronger the more desperate we become. Consider Rei Terada's critique of Martha Banta's argument in *PMLA* when she talks about the crisis facing the humanities.[27] In a column, Banta had expressed concerns that the humanities are increasingly tasked to fit neoliberal dictates and to prove their usefulness through instrumental metrics such as "system performance-based assessment," "costs and benefits," and "timely profit and loss."[28]

Such concerns are not atypical of the field, but as Terada points out, the problem appears when Banta uses "passion"—"the swell of intellectual joy" from reading, writing, and theorizing—as compensation. Passion in the last instance describes a compromise in desperate times, and in being made a compromise, the demands for its existence can become harsher. As Banta moves toward the end of her argument, she switches in tone. Passion is not just a bribe for one's endurance of neoliberalism; it also becomes something that one has to have: "Joy: remember that feeling? If you do not, try to regain it. If you never had it, then you ought not to be in this business."[29] Passion changes from compromise to requirement. How does one endure without passion when other rewards are absent? *Why* does one even want to endure without passion? The desperation presented in the grip of passion can take shape as endurance, as a call for one to stick to the path and to take on more, to hang on as one makes do with how things are. This argument is striking for its refusal of regret. For Banta, the call for passion is related to the will to rationalize the choice of sticking with the humanities. I suspect that this call for passion is likely familiar to many readers. The nature of academia easily lends itself to the encouragement of passion, expressed when one is overworked or faced with institutional and structural hurdles.

But what are costs of this refusal of regret? It is in this aspect that Brian Price's moral philosophy is instructive. Price explains that regret is a sentiment commonly used to express the indignation of making a bad choice that grants less utility.[30] This usually happens when someone chooses an option that yields a bad outcome, and when it is followed by a fantasy of the better state that would have resulted had a different option been chosen. The predication of regret on options shows how regret is related to the will. A choice can be regretted only if someone has the ability to embark on a different path; should a choice be nonvoluntary then it cannot be regretted, at least meaningfully, no matter how badly it turns out.

It is in this context that the political value in regret appears. Regret can become politically efficacious when it makes us aware of a perceptual habit—when it forces us to recognize that a bad outcome could have had a different possibility. Our tendency, however, is to make regret impossible even in a scene of a bad choice. Price uses the illustration of a house that burned down following the eruption of a long-dormant volcano. If we purchased the house with all the information we could have had, it would be impossible to regret our decision: "The nonvoluntary relation takes on the appearance of a necessary state, much like the stone that will fall to the ground no matter how often we try to habituate it to upward movement."[31] Because the actions of the volcano appear beyond our ability to control and predict, no willful action seems possible. We might wish that we had not bought the house, but we cannot regret it, because we made the decision with all the information we had received.

Still, the truth of what happens is often more complicated than it initially seems. Perceptual habits drive us toward seeing things in a way that corroborates our desires or, more precisely, what we *are made to* desire. The "constancy of objects," as Price writes—the beautiful house, the dormancy of the volcano—creates a situation that coordinates the competing interests of both the realtor (to sell) and the buyer (to want a perfect home). Our wants are projected onto objects, leading us to see what happened as "how things are," a result of unwavering fate, rather than how they are made to be. Thus we foreclose the possibility of learning something that we previously missed or disregarded or that was deliberately concealed from us—information that could have factored into a different decision. Perceptual habits, then, make our choices nonvoluntary as opposed to involuntary, as if we never had a choice to begin with, rather being led into a decision by influences that we are unable to perceive. Price offers, "If we are capable of breaking with the perceptual habits bequeathed to us by the recurrent signs willed by another with an intention to deceive, many of the so-called nonvoluntary relations can be exposed as the dissimulations of obfuscations that they truly are, rather than evidence of our own stupidity."[32] Such admissions of stupidity might be cutting, but they open the possibility of understanding how better choices can be made.

Passion can be that which makes our decisions nonvoluntary. Notice how the interiorized logic of passions makes willing in other ways difficult: because passions come from our authentic selves, when we act according to our passions, we actually do what we "will." The will becomes synonymous with passions, as if choosing differently can only come with the cost of unhappiness, and likely regret, as we become unhappy for not choosing as our heart wills. The anticipation of regret in doing something against our passions would ironically render our choices nearly nonregrettable; pursuing what we love seems to be the only option that leads into a good life, something that we try to preserve as a right choice even when we suffer its compromises. Thus passion in the last instance becomes *lasting*—the reason for keeping us on the path that we had started on.

How do we begin to challenge this? The pedagogy of regret shows us that passion, first and foremost, needs distance from the will. I suggest that we begin with returning to the ambivalent relations of *passio*, the Latin origin of *passion*. Unlike passion, passio understands emotions and desires as external instead of internal, as forces coming upon the individual rather than forces originating from one's authentic nature.[33] My intent is not to have the external confirm the internal, or to put reason over emotion, but to use passio as a point to make manifest the relationality between social forces and desires, individuals and collectives. Denaturalizing passion as a biologically individualized affect enables the possibility of understanding how our passions are shaped. Exteriorizing passions provides room for struggle with passion, or even a struggle with the absence of passion, allowing for permission to renounce one's desire without feeling that one is denying an authentic part of the self. We can see how something external can be taken as inner desire, which also presents the self as more mutable and plastic than we have come to typically accept.

In this sense, I see passio passions as a breather, a stance of nonjudgment that finds space from the normative pressures that passion exercises. In *Looking Away*, Terada describes how an optics of instability and blurriness can constitute such relief. The world, she offers, comes as a conflation of fact and value where we are pressured to judge the seen through the norm of what it is thought to be. Take, for example, a violet flower, whose vibrancy of color urges us to admire it as beautiful. Looking away is a form of "epistemological therapeutics," giving us the possibility of reconsidering how the world is presented to us: by seeing the vibrancy of the violet flower for its color as opposed to its beauty, we reserve automatic judgment. "It isn't a new norm that's being sought here, only a vacation from orchestrated affirmation," Terada writes.[34] We can take this advice to understand that passions are not meant to be disagreed with, as the Aristotelian view leans toward. Rather, a better aesthetic category for passio might be *the interesting*, a term that describes attentiveness without a necessary normative evaluation.[35] Interesting passions are attachments we can observe without commitment. They can provide curiosity and inquisitiveness without cynicism, giving us the space to evaluate and escape the pressures of affirmation.

Viewing passion this way can help us understand it as a social force. In chapter 4 I developed an understanding of passion as a collaboration——as a construction produced through a network of human and nonhuman actors. In this understanding, passion comes as alignment between the self and the external world, such that the world can make it easier to express what one feels inside. We need not, however, read passions as wholly interior. Like the afflictions of passio, passions can represent forces in a social field, conducted through bodies and things that we can situate ourselves within to ally with and expand on, or to dampen and attenuate. Proceeding with a nonsovereign reading of passion would task us with developing what Anna Lowenhaupt Tsing calls the "arts of noticing," a way of attuning to the relational worlds through which our choices of investment reverberate.[36] In this way, we can be made more attentive to new openings and connections, understanding too that investments shift how we can come to notice the world: "We are contaminated by our encounters; they change who we are as we make way for others. As contamination changes world-making projects, mutual worlds—and new directions—may emerge."[37] This perspective on passions can open a different praxis. Our choices here are not governed by a desire to remold the world to any fixed model or to buy us security. Rather, they are invested based on a want for lives to be lived more expansively and creatively, a commitment to the interdependencies that characterize the social world.

The desire for a nonsovereign approach to passion may be sensed from the ambivalent situation of suspension. In *Crowds and Party*, Jodi Dean highlights the political potential in suspension by pointing to the pervasive use of social media. She cites but inverts Sherry Turkle, who sees the compulsive use of social media as evidence of people's addiction to the suspended self-consciousness of flow. For Dean, the compulsion to social media hints at something else: a longing for a more fulfilling kind of collectivity, one that cannot be fulfilled by the culturally dominant ideas of sociality: "We may be coming to prefer the crowd, the presence of many that opens us to collectivity and relieves us of anxiety. One-on-one conversations may feel too constraining insofar as they enclose us back in an individual form. . . . The experience of flow that overwhelms the conscious experience of self that Turkle finds so threatening, then, might also be understood as a breaking out of the illusion that the individual is and can be a subject of action (rather than a form of enclosure and containment) and a giving-over to a crowd."[38]

Dean's insight is that suspension may not be merely escapist, or that even if subjects do use social media to escape the banal, such a desire is not necessarily one that can be reduced to an addiction. Instead, the draw of suspension comes from the aesthetics it affords, a chance for an affective sense of positive collectivity. In my discussion of hopeful suspension (chapter 3), I closed by describing the dangerous hope that surveillance industries offer with paternalistic, empowered suspension. Dean's argument leads us to see that what we need might not be hope as it is conventionally understood, but a sense of potential, a feeling of difference that can come in myriad forms.

Directing passions away from the interiority of the body tears us away from an egocentric way of apprehending the world, opening room for more varied, collaborative attachments. Taking the body to be "site of passage and porosity, the evidence of an openness to alterity," as Judith Butler explains in her work on nonviolence, helps redefine the terms of equality.[39] Instead of looking to compartmentalized bodies, trying to understand the equality of treatment in those terms, we look toward the conditions that sustain the relations between bodies, understanding that our world is characterized by a fundamental quality of social interdependence. "Equal treatment," she continues, "is not possible outside of a social organization of life in which material resources, food distribution, housing, work, and infrastructure seek to achieve equal conditions of livability."[40] An attunement to passions as a social force directs our attention to the bonds that make up the survivability that grounds all bodies in the biosphere.

Passio passions create room for this attentiveness to forces that make up the conditions of existence; and by virtue of being external and collective, they also encourage a more provisional and self-critical inquiry into our attachments. Passio passions are forces meant to be passed on, to matter as collective inheritance, to be picked up and let go, given to others, and perhaps picked up again in the future. They remind us of the importance of coming together and of the political force involved in obstruction and in maintaining it. Passio passions are not without potential for violence, but they urge a different ethics of relationality: a will to reach out rather than a tendency to guard, securitize, and protect.

The range and possibility of such approaches to passion extend beyond what I offer. It remains to others to pick up and reflect on the variety of styles that investment can take, for which the hegemonic notions of passionate work can be troubled. My only reminder is that we need to have a willingness to live with the ambivalences of passion, accepting even a struggle with struggle; to have a willingness that makes space even for the absence of passion, such that desperation does not force the grasp on an authentic self of realizable inner needs. Such a stance may not be revolutionary. It might not even desire revolution. However, being able to frankly claim the absence of passion is a relief in a moment where passion is demanded as what makes for a good life.

NOTES

Introduction. Passionate Work and the Good Life

1 Sennett, *Craftsman*, 9.
2 Henricks, *Play Reconsidered*, 36.
3 Henricks, *Play Reconsidered*, 37.
4 Henricks, *Play Reconsidered*, 37.
5 This is noticeable especially in Marx's shift toward a structural explanation of capitalism in his later books. See Marx, *Capital*; Sennett, *Fall of Public Man*.
6 Lam, "Why 'Do What You Love' Is Pernicious."
7 Jobs, Address.
8 Kjerulf, "Why Every Company Should Have a CHO."
9 B. Taylor, "Why Amazon Is Copying Zappos."
10 Wayfinding Academy, "Wayfinding Academy."
11 Lazzarato, "Immaterial Labor."
12 Braverman, *Labor and Monopoly Capital*, 83. In the 1970s, David Noble's critique of cybernetic factories tackled this issue from a slightly different position. He offers that the penchant for technology has led to the ascendancy of things over people, leading over time to the degradation of skills. See Noble, *Forces of Production*. These concerns relate also to the Italian *operaismo* political movements of the 1960s and 1970s, which refused work as a way of reclaiming a different possibility of an existence outside waged labor and capitalism. Work is a space of struggle over knowledge and affect, where concerns are centered not just on the wage but on cooperativeness, skills, and the will necessary for people to exist outside the reliance on paid labor.
13 Dyer-Witheford and de Peuter, *Games of Empire*.
14 Hardt and Negri, *Multitude*; Lazzarato, "Immaterial Labor."

15 See, for example, Ashton, "Upgrading the Self"; Cohen, "Cultural Work"; de Peuter, "Creative Economy and Labor Precarity"; Duffy, *Remake, Remodel*; Dyer-Witheford and de Peuter, "'EA Spouse'"; Gill and Pratt, "In the Social Factory?"; McRobbie, *Be Creative*; Ross, *No Collar*.

16 Hesmondhalgh and Baker, "'Very Complicated Version,'" 16.

17 Ross, *No Collar*, 20.

18 For a review of the various issues surrounding digital labor, see Andrejevic et al., "Participations Part 2." See also, for example, Fast, Örnebring, and Karlsson, "Metaphors of Free Labor"; Hong, "Game Modding"; Perlin, *Intern Nation*; Terranova, "Free Labor."

19 Lam, "Why 'Do What You Love' Is Pernicious Advice;" Tokumitsu, "In the Name of Love"; Griffith, "Why Are Young People Pretending to Love Work?"; Jachimowicz and McNerney, "Problem"; Newport, "Solving Gen Y's Passion Problem."

20 Kantor and Streitfeld, "Inside Amazon."

21 Newport, *So Good*.

22 Malesic, "Don't Search for 'Purpose.'"

23 See Duffy, *(Not) Getting Paid*; Kuehn and Corrigan, "Hope Labor"; Neff, *Venture Labor*; Rosenblat, *Uberland*.

24 See, for instance, Duffy, *(Not) Getting Paid*; Hochschild, *Managed Heart*.

25 Terranova, "Free Labor," 33.

26 Davidson, *Passion Economy*.

27 Stewart, *Ordinary Affects*, 5.

28 Alberti, *Biology of Loneliness*, 16.

29 Ahmed, *Cultural Politics*, 7.

30 Terada, *Feeling in Theory*, 3.

31 Williams, *Politics and Letters*, 159. For a development of the concept, see Williams, *Marxism and Literature*.

32 Berlant, *Cruel Optimism*, 196.

33 Berlant, *Cruel Optimism*, 48.

34 Ahmed, *Promise of Happiness*.

35 Illouz, *Cold Intimacies*, 2. The link between emotions and actions might also be understood through the work of Antonio Damasio. As a neuroscientist, Damasio would argue that emotions are key to producing behavior—being unable to feel can impede even the simplest of actions. See Damasio, *Descartes' Error*.

36 Lawrie, "Passion," 114.

37 Rabinbach, *Eclipse*.

38 For one of the more sympathetic views on Taylorism, see Schachter, *Frederick Taylor*. More recently, Melissa Gregg's work on domestic productivity also highlights the hope that is placed in efficiency. See Gregg, *Counterproductive*.

39 See Halpern, *Beautiful Data*; Turner, *Democratic Surround*.

40 Maslow's work will be elaborated on in chapter 1. Mark Lepper's conceptual separation of intrinsic and extrinsic motivations condenses the cultural

value of personhoods in a binary that has resonated with ideas of American individualism—this binary distinguishes between dependency and conformity on one end and independence and individualism on the other. Talking about the history of psychological motivation, he explains that the extrinsically motivated were largely understood as "pawns of external environmental forces" and the intrinsically motivated as "origins of their own purposeful actions." See Lepper et al., "Instrinsic and Extrinsic Motivation," 25; Maslow, *Motivation and Personality*.

41 Maslow, *Motivation and Personality*, 46.

42 Maslow, *Motivation and Personality*, 49.

43 See Dixon, *From Passions to Emotions*; James, *Passion and Action*.

44 Susan James, *Passion and Action*, 42.

45 Rorty, "From Passions to Emotions," 159. As Page du Bois notes, when the Christian belief entered in, passion took on the connotations of bodily aguish and affliction. In time, this too was revised, and passion became akin to desire. "The meaning has thus changed from passive experience—suffering in the sense of enduring, or being the object of action—to physical suffering and, finally, to the contrary of pathos or passivity, that is, to active desire" (du Bois, "Passion for the Dead," 270).

46 Dixon, *From Passions to Emotions*.

47 Averill, "Inner Feelings." Rei Terada provides a good discussion of the relationship between feeling and expression: "It is through what we have said of expression that we can gain an idea of the primordial reality of affective quality, wherein that part belonging to the subject and that belonging to the object are still indistinguishable. In fact, expression is that which reveals affective quality as total and undifferentiated. Expression exists prior to the distinction between body and soul, exterior and interior" (Terada, *Feeling in Theory*, 13).

48 C. Campbell, *Romantic Ethic*.

49 Averill, "Inner Feelings," 112.

50 Angela McRobbie also uses the Romantic ethic to describe the passionate work ethos of creative workers. The Romantic mode of production, she explains, has allowed creativity and pleasure to be taken as a barometer of an idealized expression of labor. Inner dreams and fantasies are to be read as fonts of "uniqueness and creative genius" (McRobbie, *Be Creative*, 107). See also Streeter, "Steve Jobs."

51 Ahmed, *Cultural Politics*, 7.

52 Brennan, *Transmission of Affect*, 77.

53 Currier and Elmi, "State of the Union."

54 Articles addressing the coronavirus and passion abound. See, for example, Levoy, "Coronavirus as a Calling"; Maughan, "Using Behavioral Science"; Regester, "Passion Industry."

55 Berardi, *Soul at Work*, 213.

56 Berardi, *Soul at Work*, 220.

57 Virno, "Ambivalence of Disenchantment," 12.

58 Fleming, *Mythology of Work*.

59 M. Fisher, *Capitalism Realism*.

60 Cazdyn, *Already Dead*.

61 Sharma, *In the Meantime*.

62 N. Fraser, "Contradictions."

63 Federici, *Revolution at Point Zero*, 7.

64 This condensed description cannot do justice to the extensive work done on social reproduction. For an overview, see Bakker and Gill, "Ontology, Method, and Hypotheses"; Delphy, *Close to Home*; Laslett and Brenner, "Gender and Social Reproduction"; Vogel, *Marxism and the Oppression of Women*. For one of the most updated uses of the concept, see Oksala, "Affective Labor and Feminist Politics."

65 N. Fraser, "Contradictions," 102.

66 The Wages for Housework campaign that Federici advanced, for instance, was an attempt to reveal the discounts that unpaid social reproductive work has provided for capitalist development. "We recognized that capitalism requires unwaged reproductive labor in order to contain the cost of labor power," Federici writes, "and we believed that a successful campaign draining the source of this unpaid labor would break the process of capital accumulation and confront capital and the state on a terrain common to most women" (Federici, *Revolution at Point Zero*, 8–9). Social reproduction is read as a powerful site of revolutionary potential because any address to it reverberates across the chain of production. In *Finite Media*, Sean Cubitt carries this discussion into ecological systems, noting that under capitalism, the commons has become a negative holder for what is externalized by the economic cycle. Something that is "common" cedes financial responsibility; it becomes something external to economic processes that can be neatly forgotten and exploited without end, just as the oceans may be filled with trash and the air pumped with toxic smog. Similarly, social reproduction is not simply a site for potentializing production; it is a machinery for hiding the concessions to production. It is where damage, exploitation, and violence can be erased, neatly forgotten, externalized, and removed from utilitarian calculations of profits and losses.

67 Vogel, *Marxism and the Oppression of Women*.

68 Federici, *Revolution at Point Zero*, 8–9.

69 In considering this I am influenced by the scholarship on resilience and its strong preoccupation with damage and recuperation. See Cazdyn, *Already Dead*; Evans and Reid, *Resilient Life*; Robin James, *Resilience and Melancholy*.

70 Grossberg's concept of the mattering map has stuck with me in the process of writing. He notes, "These 'mattering maps' are like investment portfolios: there are not only different and changing investments but different intensities

or degrees of investment. There are not only different places marked out (practices, pleasures, meanings, fantasies, desires, relations, etc.) but different purposes which these investments can play. Mattering maps define different forms, quantities and places of energy. They 'tell' people how to use and how to generate energy, how to navigate their way into and through various moods and passions, and how to live within emotional and ideological histories" (Grossberg, *We Gotta Get Out*, 82). There is a cartographic imagery in this that I find both useful and limiting. On the one hand, it shows how investments can shift, but on the other hand, it does not do nearly enough in showing the nebulous character of affective investment. It holds investment too clearly, as if we know what we are investing in, as if attachments are binding. My hope is to unbind some of these structures so we can find a space of relief in treating our investments.

Chapter 1. From Happiness to Passion

1 Arendt, *Human Condition*, 115.
2 Arendt, *Human Condition*, xii.
3 Drucker, *Practice of Management*, 293.
4 Drucker, *Practice of Management*, 304.
5 Arendt indicates this in her critique of the technological argument that "every tool and implement is primarily designed to make human life easier and human labor less painful." She writes that this perspective understands the usefulness of technology "exclusively in this anthropocentric sense" and that the "*homo faber*, the toolmaker, invented tools and implements in order to erect a world, not—at least, not primarily—to help the human life process" (Arendt, *Human Condition*, 151). I take this to mean that Arendt's concern is more generally structural than psychic.
6 I have found Micki McGee, in her study of American self-help literature, to be a useful interlocutor. McGee offers that much of self-help can be categorized into the binary of endless effort and absolute effortlessness. In the former, readers seek self-mastery through the effortful care of the self; in the latter, readers turn to New Age mysticism to seek out a kind of effortless mastery. In both cases, however, readers are devoted to self-transformation and self-interest rather than a collective future that is shared. See McGee, *Self-Help, Inc.*
7 O'Toole et al., *Work in America*, 5–6.
8 Boltanski and Chiapello, *New Spirit of Capitalism*, 415.
9 Marx, *Capital*, 415.
10 Lazzarato, "Immaterial Labor," 143.
11 Massumi, *Parables for the Virtual*, 92.
12 Massumi, *Politics of Affect*, 56–57.
13 Reddy, *Navigation of Feeling*. See also Reddy, "Against Constructionism."
14 Reddy, *Navigation of Feeling*, 55.

15 Rosenwein, *Emotional Communities*, 19.

16 Reddy conceptualizes the alternative to emotional regimes as "emotional refuge." See Reddy, *Navigation of Feeling*.

17 As Foucault offers, self-knowledge comes out of a "crisis of subjectiviza-tion" rather than a "crisis of the subject." Affective structures of happiness and passion expand the modalities by which emotional recognition will come into existence. In particular, the seemingly straightforward want for wages becomes complexified through the psychological sciences, which turn to an evidence of deep-seated, unfulfilled psychological needs that warrant address, treatment, and readjustment (Foucault, *History of Sexuality*, 95).

18 Rose, *Governing the Soul*.

19 Boltanski and Chiapello, *New Spirit of Capitalism*, 8.

20 O'Toole et al., *Work in America*, 13.

21 See Mandell, *Corporation as Family*; Tone, *Business of Benevolence*.

22 See Burawoy, *Manufacturing Consent*; Willis, *Learning to Labor*.

23 Bendix, *Work and Authority in Industry*.

24 Bendix, *Work and Authority in Industry*, 284–85.

25 The experiments characteristic of welfare capitalism, which beautify the environs of the workplace and improve workplace amenities, draw inspira-tion from consumption. See Mandell, *Corporation as Family*; Tone, *Business of Benevolence*. The spiritual element of work is most clearly discussed in Weber, *Protestant Ethic*.

26 These amount to forty-eight books across the period from 1930 to 1980. The management books were sourced in several ways. First, I used *Personnel Jour-nal*, a trade journal for personnel executives and managers, to help pick out relevant management books for analysis. Until the 1970s, *Personnel Journal* included a monthly list of new publications and a robust review of books, which were helpful in selecting materials for analysis. Second, several books in the 1930s and 1940s include comprehensive bibliographies, which were helpful for sourcing new materials. Third, I noted books repeatedly referenced in management texts and adopted them for analysis. These in-clude popular management texts such as Douglas McGregor's *The Human Side of Enterprise* but also popular best sellers such as William Whyte's *The Organization Man* and Studs Terkel's *Working*. This eclectic archive reflects the nature of management discourse: it is responsive to popular opinion and changes within the economy and society. Writers of these texts range from academics to public intellectuals and from high-status professionals to con-sultants for major firms—with many having two roles or more.

27 To highlight the shifts in affective structure and to situate its achievement in the present, I have favored the use of broad historical strokes over the careful dissection of individual cases in history. This genealogical analysis does not claim to be a comprehensive history of management ideas, but it does attempt

to illuminate changes in the underlying politics of the good life that work proposes to offer.

28 Halsey, *How to Be a Leader*, xi.

29 Halsey, *How to Be a Leader*, 31.

30 Wren and Bedeian, *Evolution of Management Thought*, 303.

31 Mayo, *Human Problems*. Mayo was the key interpreter of what the Hawthorne results meant for management, though the data from the experiment were not his. For a summary of Mayo's involvement in the research at the Hawthorne plant, see Trahair, *Elton Mayo*; Wren and Bedeian, *Evolution of Management Thought*.

32 Mayo, *Human Problems*, 36.

33 In the foreword to *The Human Problems of an Industrial Civilization*, Fritz Roethlisberger, Mayo's protégé, writes that Mayo had a "mutually interdependent" view of things: "The behavior of workers, to take an example, cannot be studied fruitfully apart from the behavior of management; one affects and is affected by the other" (Mayo, *Human Problems*, xii).

34 Mayo, *Human Problems*, 87, 100.

35 Mayo, *Human Problems*, 81.

36 For the controversies in interpretation, see Gillespie, *Manufacturing Knowledge*. Some key accounts include Carey's "Hawthorne Studies" and Franke and Kaul's "Hawthorne Experiments."

37 Roethlisberger, *Elusive Phenomena*, 50–51.

38 Zaleznik, "Foreword," 9. See also Wren and Bedeian, *Evolution of Management Thought*.

39 Mayo, *Human Problems*, 125.

40 Dingley, "Durkheim, Mayo."

41 Illouz, *Saving the Modern Soul*.

42 Gillespie, *Manufacturing Knowledge*, 73.

43 Houser, *What People Want from Business*.

44 See also Erwin Schell and Gilmore, *Manual for Executives and Foremen*, 81.

45 Houser, *What People Want from Business*, 73.

46 Gerard Hanlon, *Dark Side of Management*.

47 Ahmed, *Willful Subjects*, 4.

48 Halsey, *How to Be a Leader*, x.

49 Halsey, *How to Be a Leader*, 9.

50 Halsey, *How to Be a Leader*, 8.

51 Tead, *Human Nature and Management*, 4.

52 Tead, *Human Nature and Management*, 63.

53 Ahmed, *Willful Subjects*, 17.

54 Laird, *Psychology of Selecting Employees*, 22.

55 Laird, *Psychology of Selecting Employees*, 24.

56 Marchand, *Creating the Corporate Soul*.

57 Beckman, *How to Train Supervisors*, 27.

58 Tead, *Art of Leadership*, 90–91.
59 See Beckman, *How to Train Supervisors*; Halsey, *How to Be a Leader*; Erwin Schell, *Technique of Executive Control*; Tead, *Art of Leadership*.
60 Niles, *Middle Management*, 89.
61 Wilson, *Getting Things Done in Business*; A. Cooper, *Employee Training*; Heyel, *Human-Relations Manual for Executives*.
62 Chapple and Wright, *Guide for Supervisors*, 11.
63 Carnegie, *How to Win Friends*, 13.
64 E. Schell, *Technique of Executive Control*, 15.
65 E. Schell, *Technique of Executive Control*, 13.
66 Wilson, *Getting Things Done in Business*, 223.
67 E. Schell, *Technique of Executive Control*, 13.
68 Beckman, *How to Train Supervisors*, 90.
69 Halsey, *How to Be a Leader*, 14.
70 Wilson, *Getting Things Done in Business*, 17.
71 Bendix, *Work and Authority in Industry*, 314.
72 Mills, *Sociological Imagination*, 172.
73 Turner, *Democratic Surround*, 3.
74 The fear of conformity has had an important influence in many fields. See Frank, *Conquest of Cool*; Ogata, *Designing the Creative Child*.
75 See Mills, *White Collar*; Riesman, Glazer, and Denney, *Lonely Crowd*; Whyte, *Organization Man*.
76 Whyte, *Organization Man*, 35–36.
77 Whyte, *Organization Man*, 349.
78 Whyte, *Organization Man*, 151.
79 Riesman, Glazer, and Denney, *Lonely Crowd*, 266.
80 Frank, *Conquest of Cool*, 28.
81 Roszak, *Making of a Counter Culture*, 4. See also Reich, *Greening of America*.
82 Argyris, *Personality and Organization*, 92.
83 Argyris, *Personality and Organization*, 90.
84 Argyris, *Personality and Organization*, 121.
85 Maslow, *Motivation and Personality*, 46.
86 Herzberg, Mausner, and Snyderman, *Motivation to Work*, 111.
87 Herzberg, Mausner, and Snyderman, *Motivation to Work*, 109.
88 Herzberg, Mausner, and Snyderman, *Motivation to Work*, 114.
89 Dimock, *Philosophy of Administration*, 6.
90 Dimock, *Philosophy of Administration*, 71.
91 Steckle, *Man in Management*, 131.
92 Dimock, *Philosophy of Administration*, 73.
93 Steckle, *Man in Management*, 59.
94 McGregor, *Human Side of Enterprise*, 125.
95 McGregor, *Human Side of Enterprise*, 125.
96 McGregor, *Human Side of Enterprise*, 174.

97   McGregor, *Human Side of Enterprise*, 174.

98   McGregor, *Human Side of Enterprise*, 140.

99   Spates, *Human Values Where People Work*, 185.

100 Spates, *Human Values Where People Work*, 185.

101 Drucker, *Practice of Management*.

102 Sheppard and Herrick, *Where Have All the Robots Gone?*, xiii.

103 Gooding, *Job Revolution*, 2, 6.

104 Gooding, *Job Revolution*, 6.

105 *Work in America* was one of the most significant probes into working life organized by the US Department of Labor. See Davis and Cherns, *Quality of Working Life*.

106 Sheppard and Herrick, *Where Have All the Robots Gone?*

107 O'Toole et al., *Work in America*, 13.

108 Nader, "Afterwords," in Lasson, *Workers*, 261.

109 Davis and Cherns, *Quality of Working Life*, 2.

110 Terkel, *Working*, xiii.

111 Terkel, *Working*, xiii.

112 Terkel, *Working*, xiii.

113 Gooding, *Job Revolution*, 77.

114 Westley and Westley, *Emerging Worker*, 92.

115 Conference Board, *Job Design for Motivation*.

116 Vough, *Tapping the Human Resource*.

117 Vough, *Tapping the Human Resource*, 81.

118 Levitan and Johnston, *Work Is Here to Stay*, 79.

119 Gooding, *Job Revolution*.

120 Irish, *If Things Don't Improve Soon*, 49.

121 Irish, *If Things Don't Improve Soon*, 7.

122 Irish, *If Things Don't Improve Soon*, 20.

123 Conference Board, *Job Design for Motivation*, 28.

124 Conference Board, *Job Design for Motivation*, 29.

125 Weeks, *Problem with Work*, 90.

126 Taking on Marx's concept of false consciousness, Ahmed writes of how historical amnesia can lead to the wrong identification of the cause of suffering: "False consciousness is that which sustains an affective situation (the workers and the natives suffer) but misrecognizes the cause, such that the misrecognition allows the cause to 'cause' suffering" (Ahmed, *Promise of Happiness*, 168).

127 Terada, *Looking Away*, 3.

Chapter 2. Jobless, Undamaged, Resilient

1   See Dargis, "George Clooney and Vera Farmiga"; Morgenstern, "In the Air."

2   A. Thompson, "20 Questions."

3   I. Fraser, "Affective Labor and Alienation."

4 Popsugar, "Buzz Interview."

5 Gross, "For Reitman."

6 Notably, the sense of loss here is recovered through a normative notion of the family and heterosexual romance. James Hoberman writes in the *Village Voice*, "As articulated by the movie's several subplots and clinched with a concluding rainbow montage in which the unemployed extol the comfort of their loved ones, the cruelties of the free market can be ameliorated by a sentimental faith in Family Values. *Up in the Air* warns that you can't go home again—and then, full of false cheer and false consciousness, pretends you can" (Hoberman, "George Clooney").

7 Benanav, *Automation*.

8 Rugaber, "U.S. Unemployment Rate Falls to 50-Year Low."

9 DeSilver, "For Most U.S. Workers."

10 Ivanova, "Unemployment Rate Could Hit 25%."

11 See Fox, "What's Really Wrong with the Unemployment Rate"; Gregory, "America's Hidden Unemployment Crisis"; Wells, "Government Says Unemployment Is at 5%."

12 Glaude, *Democracy in Black*.

13 Glinton, "Unemployment May Be Dropping"; White, "Racial Gaps."

14 Kendzior, "Geography"; Schwartz, "Poorest Areas." This sense of divided enfranchisement is particularly evident—and growing—along the lines of political affiliation.

15 Walters, "Demise of Unemployment?"

16 Sharone, Blustein, and Van Horn, "Long-Term Unemployment," 552.

17 Krueger et al., "Are the Long-Term Unemployed on the Margins."

18 Barnichon and Zylberberg, "Underemployment"; Katz and Krueger, "Role of Unemployment."

19 Barnichon and Zylberberg, "Underemployment."

20 Kalleberg, "Job Quality," 429.

21 Kalleberg, *Good Jobs, Bad Jobs*.

22 By the early 2000s, this view of workers was encapsulated in a popular business catchphrase called the seven percent rule. "According to this 'rule,'" Erin Hatton writes, "if a company announced major layoffs, its stock price would jump seven percent" (Hatton, *Temp Economy*). See also Hyman, *Temp*.

23 For an illustration of the routine nature of firing, see Grote, "Step-by-Step Guide," which appears in the *Harvard Business Review*. The need to maintain professional contacts can be understood through the larger discourse on "burning bridges," advice that also structures the process of quitting. See Castrillon, "5 Tips."

24 Lane, *Company of One*, 39.

25 US Bureau of Labor Statistics data retrieved from the Federal Bank of St. Louis.

26 Randstad, "Art of the Job Hunt."

27 Beshara, *Job Search Solution*, 19.

28 Oxford English Dictionary, "Employ."

29 Lazzarato, "Neoliberalism in Action," 111.

30 See Walters, *Unemployment and Government*; Welshman, "Concept of the Unemployable."

31 Cole, "Re-Thinking Unemployment."

32 Cole, "Re-Thinking Unemployment," 1133.

33 Jahoda, Lazarsfeld, and Zeisel, *Marienthal*.

34 Jahoda, Lazarsfeld, and Zeisel, *Marienthal*, 3.

35 Jahoda, Lazarsfeld, and Zeisel, *Marienthal*, xi.

36 Jahoda, Lazarsfeld, and Zeisel, *Marienthal*, vii.

37 Jahoda, Lazarsfeld, and Zeisel, *Marienthal*, vii.

38 See Peter Miller, "Psychotherapy of Work"; Walters, *Unemployment and Government*.

39 Walters, *Unemployment and Government*, 85.

40 Oxford English Dictionary, "Apathy."

41 Grossberg writes of affect, "These formations define the meaningfulness of the world, in the sense of significance—importance—rather than of signifying" (Grossberg, *Cultural Studies*, 194). See also Gregg and Seigworth, *Affect Theory Reader*, 1.

42 Baudrillard, "Masses."

43 Cole, "Re-Thinking Unemployment," 1136.

44 Cole, "Re-Thinking Unemployment," 1135. The larger arc of Jahoda's work supports this evaluation. In *Employment and Unemployment*, she states that the norm of paid work is so total that it would be "pointless" to blame the unemployed for being depressed and ineffective: "It would amount to asking that they single-handedly overthrow the compelling social norms under which we all live" (23).

45 See Burchell, "Effects"; Cole, "From Employment Exchange."

46 See also Weeks, *Problem with Work*.

47 Jahoda, Lazarsfeld, and Zeisel, *Marienthal*, 53.

48 Jahoda, Lazarsfeld, and Zeisel, *Marienthal*, 47–48.

49 Jahoda, Lazarsfeld, and Zeisel, *Marienthal*, 87.

50 This is why Lafargue views laziness as a political stance: it rejects the call for productivity at all fronts. See Lafargue, *Right to Be Lazy*; Weeks, *Problem with Work*.

51 Jahoda, Lazarsfeld, and Zeisel, *Marienthal*, 61–62.

52 For a discussion on the impact on youths, see Jahoda, *Employment and Unemployment*. She mentions that few can manage a life of unemployment "psychologically for any length of time." Most would turn to drugs or other self-destructive behaviors (92).

53 Jahoda, *Employment and Unemployment*, 70–71.

54 Cole, "Re-Thinking Unemployment," 1137. As Lazarsfeld argues, the apathy produced through unemployment causes a "reduction of a man's effective scope," a term he primarily uses to show how the unsophisticated consumptive patterns of the working class have kept them from acquiring a better life. The term *effective scope* is used in other ways as well. For instance, Lazarsfeld shows how tolerance of ideas can impair the ability of academics to offer thoughtful, bold, and revolutionary insights. Unemployment is therefore suggestive of an impairing condition, one that keeps people from behaving at their best. See Lazarsfeld, "Sociology"; Lazarsfeld and Thielens, *Academic Mind*.

55 Harvey, *Spaces of Hope*, 103.

56 Harvey, *Spaces of Hope*, xi. Temporality, of course, represents an important aspect of capitalism, and dysfunction in synchronization—whether represented as a mismatched rhythm of labor to the speed of objects on the line or the drivers' inability to keep to the time of those they are driving for—is unfit for the logistical nature of work under capitalism. For a theorization of temporal labor, see Sharma, *In the Meantime*.

57 Frey and Stutzer, "What Can Economists Learn," 419.

58 Krueger and Schkade, "Reliability"; Deaton, "Financial Crisis." For a good overview of the problems involved in the measurement of well-being in happiness economics, see Aronczyk, "Confidence Game."

59 Frey and Stutzer, "What Can Economists Learn," 419. The authors add that while there is evidence that the opposite occurs, "the main causality seems clearly to run from unemployment to unhappiness."

60 Ahmed, *What's the Use?*, 50.

61 See, for instance, Eriksson and Rooth, "Do Employers Use Unemployment"; Krueger et al., "Are the Long-Term Unemployed"; Trzebiatowski, Wanberg, and Dossinger, "Unemployed Needn't Apply."

62 Kroft, Lange, and Notowidigdo, "Duration Dependence," 1125.

63 Ghayad, "Jobless Trap."

64 For a summary of proposed reasons for this phenomenon, see Kroft, Lange, and Notowidigdo, "Duration Dependence." Economists have volunteered four possible explanations: the unemployed may be less employable because they are deemed to be less productive; their skills may be assumed to have depreciated over the unemployment spell; it may come as pure discrimination; and workers can become discouraged over time and express less enthusiasm in the employment process. Whatever the case, the eventual position—that the unemployed are less hirable—is seen to be so justified that it is flagrantly listed in job advertisements through variants of an "unemployed need not apply" clause. Over 150 job advertisements over a four-week period in 2011 required applicants to be currently employed to be considered for hire. See National Employment Law Project, "Hiring Discrimination."

65 For key works in the late 1970s, see Baily, "Some Aspects"; Flemming, "Aspects"; Shavell and Weiss, "Optimal Payment."

66 This relates to the history of unemployment, especially its logic of involuntary unemployment. See Walters, *Unemployment and Government*. The word *distortion* is also used by Hopenhayn and Nicolini in "Optimal Unemployment Insurance" to explain how the "perverse effects" need management.

67 Hopenhayn and Nicolini, "Optimal Unemployment Insurance," 414.

68 Shavell and Weiss, "Optimal Payment."

69 Flemming, "Aspects."

70 Fredriksson and Holmlund, "Optimal Unemployment Insurance Design"; Hopenhayn and Nicolini, "Optimal Unemployment Insurance"; Chetty, "Moral Hazard."

71 Not all papers define *optimal* in the same way. One recent paper that I came across, for instance, defines it in terms of "well-being," which would then (strikingly) reverse the policies invoked by other optimal unemployment insurance papers. See Shimer and Werning, "Reservation Wages."

72 For some key articles, see Feldstein and Poterba, "Unemployment Insurance"; Mortensen, "Unemployment Insurance."

73 For a development of "surplus labor" from the Marxian perspective, see Tyner, *Dead Labor*.

74 Ghayad, "Jobless Trap."

75 As an example, the Interview Guys say that while they "support taking a day or two after you're laid off for some well-deserved self-care . . . the last thing you want to do is to slide into bad habits and depression." The period of rest recommended to those who have been laid off typically does not exceed a week (Gillis, "What to Do").

76 Gray and Suri, *Ghost Work*.

77 Allan, "Volunteering as Hope Labour."

78 Davies, *Happiness Industry*.

79 Frey and Stutzer, "What Can Economists Learn," 420.

80 Mattingly, *Moral Laboratories*.

81 Binkley, *Happiness as Enterprise*.

82 Chappell, *War on Welfare*.

83 Somers and Block, "From Poverty to Perversity."

84 Mead, *From Prophecy to Charity*, 44.

85 Mead, *From Prophecy to Charity*, 14.

86 Mead, *Beyond Entitlement*.

87 Ramesh, "Does Getting Tough on the Unemployed Work?"

88 Binkley, *Happiness as Enterprise*, 163.

89 Schram, "In the Clinic," 87–88.

90 Binkley, *Happiness as Enterprise*.

91 Geier, "Shocker Stat of the Day."

92 See Gershon, *Down and Out*; Lane, *Company of One*; Sharone, *Flawed System/Flawed Self*. For studies of manufacturing jobs, see Chen, *Cut Loose*; Silva, *Coming Up Short*.

93 Freedman, "Tips."

94 I examine a total of thirty-one different titles, sourced from Amazon's categories of "job-hunting and careers" and "job-hunting" and from libraries. I favored those that were ranked high in the "new and bestselling" list on Amazon and examined only books published after 2007. Historical comparative analyses have also been done on Bolles's *What Color Is Your Parachute?* and Yate's *Knock 'em Dead*. I examined different editions of Bolles's text, from 1983 to 2020 and of Yate's from 1985 to 2016.

95 McGee, *Self-Help, Inc.* Career guidance discourse is often used by its subjects in complex ways that may even prove subversive to the message intended by its authors. I do not assume that readers will follow the advice without modification, but as a whole, the discourse speaks about individual expectations in a condition of normalized precarity. See Fogde, "Governing through Career Coaching."

96 "Employability skills" are also defined as "transferable skills"—they are largely communicative skills "that are not specific to one particular career path but are useful across all employment sectors." We can see how employability skills are largely tools of self-subjectification. Candidates are evaluated based on their ability to describe themselves through buzzwords, to speak in a language that is "industry-ready" (SkillsYouNeed, "Employability Skills"). See also Berglund, "Fighting against All Odds"; Gershon, *Down and Out*.

97 Employability is a discourse that is responsive to institutional processes. While career guides teach general approaches to self-presentation, each country's laws, on disability for instance, can influence what employability means. On the emotional labor involved for patients of mental illness to present themselves as employable in the United Kingdom, see Elraz, "'Sellable Semblance.'" For comparison, see Garsten and Jacobsson, "Sorting People In and Out," which discusses how people have to fit within the disability system in Sweden to be "employable enough."

98 Hong, "Finding Passion in Work."

99 Bolles, *What Color Is Your Parachute?* (2013 ed.), 119.

100 Hall, "Protean Career."

101 Houston, "Job-Planning Expert."

102 Bolles, *What Color Is Your Parachute?* (1983 ed.), 16.

103 The flower exercise was originally termed the "Quick Job-Hunting Map." Initially placed in the appendix, Bolles introduced it into the core of the text in the 1987 edition, spreading it across chapters 4, 5, and 6. He explained: "The reason I removed it from the Appendices is that the exercises which

are to be found in it are so essential, that in my view no conscientious reader, job-hunter, or career-changer should omit them. But because readers were not finishing the book, they often never discovered the Map. I thought I should put an end to that." Those sections mark the beginning of what would be later revised into the flower exercise. Bolles, *What Color Is Your Parachute?* (1987 ed.), xiii.

104 Bolles, *What Color Is Your Parachute?* (2020 ed.), 26–29.

105 Bolles, *What Color Is Your Parachute?* (2013 ed.), 8.

106 Bolles, *What Color Is Your Parachute?* (2013 ed.), 36.

107 Michal Fisher, *Finding Your Career Path*, 46.

108 Baur, *Eliminated!*, 38.

109 Beshara, *Job Search Solution*.

110 Philip Fisher, *Vehement Passions*, 228.

111 Philip Fisher, *Vehement Passions*, 230.

112 Rose and Lentzos, "Making Us Resilient."

113 Dardot and Laval, *New Way of the World*, 262.

114 Ahmed, *Living a Feminist Life*, 189.

115 Baur, *Eliminated!*, viii.

116 Acuff, *Do Over*, 17.

117 See Finney, *Rebound*; Schawbel, *Promote Yourself*.

118 Silva, *Coming Up Short*.

119 Acuff, *Do Over*, 212–13.

120 Dardot and Laval, *New Way of the World*.

121 Levinson and Perry, *Guerrilla Marketing*, 35–36.

122 McGee, *Self-Help, Inc.*

123 Yate, *Knock 'em Dead* (1985 ed.), 22.

124 Yate, *Knock 'em Dead* (1985 ed.), 21.

125 Yate, *Knock 'em Dead* (1994 ed.), 59.

126 Yate, *Knock 'em Dead* (1994 ed.), 62.

127 Yate, *Knock 'em Dead* (1994 ed.), 63.

128 Yate, *Knock 'em Dead* (2000 ed.), 20.

129 Breitbarth, *Power Formula*; Dalton, *2-Hour Job Search*; Schepp and Schepp, *How to Find a Job*.

130 Gerber and Paugh, *Superconnector*, 20.

131 Grant, *Give and Take*, 30.

132 Ferrazzi and Raz, *Never Eat Alone*, 46.

133 See Coburn, *Networking Is Not Working*; Gerber and Paugh, *Superconnector*; Grant, *Give and Take*; Robinett, *How to Be a Power Connector*.

134 Granovetter, "Strength of Weak Ties."

135 Grant, *Give and Take*, 10.

136 Grant defines "dormant ties" as the people whom you "used to see often or known well," but who have "since fallen out of contact." The generosity of

givers is instilled in these relationships, creating for a relationship of trust when people reconnect. See Grant, *Give and Take*, 50.

137 Granovetter, "Strength of Weak Ties: A Network Theory Revisited."
138 The literature on social capital is extensive. For an early hypothesis, see Montgomery, "Job Search and Network Composition." For a clear explanation of this effect, see Granovetter, "Strength of Weak Ties: A Network Theory Revisited." For a review of the issue, see Tassier, "Labor Market Implications."
139 Granovetter, "Strength of Weak Ties: A Network Theory Revisited," 207.
140 Granovetter, "Strength of Weak Ties."
141 Grant, *Give and Take*.
142 Freeman, *Headhunter Hiring Secrets 2.0*, 144.
143 Dalton, *2-Hour Job Search*, 92.
144 Cremin, "Never Employable Enough."
145 Bloom, "Fight for Your Alienation," 792.
146 Lorey, *State of Insecurity*.
147 Froehls, *Gift of Job Loss*, 57.
148 Finney, *Rebound*, 33. This makes good sense, as Ilana Gershon offers, because the volatile conditions of the labor market have pragmatically rationalized the amicable termination of work relationships. Since workers need recommendation letters, transition programs, and opportunities offered by those in the previous company, they have to avoid "burning bridges" and treat these work relationships as social capital even after termination. See Gershon, *Down and Out*.
149 Baur, *Eliminated!*, 6.
150 Finney, *Rebound*, 39.
151 Hill, *Panic Free Job Search*, 69.
152 Beshara, *Job Search Solution*, 10.
153 Leahy, *Keeping Your Head*; Levinson and Perry, *Guerrilla Marketing*; Martini and Reed, *Thank You for Firing Me!*; D. Miller, *48 Days*.
154 Leahy, *Keeping Your Head*, 191.
155 Leahy, *Keeping Your Head*, 169.
156 Walker, "Hiring a Coach."
157 Leahy, *Keeping Your Head*, 178.
158 Coleman, *Proximity Principle*.
159 T. Butler, *Getting Unstuck*.
160 Acuff, *Do Over*, 41; Michal Fisher, *Finding Your Career Path*, 50.
161 Levinson and Perry, *Guerrilla Marketing*, 41.
162 Ferriss, *Four-Hour Workweek*, 82.
163 Chertkovskaya et al., "Giving Notice to Employability."
164 Weeks, *Problem with Work*, 3.
165 De Peuter, "Creative Economy and Labor Precarity."
166 Fleming, *Mythology of Work*.

1 Reeves and Read, *Total Engagement*, 1.

2 Reeves and Read, *Total Engagement*, 2.

3 The final point about Jennifer's vacation is derived from the iteration that Byron Reeves related to Adam Penenberg: "The more points she scores, the more she helps her team, whose progress is expressed by how quickly its ship sails to an island, where they are rewarded with a real-world perk: free holiday airline travel." See Penenberg, "How Video Games Are Infiltrating."

4 Burke, *Gamify*.

5 *Gamification* has acquired a broad usage and has been attached to different initiatives. This chapter focuses on what is commonly called enterprise gamification or internal gamification, the kinds of gamification that are used to increase engagement of employees.

6 J. Schell, "When Games Invade Real Life."

7 McGonigal, "Gaming Can Make a Better World."

8 McGonigal, *Reality Is Broken*, 3.

9 Huizinga, *Homo Ludens*; McGonigal, "I'm Not Playful, I'm Gameful," 654.

10 McGonigal, *Reality Is Broken*, 28–29.

11 There are numerous conferences on gamification today. Back in 2011, gamification was the subject of an annual summit headed by Gabe Zichermann, one of the leaders of the movement. By 2019, however, gamification had become splintered into multiple smaller communities. Search engines reveal gamification conferences specializing in learning, serious games, enterprise motivation, and other topical areas. The Coursera class had over 80,000 students when I took it in 2013; an August class in 2021 had over 132,000 students. For more on the technology and consulting industry, see Scheiber, "How Uber Uses Psychological Tricks"; Tsotsis, "TaskRabbit Turns Grunt Work into a Game."

12 Zuboff, *Age of Surveillance Capitalism*.

13 Rosenblat, *Uberland*; Scheiber, "How Uber Uses Psychological Tricks."

14 Bucher and Fieseler, "Flow of Digital Labor."

15 Ferlazzo, "Kathy Sierra"; Ferrara, "Games for Persuasion"; Kirkpatrick, "Ludefaction"; Sicart, "Playing the Good Life"; Skipper, "Most Important Survival Skill"; Ingraham, "Serendipity as Cultural Technique"; Pedwell, "Digital Tendencies."

16 Arendt, *Human Condition*, 127.

17 Ahmed, *Willful Subjects*, 37.

18 Zichermann and Linder, *Gamification Revolution*; Paharia, *Loyalty 3.0*; Werbach and Hunter, *For the Win*; Collins, *Gamification*.

19 Dishman, "Company."

20 Zichermann and Linder, *Gamification Revolution*, 75.

21 Marczewski, "Put Up or Shut Up."

22 Marczewski, "Put Up or Shut Up."

23 Herzberg, Mausner, and Snyderman, *Motivation to Work*, 138.

24 Werbach and Hunter, *For the Win*, 54.

25 Penenberg, *Play at Work*, 192.

26 Reeves and Read, *Total Engagement*, 4.

27 Du Bois, "Passion for the Dead."

28 Nussbaum, *Political Emotions*.

29 Vogler, "Much of Madness," 30.

30 Vogler, "Much of Madness," 30.

31 Rorty, "From Passions to Emotions," 159.

32 Kahn, "Psychological Conditions." In an interview with Workforce, Kahn expresses that he was led to develop the term *employee engagement* in 1990 because he noticed how employers of the time had largely been ignorant of the "modern concepts of empowerment, and believed that motivating others was mostly a matter of hiring the right people and giving them the right incentives." It is clear how this idea of engagement—centered on the premise that "individuals can make real choices about how much of their real, personal selves they would reveal and express in their work"—dovetails with the concept of passion endorsed today. See Burjek, "Re-Engaging with William Kahn."

33 The will comes to mind when one encounters a blockage, when the will needs bending. As Ahmed writes, "Willing might be *how* we encounter an obstacle as that which is to be overcome: we might perceive the will as a resource insofar as it is bound up with a scene of overcoming" (Ahmed, *Willful Subjects*, 37). The "unwilling" is tied up with the act of willing; what gamification hopes to do is to remove the challenge of willing, so that the forced sensation of willing disappears.

34 McGonigal, *Reality Is Broken*, 28.

35 Zichermann and Linder, *Gamification Revolution*, 75.

36 Garber, "Compassion."

37 Penenberg, *Play at Work*, 192.

38 A. Smith, *Theory of Moral Sentiment*, 9.

39 A. Smith, *Theory of Moral Sentiment*, 22.

40 Edelman, "Compassion's Compulsion"; Jaggar, "Love and Knowledge."

41 See Nussbaum, *Political Emotions*; Whitebrook, "Love and Anger."

42 Berlant, *Compassion*.

43 Bogost, "Gamification Is Bullshit."

44 See Ferrara, "Games for Persuasion"; Robertson, "Can't Play, Won't Play."

45 Henricks, *Play Reconsidered*, 11.

46 McGonigal's dissertation on ubiquitous games ("This Might Be a Game") reveals her interest in the underlying properties of play. Her discussion of the "thousand-year game" with Stewart Brand also highlights her hope in the potential of what games can do. See Long Now Foundation, "Long Conversation," for her interview with Brand.

47 Nouvel, "Why Gamification Is Broken."

48 Feiler, "Jane McGonigal."

49 J. Hanlon, "Five Years Ago."

50 Snider, "Answers."

51 Frankfurt, *On Bullshit*, 52–53.

52 As Sebastian Deterding explains, gamification has had the tendency to reduce the theory of flow to a match of skills and challenges while ignoring other components, such as feedback, autonomy, and the absence of distractions. Deterding criticizes this omission as a sloppy use of theory, but it is also important to note Csíkszentmihályi's interest in simplifying his own theory. The compassionate wish to alleviate the suffering of others may lead one to simplify, universalize, and render abstract, so that the theory can be made useful for thinking. See Deterding, "Ambiguity of Games."

53 It is likely that this narrative was recorded by the Greek historian Herodotus only as a casual anecdote to enliven the history of Lydia. See Holland, "Herodotus I, 94."

54 Csíkszentmihályi, *Beyond Boredom and Anxiety*, ix.

55 McGonigal, *Reality Is Broken*, 353.

56 Csíkszentmihályi, *Beyond Boredom and Anxiety*, x.

57 Csíkszentmihályi, "Flow, the Secret to Happiness."

58 Csíkszentmihályi, *Flow: The Psychology of Optimal Experience*.

59 Flow Consciousness Institute, "Researching and Developing"; Flow Genome Project, "The Official Source for Peak Performance."

60 Csíkszentmihályi, *Beyond Boredom and Anxiety*, xii.

61 Csíkszentmihályi, *Flow: The Psychology of Optimal Experience*, 42, 39.

62 Csíkszentmihályi, *Flow: The Psychology of Optimal Experience*, 39.

63 Csíkszentmihályi, *Finding Flow*, 105.

64 J. Schell, *Art of Game Design*, 39–40.

65 Csíkszentmihályi, *Finding Flow*, 105.

66 Ross, *No Collar*.

67 Csíkszentmihályi, *Flow: The Psychology of Optimal Experience*, 9.

68 Csíkszentmihályi, "Wings of Defeat."

69 Sobel, "Interview: Mihaly Csikszentmihalyi," 76.

70 Csíkszentmihályi, "Flow, the Secret to Happiness." The World War II origins of flow are often repeated in his books and articles.

71 George Eisen documented similar instances of children surviving starvation, boredom, and anxiety through games and play. In this context, games provided what Eisen calls "psychic numbing": "Through play and games a certain buffered learning process was initiated which served to make children familiar with an otherwise alien universe and provided them with an ability to function in this universe." The make-believe of play, powerful as it was, could not bring people a fantasy of a life outside the war, but it could allow

them to deal with the stresses of their situation and assimilate into the new world that they found themselves in (Eisen, *Children and Play in the Holocaust*, 114).

72 Seligman and Csíkszentmihályi, "Positive Psychology," 6–7.

73 Csíkszentmihályi, *Flow: Psychology of Optimal Experience*; Csíkszentmihályi, *Evolving Self*.

74 Csíkszentmihályi, *Flow: The Psychology of Optimal Experience*, 92.

75 Cited in Agamben, *Remnants of Auschwitz*, 25. Levi drew this anecdote from eyewitness accounts of Miklós Nyiszli, a Jewish Hungarian physician.

76 Agamben, *Remnants of Auschwitz*, 25–26. This is a truncated account of Agamben's longer argument about the challenges of testimony and witnessing.

77 Bacigalupe, "Is Positive Psychology Only White?"; Seligman and Csíkszentmihályi, "Reply to Comments," 90.

78 Berlant, *Compassion*.

79 Woodward, "Calculating Compassion."

80 A full review of some of these observations in Csíkszentmihályi's work will distract from the overriding thesis. Suffice to say it is possible to see an individualization of blame in much of his work. In a *Chicago Tribune* article, for instance, he offers that surgeons "get a great enjoyment out of their jobs because they know what they must accomplish" and suggests that other workers improvise challenges like the surgeon's to experience happiness in their jobs. Shipping clerks need to "take each truck-loading job as a fresh challenge," possibly treating it as a puzzle and figuring out the "best arrangement of crates or boxes in the available space." Secretaries should learn "what the possibilities are with the equipment" that surrounds them, and housewives should "set standards for themselves" in their housework. "A woman," he notices, "who determines that four strokes of an iron is more economical than six strokes, feels better with her accomplishment when the job is done." Of course, he wrote all this at a different time, but it is clear here how psychological theory can legitimize the privatization of blame. See Houston, "Happy Workers to Be Studied."

81 Hage, "Waiting Out the Crisis."

82 Csíkszentmihályi, *Flow: The Psychology of Optimal Experience*.

83 Csíkszentmihályi, *Flow: The Psychology of Optimal Experience*, 38.

84 Schüll, *Addiction by Design*, 179.

85 Heller, "High Score."

86 McGonigal, *SuperBetter*.

87 Heller, "High Score."

88 Schüll, *Addiction by Design*, 13.

89 Richmond, "Vulgar Boredom," 32.

90 Crary, *Suspensions of Perception*, 47.

91 Nakamura and Csíkszentmihályi, "Concept of Flow," 92. This statement draws from George Herbert Mead's distinction between the spontaneous "I" and the social "me," the latter a reflective, thinking self that vanishes in flow.

92 Crary, *Suspensions of Perception*, 10.

93 Daston, "Mechanical Rules before Machines."

94 Jessica Riskin explains this well in her study of eighteenth- and nineteenth-century automata. As she offers, automata were often equated to "lowly people of various sorts—slaves, conscripts, workers. . . .In such conversations, machines unsurprisingly had a decidedly Cartesian meaning: they signified the lack of a rational soul, of a capacity for reason and intellect" (Riskin, *Restless Clock*, 146). See also Ngai, *Ugly Feelings*.

95 Kim, "Gamification Ethics"; Sicart, "Playing the Good Life."

96 Sicart, "Playing the Good Life," 225–26.

97 Kirkpatrick, "Ludefaction," 521.

98 Berlant, *Cruel Optimism*, 166.

99 Lawrie, "Passion."

100 Samuel, *American Dream*.

101 Morrison, *Unstick Your Stuck*.

102 O'Neill, *Space of Boredom*, 98.

103 Kingwell, *Wish I Were Here*; Johnsen, "On Boredom," 486.

104 North, *Problem of Distraction*, 62.

105 Ahmed, *What's the Use?*, 41.

106 Philip Mirowski and Edward Nik-Khah offer the strongest argument of this point. As they relate, the information revolution in the field of economics—in both orthodox and behavioral economics—has been supported by "antihumanist undercurrents" that make human rationality irrelevant. The market is envisioned as an information processor and its participants witless users who are unable to see the "big picture." Since "market participants didn't really know very well what they wanted," economists could "assert their competence to 'design' markets, with the objective of giving people what economists believed they should want" (Mirowski and Nik-Khah, *Knowledge We Have Lost*, 7). William Davies also charts the relationship between behaviorism and happiness economics. About nudges and the rule of experts, he writes, "'Nudging' has been criticized on grounds of 'paternalism,' but of course paternalism can also be comforting. The sense that someone else is taking the important decisions, that we have been relieved of full responsibility for our actions, can come as a relief" (Davies, *Happiness Industry*, 90).

107 Sloterdijk, *You Must Change Your Life*, 376.

108 My analysis here primarily draws from a case study of the Open Badges project, now headed by IMS Global, an educational technology firm that specializes in setting global standards for educational products. I reviewed different badging platforms using the Open Badges standard, examined

over twenty videos on YouTube, and looked at demos (usually webinars and livestreams) of enterprise gamification products.

109 Mozilla Foundation, Peer 2 Peer University, and MacArthur Foundation, "Open Badges for Lifelong Learning."

110 Clinton Global Initiative, "Digital Badges."

111 Clinton Global Initiative, "Digital Badges."

112 Becker, *Human Capital.*

113 Murphy, *Economization of Life*, 115.

114 Gershon, *Down and Out*, 11.

115 Urban Institute, "How Place Matters."

116 Forester, "Mozilla Open Badges 101."

117 Duncan, "Digital Badges for Learning."

118 Duncan, "Digital Badges for Learning."

119 MacArthur Foundation, "What Is a Badge?"

120 Most Open Badges workshops present an image of a badge, with metadata covering the badge name, its description, the criteria for earning the badge, the issuer, the date of expiration, evidence for the badge to be awarded, and tags that explain the badge's relationship to academic or professional standards. For more information on the underlying metadata for badges, see Badge Wiki, "Guide to Writing." For more on how badges are not just metadata but also a compressed "powerful behavioral tool," see Fanfarelli and McDaniel, *Designing Effective Digital Badges*, 15.

121 Galloway, *Protocol*, 7.

122 At the point of writing, this is more theoretical than an actual possibility. Digital badges are built on the same standards as Open Badges, which should make it technically possible to move information from one platform to another to recognize the badges earned. To date, badge platforms have not made such a commitment. Hence, though they are theoretically "interoperable," badge platforms still do not support the kinds of fluidity expressed in the promotional videos of Open Badges.

123 Seitzinger, "Open Badges."

124 Credly, "Design. Launch. Success."

125 Suriano, *Office Arcade*, 107.

126 Badgeville, "Badgeville for Salesforce Demo."

127 Badgeville, "Visualize the Future of Work."

128 Berlant, *Cruel Optimism*, 164.

129 Galloway, *Gaming.*

130 Bunchball, "Introducing Nitro 5.0."

131 See, for example, Marczewski, "Put Up or Shut Up"; Nouvel, "Why Gamification Is Broken"; Zichermann and Linder, *Gamification Revolution.*

132 Suriano, *Office Arcade*, 107.

133 See Griswold, "How Uber Gamified Work"; Scheiber, "How Uber Uses Psychological Tricks."

134 Wark, *Gamer Theory.*
135 Sloterdijk, *You Must Change Your Life,* 376.
136 See Dean, "Communicative Capitalism"; Pfaller, *Interpassivity.*

Chapter 4. Urban Preserves

1 Clive Wilkinson Architects, "Endless Workspace."
2 McKnight, "Clive Wilkinson Suggests 'Carpet Bombing.'"
3 Jha, "Endless Workspace."
4 Brownlee, "Office the Size of a City."
5 Graham and Marvin, *Splintering Urbanism.*
6 Miller, Casey, and Konchar, *Change Your Space,* 16.
7 Miller, Casey, and Konchar, *Change Your Space,* 18.
8 Berlant, *Cruel Optimism,* 196.
9 These arguments are made through fieldwork and interviews, as well as a discourse analysis of media articles and forums on coworking. I took time from 2016 to 2019 to intermittently visit and work in coworking spaces across California and in Bali, Indonesia. During this time, I observed the interactions of coworkers within the spaces and the designs of the interiors and interviewed space operators and hosts, as well as coworking members. I also had the opportunity to participate in the Global Coworking Unconference Conference (GCUC), a major coworking conference, held in Los Angeles in 2016, and examined the uploaded video materials for the conferences in 2019 and 2020. The data collected there supplemented other materials of analysis, including books and media articles that either addressed coworking or were published by coworking space operators advancing the values that the movement supports; conversations found in the public coworking Google Group; videos and webinars produced by coworking businesses; and blog posts of prominent members of the movement.
10 Kessler, "Adam Neumann's $16 Billion Neo-Utopian Play."
11 De Peuter, "Creative Economy and Labor Precarity." A recent survey indicates that coworking spaces are starting to function like satellite work locations—spaces where employees of established firms can work. This is partly a cost-cutting measure (rent at coworking spaces tends to be cheaper) and also a way of tapping into the "synergies" of coworking sites.
12 Osnowitz, *Freelancing Expertise.*
13 Gayle, "US Gig Economy."
14 Upwork, "Freelancing in America."
15 Miller and Miller, "Rise of the Supertemp."
16 See Cohen, "Cultural Work"; de Peuter, "Creative Economy and Labor Precarity"; Osnowitz, *Freelancing Expertise.*
17 Horowitz and Poynter, *Freelancer's Bible.*
18 Upwork, "Freelancing in America."

19 Hillman and Hoy, "Bootstrapping, Community and Quality of Life."

20 Dullroy, "Coworking Began at Regus."

21 Battelle, "Scaling through Culture."

22 Clark, "Co-Working Spaces."

23 Hillman, email to author, March 28, 2016.

24 Coonerty and Neuner, *Rise of the Naked Economy*, 148.

25 Foertsch, "Coworking in the USA 2016."

26 Turnstone, "Why Coworking."

27 De Peuter, "Creative Economy and Labor Precarity."

28 Neuberg, "Start of Coworking."

29 Ahmed, *Promise of Happiness.*

30 L. C. Johnson, *Co-Workplace.*

31 C. Johnson, "Look Out Coworking."

32 Cadwalladr, "WeWork."

33 Rice, "Is This the Office."

34 Collective Agency, "Community Mission Statement."

35 Spreitzer, Bacevice, and Garrett, "Why People Thrive."

36 Dorsch, "To What Extent."

37 Sophie, "Getting Rid of the 'Co-Working' Hyphen."

38 GCUC Radio, "Episode 01."

39 Parry, "Is Freelancing a Lonely Business?"; Spencer, "29 Easy Ways"; Giang, "'Modern' Workplace."

40 This comes from another research project that I have developed on telecommuting in the 1980s. Many self-help texts of the period warned readers about the isolation of working from home, even describing it as the main challenge they would face as they remove themselves from the physical workplace. Debra Schepp and Brad Schepp's *The Telecommuter's Handbook*, for instance, tells readers to "plan ahead" to combat such "isolation," to schedule "lunch dates, make phone calls, and get out and contact people" (29).

41 Pomeroy, "Loneliness Is Harmful." For a summary of the tumultuous minister of loneliness position from 2018 to 2020, see Birnstengel, "Two Years after Hiring."

42 Murthy, *Together*, xv. See also Barry, "Former Surgeon General Vivek Murthy."

43 Murthy, *Connecting at Work*, 6.

44 Murthy, *Connecting at Work*, 7.

45 Alberti, *Biography of Loneliness.*

46 Svendsen, *Philosophy of Loneliness*, 1.

47 Lepore, *History of Loneliness*, n.p.

48 Entis, "Big Business of Loneliness."

49 Bacigalupo and Proctor, "Community."

50 King, "Coworking Is Not about Workspace."

51 Clark, "Co-Working Spaces."

52 Oren.S, "Infuriating Article."

53 Hillman, "What to Do."

54 Hillman, "What to Do."

55 Arendt, *Origins of Totalitarianism*, 475.

56 Hillman, "Why Do Some Freelancers Work."

57 Oldenburg, *Great Good Place*.

58 Gandini, "Rise of Coworking Spaces."

59 Horowitz and Poynter, *Freelancer's Bible*, 101.

60 Osnowitz, *Freelancing Expertise*, 121.

61 Arvidsson, *Brands*, 9. See also Storper and Venables, "Buzz"; Terranova, "Free Labor."

62 Horowitz and Poynter, *Freelancer's Bible*.

63 See Foertsch, "Advantages of Coworking Spaces"; Neuberg, "Start of Coworking"; Spreitzer, Bacevice, and Garrett, "Why People Thrive."

64 Dumm, *Loneliness*, 22.

65 Arendt, *Origins of Totalitarianism*, 475.

66 Arendt, *Origins of Totalitarianism*, 476.

67 Dyer-Witheford citing Marx, *Cyber-Proletariat*, 12.

68 J. Butler, *Force of Nonviolence*.

69 Stauffer, *Ethical Loneliness*, 19.

70 Stauffer, *Ethical Loneliness*, 20.

71 Stauffer, *Ethical Loneliness*, 19.

72 Dumm, *Loneliness*, 40.

73 We see why loneliness is understood as the opposite of solitude here: the latter leads to a generative spark of creativity; the former, a withdrawal from it.

74 Cozier, "Coworking Spaces"; Solman, "Selling Office Space"; Suarez, *Coworking Handbook*; Chan, "Co-Working Spaces."

75 Kwiatkowski, "Coworking and Suicide."

76 Merkel, "Coworking in the City," 124.

77 Merkel, "Coworking in the City," 131.

78 Kwiatkowski and Buczynski, *Coworking*, intro, loc. 32.

79 Coonerty and Neuner, *Rise of the Naked Economy*, 125.

80 Carroll, "Lonely Affects."

81 Chan, "Co-Working Spaces."

82 Illouz, *Saving the Modern Soul*.

83 Lewis, "WeWork Cleaners."

84 O'Connor, "Workers behind WeWork."

85 Silver-Greenberg and Corkery, "Start-Ups Embrace Arbitration."

86 Suarez, *Coworking Handbook*, 40.

87 Carroll, "Lonely Affects," 9.

88 Tafuri, *Architecture and Utopia*, 36–37.

89 Tafuri, *Architecture and Utopia*, 46.

90 Mozingo, *Pastoral Capitalism*.

91 Lange, *Dot-Com City*, 5.

92 Zukin, *Naked City*.

93 Jones, *Fifth Age of Work*; Miller, Casey, and Konchar, *Change Your Space*.

94 Neuberg, "Start of Coworking."

95 Spreitzer, "'Coworking' Grows."

96 Gandini, "Rise of Coworking Spaces."

97 Greenberg, *Branding New York*.

98 Gandini, "Rise of Coworking Spaces"; Peck, "Cult of Urban Creativity"; Peck, "Struggling with the Creative Class"; Pratt, "Creative Cities."

99 Florida, *Rise of the Creative Class*, 75.

100 Harvey, "Globalization and the Spatial Fix."

101 Harvey, "Globalization and the Spatial Fix," 25.

102 Florida, *Great Reset*, 5.

103 Florida, *Great Reset*, 7.

104 Florida, *Great Reset*, 8–9.

105 Florida, *Great Reset*, 137.

106 Florida, *Great Reset*, 148–49.

107 Botsman and Rogers, *What's Mine Is Yours*, xix.

108 Botsman and Rogers, *What's Mine Is Yours*, 45.

109 Botsman and Rogers, *What's Mine Is Yours*, 175.

110 Horowitz and Poynter, *Freelancer's Bible*, 319.

111 Kasriel, "Four Trends."

112 Boyer, "Leading Edge."

113 Gregg, *Work's Intimacy*. See also work on social reproduction, including Lorey, *State of Insecurity*; Vogel, *Marxism and the Oppression of Women*.

114 Martin, *Organizational Complex*.

115 Tolentino, "Gig Economy."

116 Stauffer, *Ethical Loneliness*, 20.

117 Scannell, *Television*, 25.

118 Bacevice, "Why Coworking Is Hot."

119 Miles, *Spaces for Consumption*, 15.

120 Foertsch, "What Coworking Members Want."

121 R. Campbell, "Why I Ditched My Co-Working Space."

122 Miles, "Neoliberal City," 225.

123 Rice, "Is This the Office."

124 Klingmann, *Brandscapes*.

125 March, "The Future of Workplace."

126 Liu, *Laws of Cool*, 163–64.

127 Carr, "Modern Office Design."

128 Thrift, *Non-Representational Theory*, 297.

129 Potts, "Life Hacking and Everyday Rhythm."

130 C. Taylor, *Modern Social Imaginaries*, 168.

131 Solman, "Selling Office Space."

132 Foertsch, "Advantages of Coworking Spaces."
133 Comparably, "WeWork Mission Statement"; Opodz, "Build It Together."
134 Ahmed, *Promise of Happiness.*
135 Thrift, *Non-Representational Theory*, 297.
136 Osnowitz, *Freelancing Expertise.*
137 Crang, "Public Space."
138 Skeates, "Infinite City."
139 C. Johnson, "Look Out Coworking."
140 Harvey, *Spaces of Hope.*
141 D. Cooper, *Everyday Utopias*, 18.
142 D. Cooper, *Everyday Utopias*, 25.

Conclusion. Passion in the Last Instance

1 Fernandez, "Best Route."
2 Sin, "Technology Kills Jobs?"
3 Doorley, "Stanford 2025."
4 Neff, *Venture Labor.* Unsurprisingly, there are strong similarities between these personhoods and the entrepreneurial ethos of Stanford's Silicon Valley neighbors. Stanford has been described as "Silicon Valley's queen mother" and "handmaiden," an incubator for the tech companies in the valley. See N. Thompson, "Stanford and Its Startups."
5 Berlant, *Cruel Optimism.*
6 For examples of such works, see Duffy, *(Not) Getting Paid*; Dyer-Witheford and de Peuter, "'EA Spouse'"; Kuehn and Corrigan, "Hope Labor"; McRobbie, *Be Creative*; Ross, *No Collar.*
7 Duffy, *(Not) Getting Paid.*
8 Tokumitsu, *Do What You Love.*
9 Ahmed, *Promise of Happiness.*
10 Lorey, *State of Insecurity.*
11 For examples, see Jachimowicz and McNerney, "Problem with Following Your Passion"; Lam, "Why 'Do What You Love' Is Pernicious"; Newport, *So Good*; Tokumitsu, "In the Name of Love."
12 Marx, "Economic and Philosophical Manuscripts," 82.
13 Marx, "Economic and Philosophical Manuscripts," 104–5.
14 Ahmed, *Promise of Happiness*, 167.
15 Ahmed, *Promise of Happiness*, 168.
16 Averill, "Inner Feelings."
17 Terranova, "Free Labor."
18 M. Smith, "Amazon Retaliation."
19 Bellafante, "'We Didn't Sign Up for This.'"
20 Bensinger, "Don't Look Away."
21 Pan, "Our Summer of Financial Ruin."

22 Arias, Tejada-Vera, and Ahmad, *Provisional Life Expectancy Estimates.*
23 Szalavitz, "Pain and Isolation."
24 Tyner, *Dead Labor*, xiii.
25 Berardi, *Soul at Work*, 219.
26 Raventós and Wark, *Against Charity*; Weeks, *Problem with Work.*
27 Terada, "Passion and Mental Work."
28 Banta, "Mental Work, Metal Work," 205.
29 Banta, "Mental Work, Metal Work," 206.
30 Price, *Theory of Regret.*
31 Price, *Theory of Regret,* 38.
32 Price, *Theory of Regret,* 50.
33 Brennan, *Transmission of Affect*; Susan James, *Passion and Action*; Rorty, "From Passions to Emotions."
34 Terada, *Looking Away,* 32.
35 Ngai, *Our Aesthetic Categories.*
36 Tsing, *Mushroom,* 17.
37 Tsing, *Mushroom,* 27.
38 Dean, *Crowds and Party,* 43–44.
39 J. Butler, *Force of Nonviolence,* 16.
40 J. Butler, *Force of Nonviolence,* 17.

BIBLIOGRAPHY

Acuff, Jon. *Do Over: Rescue Monday, Reinvent Your Work and Never Get Stuck.* New York: Portfolio/Penguin, 2015.

Acuff, Jon. *Quitter: Closing the Gap between Your Day Job and Your Dream Job.* Brentwood, TN: Lampo, 2011.

Agamben, Giorgio. *Remnants of Auschwitz: The Witness and the Archive.* Translated by Daniel Heller-Roazen. New York: Zone, 1999.

Ahmed, Sara. *The Cultural Politics of Emotion.* London: Routledge, 2004.

Ahmed, Sara. *Living a Feminist Life.* Durham, NC: Duke University Press, 2016.

Ahmed, Sara. *The Promise of Happiness.* Durham, NC: Duke University Press, 2010.

Ahmed, Sara. "Selfcare as Warfare." *Feministkilljoys* (blog), August 25, 2014. https://feministkilljoys.com/2014/08/25/selfcare-as-warfare/.

Ahmed, Sara. *What's the Use? On the Uses of Use.* Durham, NC: Duke University Press, 2019.

Ahmed, Sara. *Willful Subjects.* Durham, NC: Duke University Press, 2014.

Alberti, Fay Bound. *A Biography of Loneliness: The History of an Emotion.* Oxford: Oxford University Press, 2019.

Allan, Kori. "Volunteering as Hope Labour: The Potential Value of Unpaid Work Experience for the Un- and Under-Employed." *Culture, Theory and Critique* 60, no. 1 (January 2019): 66–83.

Andrejevic, Mark, John Banks, John Edward Campbell, Nick Couldry, Adam Fish, Alison Hearn, and Laurie Ouellette. "Participations Part 2: Labor." *International Journal of Communication* 8 (March 2014): 1089–1106.

Arendt, Hannah. *The Human Condition.* Chicago: University of Chicago Press, 1998.

Arendt, Hannah. *The Origins of Totalitarianism.* San Diego, CA: Harvest, 1979.

Argyris, Chris. *Personality and Organization: The Conflict between System and the Individual.* New York: Harper, 1957.

Arias, Elizabeth, Betzaida Tejada-Vera, and Farida Ahmad. *Provisional Life Expectancy Estimates for January through June, 2020.* CDC Vital Statistics Rapid Release, February 2021. https://www.cdc.gov/nchs/data/vsrr/VSRR10-508.pdf.

Aronczyk, Melissa. "Confidence Game: Marketing Well-Being in Economic Surveys." *European Journal of Cultural Studies* 17, no. 3 (June 2014): 244–57.

Arvidsson, Adam. *Brands: Meaning and Value in Media Culture.* London: Routledge, 2006.

Ashton, Daniel. "Upgrading the Self: Technology and the Self in the Digital Games Perpetual Innovation Economy." *Convergence* 17, no. 3 (August 2011): 307–21.

Averill, James R. "Inner Feelings, Works of the Flesh, the Beast Within, Diseases of the Mind, Driving Force, and Putting on a Show: Six Metaphors of Emotion and Their Theoretical Extension." In *Metaphors in the History of Psychology*, edited by David E. Leary, 104–32. Cambridge, UK: Cambridge University Press, 1990.

Bacevice, Peter. "Why Coworking Is Hot." *Money*, November 19, 2014. https://money.com/coworking-why-it-works/.

Bacigalupe, Gonzalo. "Is Positive Psychology Only White Psychology?" *American Psychologist* 56, no. 1 (January 2001): 82–83.

Bacigalupo, Tony, and Ashley Proctor. "Community." Unrecorded session (April 15, 2019) at the 2019 Global Coworking Unconference Conference (GCUC), Denver, CO, April 15–18, 2019.

Badgeville. "Badgeville for Salesforce Demo." Video, 3:43. Accessed December 13, 2015. https://www.youtube.com/watch?v=YajwynaGCQE. Video no longer available; copy in the collection of author.

Badgeville. "Visualize the Future of Work." Accessed January 14, 2016. https://web.archive.org/web/20160111043057/https://badgeville.com/.

Badge Wiki. "A Guide to Writing Open Badge Metadata." Last edited March 1, 2019. https://badge.wiki/wiki/A_Guide_to_Writing_Open_Badge_Metadata.

Baily, Martin Neil. "Some Aspects of Optimal Unemployment Insurance." *Journal of Public Economics* 10, no. 3 (1978): 379–402.

Bakker, Isabella, and Stephen Gill. "Ontology, Method, and Hypotheses." In *Power, Production and Social Reproduction: Human In/security in the Global Political Economy*, edited by Isabella Bakker and Stephen Gill, 17–41. New York: Palgrave Macmillan, 2003.

Banta, Martha. "Mental Work, Metal Work." PMLA 113, no. 2 (March 1998): 199–211.

Barnichon, Regis, and Yanos Zylberberg. "Underemployment and the Trickle-Down of Unemployment." *American Economic Journal: Macroeconomics* 11, no. 2 (April 2019): 40–78.

Barry, Colleen. "Former Surgeon General Vivek Murthy and Colleen Barry on Loneliness and Health." *Hopkins Bloomberg Public Health Magazine*, February 17, 2020. https://magazine.jhsph.edu/2020/former-surgeon-general-vivek-murthy-and-colleen-barry-loneliness-and-health.

Battelle, John. "Scaling through Culture: WeWork and Blue Bottle (vs. Regus and Starbucks)." *John Battelle's Searchblog*, June 17, 2015. http://battellemedia.com /archives/2015/06/scaling-through-culture-wework-and-blue-bottle-vs-regus -and-starbucks.php.

Baudrillard, Jean. "The Masses: The Implosion of the Social in the Media." *New Literary History* 16, no. 3 (1985): 577–89.

Baur, Jean. *Eliminated! Now What?* Indianapolis: Jist Works, 2011.

Becker, Gary S. *Human Capital: A Theoretical and Empirical Analysis, with Special Reference to Education.* Chicago: University of Chicago Press, 2009.

Beckman, R. O. *How to Train Supervisors: Manual and Outlines for Determinate Discussion.* New York: Harper, 1944.

Bellafante, Ginia. "'We Didn't Sign Up for This': Amazon Workers on the Front Lines." *New York Times*, February 18, 2021. https://www.nytimes.com/2020/04 /03/nyregion/coronavirus-nyc-chris-smalls-amazon.html.

Bendix, Reinhard. *Work and Authority in Industry: Managerial Ideologies in the Course of Industrialization.* New Brunswick, NJ: Transaction, 2001.

Bensinger, Greg. "Don't Look Away from Amazon Workers' Latest Union Drive." *New York Times*, February 17, 2021. https://www.nytimes.com/2021/02/17 /opinion/amazon-workers-union.html.

Berardi, Franco "Bifo." *The Soul at Work: From Alienation to Autonomy.* Translated by Francesca Cadel and Giuseppina Mecchia. Los Angeles: Semiotext, 2009.

Berglund, Karin. "Fighting against All Odds: Entrepreneurship Education as Employability Training." *Ephemera: Theory and Politics in Organization* 13, no. 4 (2013): 717–35. http://www.ephemerajournal.org/contribution/fighting-against -all-odds-entrepreneurship-education-employability-training.

Berlant, Lauren, ed. *Compassion: The Culture and Politics of an Emotion.* New York: Routledge, 2004.

Berlant, Lauren. *Cruel Optimism.* Durham, NC: Duke University Press, 2011.

Beshara, Tony. *The Job Search Solution: The Ultimate System for Finding a Great Job Now!* New York: AMACOM, 2012.

Binkley, Sam. *Happiness as Enterprise: An Essay on Neoliberal Life.* Albany: State University of New York Press, 2014.

Birnstengel, Grace. "Two Years after Hiring a Minister of Loneliness, People in the U.K. Are Still Lonely." MarketWatch, January 29, 2020. https://www .marketwatch.com/story/two-years-after-hiring-a-minister-of-loneliness -people-in-the-uk-are-still-lonely-2020-01-29.

Bloom, Peter. "Fight for Your Alienation: The Fantasy of Employability and the Ironic Struggle for Self-Exploitation." *Ephemera: Theory and Politics in Organization* 13, no. 4 (2013): 785–807.

Bogost, Ian. "Gamification Is Bullshit." August 8, 2011. http://bogost.com/writing /blog/gamification_is_bullshit/.

Bolles, Richard N. *What Color Is Your Parachute? A Practical Manual for Job-Hunters and Career-Changers.* New York: Ten Speed, 1983.

Bolles, Richard N. *What Color Is Your Parachute? A Practical Manual for Job-Hunters and Career-Changers*. 1987 ed. New York: Ten Speed, 1987.

Bolles, Richard N. *What Color Is Your Parachute? A Practical Manual for Job-Hunters and Career-Changers*. 2013 ed. New York: Ten Speed, 2012.

Bolles, Richard N. *What Color Is Your Parachute? A Practical Manual for Job-Hunters and Career-Changers*. 2020 ed. New York: Ten Speed, 2019.

Boltanski, Luc, and Eve Chiapello. *The New Spirit of Capitalism*. Translated by Gregory Elliott. London: Verso, 2005.

Botsman, Rachel, and Roo Rogers. *What's Mine Is Yours: The Rise of Collaborative Consumption*. New York: HarperCollins, 2010.

Boyer, Bryan. "The Leading Edge: Independents Are an Early Warning System for the Economy." Dash Marshall/Civic Futures, July 15, 2014. https://medium.com/@bryan/the-leading-edge-81485feb3ef0.

Braverman, Harry. *Labor and Monopoly Capital: The Degradation of Work in the Twentieth Century*. New York: Monthly Review, 1998.

Breitbarth, Wayne. *The Power Formula for LinkedIn Success: Kick-Start Your Business, Brand, and Job Search*. Austin, TX: Greenleaf, 2011.

Brennan, Teresa. *The Transmission of Affect*. Ithaca, NY: Cornell University Press, 2004.

Brownlee, John. "An Office the Size of a City: Googleplex Designer's Latest Zany Idea." *Fast Company*, December 11, 2015. http://www.fastcodesign.com/3054263/the-googleplex-designers-latest-idea-an-office-that-never-ends.

Bucher, Eliane, and Christian Fieseler. "The Flow of Digital Labor." *New Media and Society* 19, no. 11 (November 2017): 1868–86.

Bunchball. "Introducing Nitro 5.0 from Bunchball." March 23, 2013. Video, 2:13. https://www.youtube.com/watch?v=BD6z1RwNgSM.

Burawoy, Michael. *Manufacturing Consent: Changes in the Labor Process under Monopoly Capitalism*. Chicago: University of Chicago Press, 1982.

Burchell, Brendan. "The Effects of Labor Market Position, Job Security, and Unemployment on Psychological Health." In *Social Change and the Experience of Unemployment*, edited by Duncan Gallie, Catherine Marsh, and Carolyn Vogler, 188–212. Oxford: Oxford University Press, 1994.

Burjek, Andie. "Re-Engaging with William Kahn 25 Years after He Coined Term Employee Engagement." *Workforce*, December 14, 2015. https://www.workforce.com/2015/12/14/re-engaging-with-william-kahn-25-years-after-he-coined-term-employee-engagement/.

Burke, Brian. *Gamify: How Gamification Motivates People to Do Extraordinary Things*. New York: Routledge, 2016.

Butler, Judith. *The Force of Nonviolence: The Ethical in the Political*. London: Verso, 2020.

Butler, Timothy. *Getting Unstuck: How Dead Ends Become New Paths*. Boston: Harvard Business Press, 2007.

Cadwalladr, Carole. "WeWork: They've Transformed the Office, Now It's Time for Your Home." *Guardian*, January 11, 2016. http://www.theguardian.com

/global/2016/jan/11/wework-transforming-office-life-and-home-life-carole
-cadwalladr.

Campbell, Colin. *The Romantic Ethic and the Spirit of Modern Consumerism*. New York: Palgrave Macmillan, 2018.

Campbell, Rebekah. "Why I Ditched My Co-Working Space." *New York Times*, July 8, 2014. http://boss.blogs.nytimes.com/2014/07/08/why-i-ditched-my-co-working-space/.

Carey, Alex. "The Hawthorne Studies: A Radical Criticism." *American Sociological Review* 32, no. 3 (1967): 403–16.

Carnegie, Dale. *How to Win Friends and Influence People*. New York: Simon and Schuster, 1981.

Carr, Robert. "Modern Office Design Must Focus on 'Sense of Purpose' Ideal." *National Real Estate Investor*, January 29, 2016. http://nreionline.com/office/modern-office-design-must-focus-sense-purpose-ideal.

Carroll, Melissa. "Lonely Affects and Queer Sexualities: A Politics of Loneliness in Contemporary Western Culture." PhD diss., McMaster University, 2013.

Castrillon, Caroline. "5 Tips to Quit Your Job without Burning Bridges." *Forbes*, October 27, 2019. https://www.forbes.com/sites/carolinecastrillon/2019/10/27/5-tips-to-quit-your-job-without-burning-bridges/.

Cazdyn, Eric. *The Already Dead: The New Time of Politics, Culture, and Illness*. Durham, NC: Duke University Press, 2012.

Chan, Nathan. "Co-Working Spaces = Higher Success for Your Startup." *Foundr*, December 23, 2014. https://foundr.com/articles/building-a-business/co-working-spaces-higher-success-startup.

Chappell, Marisa. *The War on Welfare*. Philadelphia: University of Pennsylvania Press, 2010.

Chapple, Eliot Dismore, and Edmond F. Wright. *A Guide for Supervisors on How to Understand People and Control Their Behavior*. New York: National Foreman Institute, 1946.

Chen, Victor Tan. *Cut Loose: Jobless and Hopeless in an Unfair Economy*. Oakland: University of California Press, 2015.

Chertkovskaya, Ekaterina, Peter Watt, Stefan Tramer, and Sverre Spoelstra. "Giving Notice to Employability." *Ephemera: Theory and Politics in Organization* 13, no. 4 (2013): 701–16.

Chetty, Raj. "Moral Hazard vs. Liquidity and Optimal Unemployment Insurance." National Bureau of Economic Research Working Paper Series 13967, Cambridge, MA, April 1, 2008.

Clark, Patrick. "Co-Working Spaces: An Expensive Cure for Loneliness." Bloomberg, February 2, 2015. http://www.bloomberg.com/news/articles/2015-02-02/co-working-spaces-an-expensive-cure-for-loneliness.

Clinton Global Initiative. "Digital Badges: Unlocking Two Million Better Futures—CGI America 2013." June 21, 2013. Video, 4:06. https://www.youtube.com/watch?v=1Qq7emqbzcA.

Clive Wilkinson Architects. "The Endless Workplace." October 16, 2015. http://www.clivewilkinson.com/the-endless-workplace/.

Coburn, Derek. *Networking Is Not Working: Stop Collecting Business Cards and Start Making Meaningful Connections.* Washington, DC: Ideapress, 2014.

Cohen, Nicole S. "Cultural Work as a Site of Struggle: Freelancers and Exploitation." *TripleC: Communication, Capitalism and Critique; Open Access Journal for a Global Sustainable Information Society* 10, no. 2 (May 2012): 141–55.

Cole, Matthew. "From Employment Exchange to Jobcentre Plus: The Changing Institutional Context of Unemployment." *History of the Human Sciences* 20, no. 4 (November 2007): 129–46.

Cole, Matthew. "Re-Thinking Unemployment: A Challenge to the Legacy of Jahoda et al." *Sociology* 41, no. 6 (December 2007): 1133–49.

Coleman, Ken. *The Proximity Principle: The Proven Strategy That Will Lead to the Career You Love.* Brentwood, TN: Ramsey, 2019.

Collective Agency. "Community Mission Statement." Accessed July 26, 2021. https://collectiveagency.co.

Collins, Chris. *Gamification: Playing for Profits; A Book of Sales Games and Motivational Tools.* Middletown, DE: CreateSpace, 2015.

Comparably. "WeWork Mission Statement." Accessed July 26, 2021. https://www.comparably.com/companies/wework/mission

Conference Board. *Job Design for Motivation.* New York: Conference Board, 1971.

Coonerty, Ryan, and Jeremy Neuner. *The Rise of the Naked Economy: How to Benefit from the Changing Workplace.* New York: St. Martin's, 2013.

Cooper, Alfred M. *Employee Training.* McGraw-Hill, 1942.

Cooper, Davina. *Everyday Utopias: The Conceptual Life of Promising Spaces.* Durham, NC: Duke University Press, 2014.

Cozier, Tamy. "Coworking Spaces Combat the Work-at-Home Blues." *Metropolis,* August 4, 2015. http://www.metropolismag.com/Point-of-View/August-2015/Coworking-Spaces-Combat-the-Work-At-Home-Blues/.

Crabtree, Steve. "A Good Job Means a Good Life." *Gallup Business Journal,* April 11, 2011. https://news.gallup.com/businessjournal/147443/Good-Job-Means-Good-Life.aspx.

Crang, Mike. "Public Space, Urban Space and Electronic Space: Would the Real City Please Stand Up?" *Urban Studies* 37, no. 2 (February 2000): 301–17.

Crary, Jonathan. *Suspensions of Perception: Attention, Spectacle, and Modern Culture.* Cambridge, MA: MIT Press, 1999.

Credly. "Design. Launch. Success." Accessed June 25, 2020. https://web.archive.org/web/20200604141250/https://info.credly.com/.

Cremin, Colin. "Never Employable Enough: The (Im)Possibility of Satisfying the Boss's Desire." *Organization* 17, no. 2 (September 2009): 131–49.

Csíkszentmihályi, Mihály. *Beyond Boredom and Anxiety: Experiencing Flow in Work and Play.* San Francisco: Jossey-Bass, 1975.

Csíkszentmihályi, Mihály. *The Evolving Self: A Psychology for the Third Millennium.* New York: HarperCollins, 1990.

Csíkszentmihályi, Mihály. *Finding Flow: The Psychology of Engagement with Everyday Life.* New York: Basic, 1997.

Csíkszentmihályi, Mihály. *Flow: The Psychology of Optimal Experience.* New York: Harper, 1990.

Csíkszentmihályi, Mihály. "Flow, the Secret to Happiness." Filmed February 2004 in Monterey, CA. TED video, 18:42. https://www.ted.com/talks/mihaly _csikszentmihalyi_on_flow?language=en.

Csíkszentmihályi, Mihály. "Play and Intrinsic Rewards." *Journal of Humanistic Psychology* 15, no. 3 (July 1975): 41–63.

Csíkszentmihályi, Mihály. "The Wings of Defeat." *New Yorker*, September 15, 1962.

Cubitt, Sean. *Finite Media: Environmental Implications of Digital Technologies.* Durham, NC: Duke University Press, 2017.

Currier, Erin, and Sheida Elmi. "State of the Union 2016: Securing the American Dream." Pew Charitable Trusts, January 13, 2016. http://pew.org/1N83GVf.

Dalton, Steve. *The 2-Hour Job Search: Using Technology to Get the Right Job Faster.* Berkeley, CA: Ten Speed Press, 2012.

Damasio, Antonio R. *Descartes' Error: Emotion, Reason and the Human Brain.* New York: Avon, 1994.

Dardot, Pierre, and Christian Laval. *The New Way of the World: On Neoliberal Society.* London: Verso, 2014.

Dargis, Manohla. "George Clooney and Vera Farmiga as High Fliers." *New York Times*, December 3, 2009. http://www.nytimes.com/2009/12/04/movies /04upinair.html.

Daston, Lorraine. "Mechanical Rules before Machines." 2019 Social Science Research Council Fellow Lecture, Roosevelt House Public Policy Institute, Hunter College, New York, February 13, 2019. Video, 1:53:03. https://www .youtube.com/watch?v=6xErFnyjMAA.

Davidson, Adam. *The Passion Economy: The New Rules for Thriving in the Twenty-First Century.* New York: Knopf, 2020.

Davies, William. *The Happiness Industry: How the Government and Big Business Sold Us Well-Being.* London: Verso, 2015.

Davis, Louis E., and Albert Cherns. *The Quality of Working Life*, vol. 1. New York: Free Press, 1975.

Dean, Jodi. "Communicative Capitalism: Circulation and the Foreclosure of Politics." *Cultural Politics* 1, no. 1 (2005): 51–74.

Dean, Jodi. *Crowds and Party.* London: Verso, 2016.

Deaton, Angus. "The Financial Crisis and the Well-Being of Americans." *Oxford Economic Papers* 64, no. 1 (January 2012): 1–26.

Delphy, Christine. *Close to Home: A Materialist Analysis of Women's Oppression.* Translated by Diana Leonard. London: Verso, 2016.

De Peuter, Greig. "Creative Economy and Labor Precarity: A Contested Convergence." *Journal of Communication Inquiry* 35, no. 4 (August 2011): 417–25.

DeSilver, Drew. "For Most U.S. Workers, Real Wages Have Barely Budged in Decades." Pew Research Center, August 7, 2018. https://www.pewresearch.org /fact-tank/2018/08/07/for-most-us-workers-real-wages-have-barely-budged -for-decades/.

Deterding, Sebastian. "The Ambiguity of Games: Histories and Discourses of a Gameful World." In *The Gameful World: Approaches, Issues, Applications*, edited by Steffen P. Walz and Sebastian Deterding, 225–44. Cambridge, MA: MIT Press, 2014.

Dimock, Marshall. *A Philosophy of Administration toward Creative Growth*. New York: Harper, 1958.

Dingley, James C. "Durkheim, Mayo, Morality and Management." *Journal of Business Ethics* 16, no. 11 (August 1997): 1117–29.

Dishman, Lydia. "The Company That's Figured Out How to Help Call Center Employees Not Hate Their Jobs." *The Future of Work* (blog), *Fast Company*, July 24, 2015. http://www.fastcompany.com/3048697/the-future-of-work/how -social-physics-is-helping-call-center-employees-not-hate-their-jobs.

Dixon, Thomas. *From Passions to Emotions: The Creation of a Secular Psychological Category*. Cambridge, UK: Cambridge University Press, 2006.

Doorley, Scott. "Stanford 2025—Scott Doorley." Stanford University, November 14, 2015. Video, 18:56. https://www.youtube.com/watch?v=wadb6A6rh1E.

Dorsch, Susan. "To What Extent Have You Articulated Your Higher Purpose?" Google Groups, July 4, 2014. https://groups.google.com/forum/#!msg /coworking/CFsjTAEPP2g/OdcREN91N6gJ.

Drucker, Peter. *The Practice of Management*. New York: Harper and Row, 1954.

Du Bois, Page. "A Passion for the Dead: Ancient Objects and Everyday Life." In *Representing the Passions: Histories, Bodies, Visions*, edited by R. Meyer, 270–88. Los Angeles: Getty, 2003.

Duffy, Brooke Erin. *(Not) Getting Paid to Do What You Love: Gender, Social Media, and Aspirational Work*. New Haven, CT: Yale University Press, 2017.

Duffy, Brooke Erin. *Remake, Remodel: Women's Magazines in the Digital Age*. Champaign: University of Illinois Press, 2013.

Dullroy, Joel. "Coworking Began at Regus . . . but Not the Way They Think." *Deskmag*, April 4, 2012. http://www.deskmag.com/en/coworking-did-begin-at -regus-but-not-the-way-they-think-362.

Dumm, Thomas L. *Loneliness as a Way of Life*. Cambridge, MA: Harvard University Press, 2009.

Duncan, Arne. "Digital Badges for Learning." Speech presented at the fourth annual launch of the MacArthur Foundation Digital Media and Lifelong Learning Competition, Hirshhorn Museum, Washington DC, September 15, 2011. https:// web.archive.org/web/20111229000911/http://www.ed.gov/news/speeches/digital -badges-learning.

Dyer-Witheford, Nick. *Cyber-Proletariat: Global Labour in the Digital Vortex.* Toronto: Pluto, 2015.

Dyer-Witheford, Nick, and Greig de Peuter. "'EA Spouse' and the Crisis of Video Game Labour: Enjoyment, Exclusion, Exploitation, and Exodus." *Canadian Journal of Communication* 31, no. 3 (October 2006): 599–617. http://www.cjc -online.ca/index.php/journal/article/view/1771.

Dyer-Witheford, Nick, and Greig de Peuter. *Games of Empire: Global Capitalism and Video Games.* Minneapolis: University of Minnesota Press, 2009.

Edelman, L. "Compassion's Compulsion." In *Compassion: The Culture and Politics of an Emotion,* edited by Lauren Berlant, 159–86. New York: Routledge, 2004.

Eisen, George. *Children and Play in the Holocaust: Games among the Shadows.* Amherst: University of Massachusetts Press, 1990.

Elraz, Hadar. "The 'Sellable Semblance': Employability in the Context of Mental-Illness." *Ephemera: Theory and Politics in Organization* 13, no. 4 (2013): 809–24.

Entis, Laura. "The Big Business of Loneliness." *Vox,* April 29, 2019. https://www .vox.com/the-highlight/2019/4/29/18511580/loneliness-co-living-coworking -friend-app-tribe-wework.

Eriksson, Stefan, and Dan-Olof Rooth. "Do Employers Use Unemployment as a Sorting Criterion When Hiring?" *American Economic Review* 104, no. 3 (March 2014): 1014.

Evans, Brad, and Julian Reid. *Resilient Life: The Art of Living Dangerously.* Cambridge, UK: Polity, 2014.

Fanfarelli, Joey R., and Rudy McDaniel. *Designing Effective Digital Badges: Applications for Learning.* New York: Routledge, 2019.

Fast, Karin, Henrik Örnebring, and Michael Karlsson. "Metaphors of Free Labor: A Typology of Unpaid Work in the Media Sector." *Media, Culture and Society* 38, no. 7 (October 2016): 963–78.

Federici, Silvia. *Revolution at Point Zero: Housework, Reproduction, and Feminist Struggle.* Oakland, CA: PM Press, 2012.

Feiler, Bruce. "Jane McGonigal, Designer of Superbetter, Moves Games Deeper into Daily Life." *New York Times,* April 27, 2012. http://www.nytimes.com/2012 /04/29/fashion/jane-mcgonigal-designer-of-superbetter-moves-games-deeper -into-daily-life.html.

Feldstein, Martin, and James M. Poterba. "Unemployment Insurance and Reservation Wage." *Business Economics* 55, no. 2 (April 2020): 67–68.

Ferlazzo, Larry. "Kathy Sierra on Gamification in Education." *Larry Ferlazzo's Websites of the Day* (blog), February 26, 2012. http://larryferlazzo.edublogs.org /2012/02/26/kathy-sierra-on-gamification-in-education/.

Fernandez, Warren. "Best Route to the Future Is the One You Chart Yourself." *Straits Times,* April 9, 2017. http://www.straitstimes.com/opinion/best-route-to -the-future-is-the-one-you-chart-yourself.

Ferrara, John. "Games for Persuasion: Argumentation, Procedurality, and the Lie of Gamification." *Games and Culture* 8, no. 4 (July 2013): 289–304.

Ferrazzi, Keith, and Tahl Raz. *Never Eat Alone: And Other Secrets to Success, One Relationship at a Time*. New York: Doubleday, 2005.

Ferriss, Timothy. *The Four-Hour Workweek: Escape 9–5, Live Anywhere, and Join the New Rich*. New York: Crown, 2009.

Finney, Martha I. *Rebound: A Proven Plan for Starting Over after Job Loss*. Upper Saddle River, NJ: FT Press, 2009.

Fisher, Mark. *Capitalism Realism: Is There No Alternative?* Alresford, UK: Zero, 2009.

Fisher, Michal. *Finding Your Career Path without Losing Your Mind*. Seattle: Amazon Digital Services, 2013.

Fisher, Philip. *The Vehement Passions*. Princeton, NJ: Princeton University Press, 2002.

Fleming, Peter. *The Mythology of Work: How Capitalism Persists Despite Itself*. London: Pluto, 2015.

Flemming, J. S. "Aspects of Optimal Unemployment Insurance: Search, Leisure, Savings and Capital Market Imperfections." *Journal of Public Economics* 10, no. 3 (December 1978): 403–25.

Florida, Richard. *The Great Reset: How the Post-Crash Economy Will Change the Way We Live and Work*. New York: HarperCollins, 2010.

Florida, Richard. *The Rise of the Creative Class*. New York: Basic, 2014.

Flow Consciousness Institute. "Researching and Developing Cutting Edge Tools for Unlocking Human Potential." Accessed July 21, 2021. Last modified 2020. https://www.flowconsciousnessinstitute.com/.

Flow Genome Project. "The Official Source for Peak Performance and Culture." Accessed July 31, 2021. https://www.flowgenomeproject.com/.

Foertsch, Carsten. "Advantages of Coworking Spaces over Other Offices." *Deskmag*, October 11, 2012. http://www.deskmag.com/en/advantages-of-coworkig-spaces-over-traditional-and-home-offices-581.

Foertsch, Carsten. "Coworking in the USA 2016—GCUCALL 2016." SlideShare presentation. May 5, 2016. https://www.slideshare.net/carstenfoertsch/coworking-in-the-usa-2016.

Foertsch, Carsten. "What Coworking Members Want." *Deskmag*, February 23, 2012. http://www.deskmag.com/en/what-coworking-space-members-want-survey-211.

Fogde, Marinette. "Governing through Career Coaching: Negotiations of Self Marketing." *Organization* 18, no. 1 (July 2010): 62–82.

Forester, Jade. "Mozilla Open Badges 101: Digging into Badges (a Webinar)." January 30, 2014. Video, 54:04. https://www.youtube.com/watch?v=Zdv6R2BiYq4.

Foucault, Michel. *The History of Sexuality*. Vol. 3, *The Care of the Self*. Translated by Robert Hurley. Reprint ed. New York: Vintage, 1988.

Fox, Justin. "What's Really Wrong with the Unemployment Rate." *Bloomberg*, August 10, 2016. https://www.bloomberg.com/view/articles/2016-08-10/what-s-really-wrong-with-the-unemployment-rate.

Frank, Thomas. *The Conquest of Cool: Business Culture, Counterculture, and the Rise of Hip Consumerism*. Chicago: University of Chicago Press, 1998.

Franke, Richard Herbert, and James D. Kaul. "The Hawthorne Experiments: First Statistical Interpretation." *American Sociological Review* 43, no. 5 (1978): 623–43.

Frankfurt, Harry G. *On Bullshit*. Princeton, NJ: Princeton University Press, 2005.

Fraser, Ian. "Affective Labor and Alienation in *Up in the Air*." In *Work in Cinema: Labor and the Human Condition*, edited by Ewa Mazierska, 29–48. New York: Palgrave Macmillan, 2013.

Fraser, Nancy. "Contradictions of Capital and Care." *New Left Review* 100 (July/August 2016): 99–117.

Fredriksson, Peter, and Bertil Holmlund. "Optimal Unemployment Insurance Design: Time Limits, Monitoring, or Workfare?" *International Tax and Public Finance* 13, no. 5 (September 2006): 565–85.

Freedman, Harry. "Tips to Help You Stay Positive While Job Hunting." *Guardian*, May 24, 2013. https://www.theguardian.com/careers/careers-blog/stay-positive -job-search.

Freeman, Skip. *Headhunter Hiring Secrets 2.0: The Rules of the Hiring Game Have Changed . . . Forever*. Charleston, SC: CreateSpace, 2016

Frey, Bruno S., and Alois Stutzer. "What Can Economists Learn from Happiness Research?" *Journal of Economic Literature* 40, no. 2 (June 2002): 402–35.

Froehls, Michael. *The Gift of Job Loss: A Practical Guide to Realizing the Most Rewarding Time of Your Life*. Texas: Peitho, 2011.

Galloway, Alexander R. *Gaming: Essays on Algorithmic Culture*. Minneapolis: University of Minnesota Press, 2006.

Galloway, Alexander R. *Protocol: How Control Exists after Decentralization*. Cambridge, MA: MIT Press, 2006.

Gandini, Alessandro. "The Rise of Coworking Spaces: A Literature Review." *Ephemera: Theory and Politics in Organization* 15, no. 1 (2015): 193–205.

Garber, Marjorie. "Compassion." In *Compassion: The Culture and Politics of an Emotion*, edited by Lauren Berlant, 15–28. New York: Routledge, 2004.

Garsten, Christina, and Kerstin Jacobsson. "Sorting People In and Out: The Plasticity of the Categories of Employability, Work Capacity and Disability as Technologies of Government." *Ephemera: Theory and Politics in Organization* 13, no. 4 (2013): 825–50. http://www.ephemerajournal.org/contribution/sorting -people-and-out-plasticity-categories-employability-work-capacity-and -disability.

Gayle, Caleb. "US Gig Economy: Data Shows 16m People in 'Contingent or Alternative' Work." *Guardian*, June 7, 2018. https://www.theguardian.com /business/2018/jun/07/america-gig-economy-work-bureau-labor-statistics.

GCUC Radio. "Episode 01: Kickoff with Tony Bacigalupo." *GCUC Coworking Podcast*, February 2, 2016. Audio, 13:12. https://soundcloud.com/gcuc/kickoff-episode.

Geier, Kathleen. "Shocker Stat of the Day: Life Expectancy Decreases by 4 Years among Poor White People in the U.S." *Washington Monthly*, September 22, 2012. http://washingtonmonthly.com/2012/09/22/shocker-stat-of-the-day-life -expectancy-decreases-by-4-years-among-poor-white-people-in-the-u-s/.

Gerber, Scott, and Ryan Paugh. *Superconnector: Stop Networking and Start Building Business Relationships That Matter.* New York: Da Capo, 2018.

Gershon, Ilana. *Down and Out in the New Economy: How People Find (or Don't Find) Work Today.* Chicago: University of Chicago Press, 2017.

Ghayad, Rand. "The Jobless Trap." 2014. https://citeseerx.ist.psu.edu/viewdoc /download?doi=10.1.1.692.6736&rep=rep1&type=pdf.

Giang, Vivian. "The 'Modern' Workplace Doesn't Just Make Us Lonely, It Can Make Us Physically Ill." *Quartz,* November 12, 2015. http://qz.com/547348/the -modern-workplace-doesnt-just-make-us-lonely-it-can-make-us-physically-ill/.

Gill, Rosalind, and Andy Pratt. "In the Social Factory? Immaterial Labour, Precariousness and Cultural Work." *Theory, Culture and Society* 25, nos. 7–8 (December 2008): 1–30.

Gillespie, Richard. *Manufacturing Knowledge: A History of the Hawthorne Experiments.* Cambridge, UK: Cambridge University Press, 1993.

Gillis, Jeff. "What to Do When You Get Laid Off." The Interview Guys, July 30, 2018. https://theinterviewguys.com/what-to-do-when-you-get-laid-off/.

Glaude, Eddie S. *Democracy in Black: How Race Still Enslaves the American Soul.* New York: Crown, 2016.

Glinton, Sonari. "Unemployment May Be Dropping, but It's Still Twice as High for Blacks." *All Things Considered,* National Public Radio. February 5, 2016. http://www.npr.org/2016/02/05/465748249/african-americans-face-uncertain -reality-despite-low-unemployment-rate.

Gooding, Judson. *The Job Revolution.* New York: Collier, 1972.

Graham, Stephen, and Simon Marvin. *Splintering Urbanism: Networked Infrastructures, Technological Mobilities and the Urban Condition.* Abingdon, UK: Routledge, 2002.

Granovetter, Mark S. "The Strength of Weak Ties." *American Journal of Sociology* 78, no. 6 (May 1973): 1360–80.

Granovetter, Mark S. "The Strength of Weak Ties: A Network Theory Revisited." *Sociological Theory* 1 (1983): 201–33.

Grant, Adam. *Give and Take: A Revolutionary Approach to Success.* New York: Viking, 2013.

Gray, Mary L., and Siddharth Suri. *Ghost Work: How to Stop Silicon Valley from Building a New Global Underclass.* Boston: Houghton Mifflin Harcourt, 2019.

Greenberg, Miriam. *Branding New York: How a City in Crisis Was Sold to the World.* New York: Routledge, 2008.

Gregg, Melissa. *Counterproductive: Time Management in the Knowledge Economy.* Durham, NC: Duke University Press, 2018.

Gregg, Melissa. *Work's Intimacy.* Cambridge, UK: Polity, 2011.

Gregg, Melissa, and Gregory J. Seigworth, eds. *The Affect Theory Reader.* Durham, NC: Duke University Press, 2010.

Gregory, Stephen. "America's Hidden Unemployment Crisis." *Epoch Times,* October 14, 2016. http://www.theepochtimes.com/n3/2163987-americas-hidden -unemployment-crisis/.

Griffith, Erin. "Why Are Young People Pretending to Love Work?" *New York Times*, February 22, 2019. https://www.nytimes.com/2019/01/26/business /against-hustle-culture-rise-and-grind-tgim.html.

Griswold, Alison. "How Uber Gamified Work." *Quartz*, October 11, 2017. https://qz.com/1098894/see-how-uber-made-driving-for-them-into-a-game/.

Gross, Terry. "For Reitman, the Best Characters Are 'Up in the Air.'" *Fresh Air*, National Public Radio, December 2, 2009. http://www.npr.org/templates/story /story.php?storyId=120993990.

Grossberg, Lawrence. *Cultural Studies in the Future Tense*. Durham, NC: Duke University Press, 2010.

Grossberg, Lawrence. *We Gotta Get Out of This Place: Popular Conservatism and Postmodern Culture*. New York: Routledge, 1992.

Grote, Dick. "A Step-by-Step Guide to Firing Someone." *Harvard Business Review*, February 17, 2016. https://hbr.org/2016/02/a-step-by-step-guide-to -firing-someone.

Hage, Ghassan. "Waiting Out the Crisis: On Stuckedness and Governmentality." In *Waiting*, 97–106. Carlton, Australia: Melbourne University Press, 2009.

Hall, Douglas T. "The Protean Career: A Quarter-Century Journey." *Journal of Vocational Behavior* 65, no. 1 (August 2004): 1–13.

Halpern, Orit. *Beautiful Data: A History of Vision and Reason since 1945*. Durham, NC: Duke University Press, 2014.

Halsey, George D. *How to Be a Leader*. New York: Harper, 1938.

Hanlon, Gerard. *The Dark Side of Management: A Secret History of Management Knowledge*. Abingdon, UK: Routledge, 2016.

Hanlon, Jay. "Five Years Ago, Stack Overflow Launched: Then, a Miracle Occurred." *The Overflow* (blog). September 16, 2013. https://blog.stackoverflow.com/2013/09 /five-years-ago-stack-overflow-launched-then-a-miracle-occurred/.

Hannon, Kerry E. *Love Your Job: The New Rules for Career Happiness*. Hoboken, NJ: Wiley, 2015.

Hardt, Michael, and Antonio Negri. *Multitude: War and Democracy in the Age of Empire*. New York: Penguin, 2004.

Harvey, David. "Globalization and the Spatial Fix." *Geographische Revue* 2, no. 3 (2001): 23–31.

Harvey, David. *Spaces of Hope*. Berkeley: University of California Press, 2000.

Hatton, Erin. *The Temp Economy: From Kelly Girls to Permatemps in Postwar America*. Philadelphia: Temple University Press, 2011.

Heller, Nathan. "High Score." *New Yorker*, September 14, 2015. https://www .newyorker.com/magazine/2015/09/14/high-score.

Henricks, Thomas S. *Play Reconsidered: Sociological Perspectives on Human Expression*. Champaign: University of Illinois Press, 2006.

Herzberg, Frederick, Bernard Mausner, and Barbara Snyderman. *The Motivation to Work*. New York: Wiley, 1959.

Hesmondhalgh, David, and Sarah Baker. "'A Very Complicated Version of Freedom': Conditions and Experiences of Creative Labour in Three Cultural Industries." *Poetics* 38, no. 1 (February 2010): 4–20.

Heyel, Carl. *Human-Relations Manual for Executives.* McGraw-Hill, 1939.

Hill, Paul. *The Panic Free Job Search: Unleash the Power of the Web and Social Networking to Get Hired.* Pompton Plains, NJ: Career, 2010.

Hillman, Alex. "What to Do When People in Your Area Don't Understand Co-working." *Alex Hillman* (blog), October 14, 2014. http://dangerouslyawesome .com/2014/10/what-to-do-when-people-dont-understand-coworking/.

Hillman, Alex. "Why Do Some Freelancers Work Out of Cafes vs. Coworking Spaces (and Vice Versa)?" *Alex Hillman* (blog), October 3, 2014. https:// dangerouslyawesome.com/2014/10/why-do-some-freelancers-work-out-of -cafes-vs-coworking-spaces-and-vice-versa/.

Hillman, Alex, and Amy Hoy. "Amy Hoy and Alex Hillman on Bootstrapping, Community and Quality of Life." Good Life Project, June 5, 2014. Video, 1:18:30. https://www.youtube.com/watch?v=NU3xkoNKZCg.

Hoberman, James. "George Clooney in Up in the Air." *Village Voice*, December 1, 2009. http://www.villagevoice.com/film/george-clooney-in-up-in-the-air-6393797.

Hochschild, Arlie Russell. *The Managed Heart: Commercialization of Human Feeling.* Berkeley: University of California Press, 1983.

Holland, Louise Adams. "Herodotus I, 94: A Phocaean Version of an Etruscan Tale." *American Journal of Archaeology* 41, no. 3 (July–September 1937): 377–82.

Hong, Renyi. "Finding Passion in Work: Media, Passion and Career Guides." *European Journal of Cultural Studies* 18, no. 2 (April 2015): 190–206.

Hong, Renyi. "Game Modding, Prosumerism and Neoliberal Labor Practices." *International Journal of Communication* 7 (April 2013): 984–1002.

Hopenhayn, Hugo A., and Juan Pablo Nicolini. "Optimal Unemployment Insurance." *Journal of Political Economy* 105, no. 2 (April 1997): 412–38.

Horowitz, Sara, and Toni Sciarra Poynter. *The Freelancer's Bible: Everything You Need to Know to Have the Career of Your Dreams—On Your Terms.* New York: Workman, 2012.

Houser, David. *What People Want from Business.* New York: McGraw-Hill, 1938.

Houston, Jack. "Happy Workers to Be Studied." *Chicago Tribune*, January 25, 1976.

Houston, Jack. "Job-Planning Expert Shows Analytical Way to Find Work." *Chicago Tribune*, May 25, 1975.

Huizinga, Johan H. *Homo Ludens: Study of the Play Element in Culture.* London: Routledge, 1980.

Hyman, Louis. *Temp: The Real Story of What Happened to Your Salary, Benefits, and Job Security.* New York: Penguin, 2018.

Illouz, Eva. *Cold Intimacies: The Making of Emotional Capitalism.* Malden, MA: Polity, 2007.

Illouz, Eva. *Saving the Modern Soul: Therapy, Emotions, and the Culture of Self-Help.* Berkeley: University of California Press, 2008.

Ingraham, Chris. "Serendipity as Cultural Technique." *Culture, Theory and Critique* 60, no. 2 (2019): 107–22.

Irish, Richard K. *If Things Don't Improve Soon I May Ask You to Fire Me: The Management Book for Everyone Who Works*. New York: Anchor, 1976.

Ivanova, Irina. "Unemployment Rate Could Hit 25%, Rivaling Great Depression, Goldman Sachs Predicts." *CBS News*, May 14, 2020. https://www.cbsnews.com/news/unemployment-rate-could-hit-25-percent-goldman-sachs-predicts/.

Jachimowicz, Jon, and Sam McNerney. "The Problem with Following Your Passion." *Washington Post*, November 6, 2015. https://www.washingtonpost.com/news/on-leadership/wp/2015/11/06/the-problem-with-following-your-passion/.

Jaggar, Alison M. "Love and Knowledge: Emotion in Feminist Epistemology." *Inquiry* 32, no. 2 (1989): 151–76.

Jahoda, Marie. *Employment and Unemployment: A Social-Psychological Analysis*. Cambridge, UK: CUP Archive, 1982.

Jahoda, Marie, Paul F. Lazarsfeld, and Hans Zeisel. *Marienthal: The Sociography of an Unemployed Community*. New Brunswick, NJ: Transaction, 2002.

James, Robin. *Resilience and Melancholy: Pop Music, Feminism, Neoliberalism*. Alresford, UK: Zero, 2015.

James, Susan. *Passion and Action: The Emotions in Seventeenth-Century Philosophy*. Oxford: Clarendon, 1997.

Jha, Antara. "The Endless Workspace." Arch2o, 2015. http://www.arch2o.com/endless-workspace-clive-wilkinson-architects/.

Jobs, Steve. Address at Stanford University's 2005 commencement ceremony. Posted March 8, 2008. Video, 15:04. https://www.youtube.com/watch?v=UF8uR6Z6KLc.

Johnsen, Ramus. "On Boredom: A Note on Experience without Qualities." *Ephemera: Theory and Politics in Organization* 11, no. 4 (2011): 482–89.

Johnson, Cat. "Look Out Coworking, Here Comes Big Money!" *Blog + Press* (blog), GCUC, May 31, 2016. http://usa.gcuc.co/look-out-coworking-here-comes-big-money-by-cat-johnson/.

Johnson, Laura C. *The Co-Workplace: Teleworking in the Neighbourhood*. Vancouver: University of British Columbia Press, 2003.

Jones, Andrew M. *The Fifth Age of Work: How Companies Can Redesign Work to Become More Innovative in a Cloud Economy*. Portland, OR: Night Owls, 2013.

Kahn, William A. "Psychological Conditions of Personal Engagement and Disengagement at Work." *Academy of Management Journal* 33, no. 4 (December 1990): 692–724.

Kalleberg, Arne L. *Good Jobs, Bad Jobs: The Rise of Polarized and Precarious Employment Systems in the United States, 1970s to 2000s*. New York: Russell Sage Foundation, 2011.

Kalleberg, Arne L. "Job Quality and Precarious Work Clarifications, Controversies, and Challenges." *Work and Occupations* 39, no. 4 (November 2012): 427–48.

Kantor, Jodi, and David Streitfeld. "Inside Amazon: Wrestling Big Ideas in a Bruising Workplace." *New York Times*, August 15, 2015. http://www.nytimes .com/2015/08/16/technology/inside-amazon-wrestling-big-ideas-in-a-bruising -workplace.html.

Kasriel, Stephane. "The Four Trends That Will Change the Way We Work by 2021." *Fast Company*, December 14, 2015. http://www.fastcompany.com/3054546 /the-future-of-work/the-four-trends-that-will-change-the-way-we-work-by -2021.

Katz, Lawrence F., and Alan B. Krueger. "The Role of Unemployment in the Rise in Alternative Work Arrangements." *American Economic Review Papers and Proceedings* 107, no. 5 (May 2017): 388–92.

Kendzior, Sarah. "Geography Is Making America's Uneven Economic Recovery Worse." *Quartz*, April 29, 2016. http://qz.com/672589/geography-is-making -americas-uneven-economic-recovery-worse/.

Kessler, Sarah. "Adam Neumann's $16 Billion Neo-Utopian Play to Turn WeWork into WeWorld." *Fast Company*, March 14, 2016. http://www.fastcompany.com /3057415/most-innovative-companies/adam-neumanns-16-billion-neo-utopian -play-to-turn-wework-into-wewo.

Kim, Tae Wan. "Gamification Ethics: Exploitation and Manipulation." Gamification Research Network CHI workshop papers. 2015. http://gamification -research.org/wp-content/uploads/2014/11/GAMICHI15_kim.pdf.

King, Steve. "Coworking Is Not about Workspace—It's about Feeling Less Lonely." *Harvard Business Review*, December 28, 2017. https://hbr.org/2017/12 /coworking-is-not-about-workspace-its-about-feeling-less-lonely.

Kingwell, Mark. *Wish I Were Here: Boredom and the Interface*. Montreal: McGill-Queen's University Press, 2019.

Kirkpatrick, Graeme. "Ludefaction: Fracking of the Radical Imaginary." *Games and Culture* 10, no. 6 (November 2015): 507–24.

Kjerulf, Alexander. "Why Every Company Should Have a CHO (Chief Happiness Officer)." *The Chief Happiness Officer Blog* (blog), April 20, 2015. http:// positivesharing.com/2015/04/why-every-company-should-have-a-chief -happiness-officer/.

Klingmann, Anna. *Brandscapes: Architecture in the Experience Economy*. Cambridge, MA: MIT Press, 2007.

Kroft, Kory, Fabian Lange, and Matthew J. Notowidigdo. "Duration Dependence and Labor Market Conditions: Evidence from a Field Experiment." *Quarterly Journal of Economics* 128, no. 3 (August 2013): 1123–67.

Krueger, Alan B., Judd Cramer, David Cho, Katharine G. Abraham, and Robert Shimer. "Are the Long-Term Unemployed on the Margins of the Labor Market? Comments and Discussion." *Brookings Papers on Economic Activity* 1 (March 2014): 229–99.

Krueger, Alan B., and David A. Schkade. "The Reliability of Subjective Well-Being Measures." *Journal of Public Economics* 92, nos. 8–9 (August 2008): 1833–45.

Kuehn, Kathleen, and Thomas F. Corrigan. "Hope Labor: The Role of Employment Prospects in Online Social Production." *Political Economy of Communication* 1, no. 1 (2013): 9–25.

Kwiatkowski, Angel. "Coworking and Suicide: What the Spirograph Can Teach Us about Community." *Cohere* (blog), Cohere Coworking. March 17, 2016. http://coherecommunity.com/blog/coworking-and-suicide-what-the -spirograph-can-teach-us-about-community.

Kwiatkowski, Angel, and Beth Buczynski. *Coworking: How Freelancers Escape the Coffee Shop Office and Tales of Community from Independents around the World.* Self-published, Amazon Digital Services, 2011. Kindle.

LaFargue, Paul. *The Right to Be Lazy.* California: AK Press, 2011.

Laird, Donald A. *The Psychology of Selecting Employees.* New York: McGraw-Hill, 1937.

Lam, Bourree. "Why 'Do What You Love' Is Pernicious Advice." *Atlantic*, August 7, 2015. http://www.theatlantic.com/business/archive/2015/08/do-what-you -love-work-myth-culture/399599/.

Lane, Carrie M. *A Company of One: Insecurity, Independence, and the New World of White-Collar Unemployment.* Ithaca, NY: ILR Press, 2011.

Lange, Alexandra. *The Dot-Com City: Silicon Valley Urbanism.* Moscow: Strelka, 2012.

Laslett, Barbara, and Johanna Brenner. "Gender and Social Reproduction: Historical Perspectives." *Annual Review of Sociology* 15, no. 1 (1989): 381–404.

Lasson, Kenneth. *The Workers: Portraits of Nine American Jobholders.* New York: Grossman, 1971.

Lawrie, Reynold. "Passion." *Philosophy and Phenomenological Research* 41, nos. 1–2 (1980): 106–26.

Lazarsfeld, Paul F. "The Sociology of Empirical Social Research." *American Sociological Review* 27, no. 6 (December 1962): 757–67.

Lazarsfeld, P. F., and Wagner Thielens. *The Academic Mind: Social Scientists in a Time of Crisis.* Glencoe, IL: Free Press, 1958.

Lazzarato, Maurizio. "Immaterial Labor." In *Radical Thought in Italy: A Potential Politics*, edited by Paolo Virno and Michael Hardt, 132–46. Minneapolis: University of Minnesota Press, 1996.

Lazzarato, Maurizio. "Neoliberalism in Action: Inequality, Insecurity and the Reconstitution of the Social." *Theory, Culture and Society* 26, no. 6 (November 2009): 109–33.

Leahy, Robert L. *Keeping Your Head after Losing Your Job: How to Survive Unemployment.* North Fayette, PA: Behler, 2014.

Lepore, Jill. "The History of Loneliness." *New Yorker*, June 4, 2020. https://www .newyorker.com/magazine/2020/04/06/the-history-of-loneliness.

Lepper, Mark R., Sheena Sethi, Dania Dialdin, and Michael Drake. "Intrinsic and Extrinsic Motivation: A Developmental Perspective." In *Developmental Psychopathology: Perspectives on Adjustment, Risk, and Disorder*, edited by Suniya S.

Luthar, Jacob A. Burack, Dante Cicchetti, and John R. Weisz, 23–50. New York: Cambridge University Press, 1997.

Levinson, Jay Conrad, and David E. Perry. *Guerrilla Marketing for Job Hunters 3.0.* Hoboken, NJ: Wiley, 2011.

Levitan, Sar A., and William G. Johnston. *Work Is Here to Stay, Alas.* Salt Lake City: Olympus, 1973.

Levoy, Gregg. "The Coronavirus as a Calling." *Passion!* (blog), *Psychology Today,* March 21, 2020. https://www.psychologytoday.com/blog/passion/202003/the -coronavirus-calling.

Lewis, Cora. "WeWork Cleaners to Protest over Wages: 'We Work Here Too.'" *BuzzFeed News,* June 18, 2015. http://www.buzzfeed.com/coralewis/wework -cleaners-push-for-raise.

Liu, Alan. *The Laws of Cool: Knowledge Work and the Culture of Information.* Chicago: University of Chicago Press, 2004.

Long Now Foundation. "Long Conversation 19 of 19 | Stewart Brand and Jane McGonigal." May 22, 2020. Video, 18:01. https://www.youtube.com/watch?v =YQVi8xiw-Js.

Lorey, Isabell. *State of Insecurity: Government of the Precarious.* Translated by Aileen Derieg. London: Verso, 2015.

MacArthur Foundation. "What Is a Badge?" June 19, 2013. Video, 3:36. https:// www.youtube.com/watch?v=RDmfEonoOJ8&feature=emb_logo.

Malesic, Jonathan. "Don't Search for 'Purpose.' You Will Fail." *New Republic,* May 28, 2015. https://newrepublic.com/article/121915/dont-search-purpose-you -will-fail.

Mandell, Nikki. *The Corporation as Family: The Gendering of Corporate Welfare, 1890–1930.* Chapel Hill: University of North Carolina Press, 2002.

March, Melissa. "The Future of Workplace UX." Unrecorded session (May 4, 2016) at the 2016 Global Coworking Unconference Conference (GCUC), Los Angeles, CA, May 3–6, 2016.

Marchand, Roland. *Creating the Corporate Soul: The Rise of Public Relations and Corporate Imagery in American Big Business.* Los Angeles: University of California Press, 1998.

Marczewski, Andrzej. "Put Up or Shut Up and Stop Moaning about Gamification." Business 2 Community, March 24, 2014. http://www.business2community .com/tech-gadgets/put-shut-stop-moaning-gamification-0819531.

Martin, Reinhold. *The Organizational Complex: Architecture, Media, and Corporate Space.* Cambridge, MA: MIT Press, 2005.

Martini, Kitty, and Candice Reed. *Thank You for Firing Me! How to Catch the Net Wave of Success after You Lose Your Job.* New York: Sterling, 2010.

Marx, Karl. *Capital: A Critique of Political Economy,* vol. 1. Translated by Samuel Moore and Edward Aveling. Moscow: Progress, 1995.

Marx, Karl. "Economic and Philosophical Manuscripts." In *Karl Marx: Selected Writings,* edited by David McLellan, 75–112. Oxford: Oxford University Press, 1977.

Maslow, Abraham H. *Motivation and Personality*. New York: Harper and Row, 1970.

Massumi, Brian. *Parables for the Virtual: Movement, Affect, Sensation*. Durham, NC: Duke University Press, 2002.

Massumi, Brian. *Politics of Affect*. Cambridge, UK: Polity, 2015.

Mattingly, Cheryl. *Moral Laboratories: Family Peril and the Struggle for a Good Life*. Oakland: University of California Press, 2014.

Maughan, Mike. "Using Behavioral Science to Help Parents Navigate a New Reality." Thrive Global, May 14, 2020. https://thriveglobal.com/stories /behavioral-science-help-parents-work-from-home-family-lessons/.

Mayo, Elton. *The Human Problems of an Industrial Civilization*. New York: Viking, 1960.

McGee, Micki. *Self-Help, Inc.: Makeover Culture in American Life*. Oxford: Oxford University Press, 2005.

McGonigal, Jane. "Gaming Can Make a Better World." Filmed February 2010 in Long Beach, CA. TED video, 20:31. https://www.youtube.com/watch?v =dE1DuBesGYM.

McGonigal, Jane. "I'm Not Playful, I'm Gameful." In *The Gameful World: Approaches, Issues, Applications*, edited by Steffen P. Walz and Sebastian Deterding, 653–58. Cambridge, MA: MIT Press, 2014.

McGonigal, Jane. *Reality Is Broken: Why Games Make Us Better and How They Can Change the World*. New York: Penguin, 2011.

McGonigal, Jane. *SuperBetter: A Revolutionary Approach to Getting Stronger, Happier, Braver and More Resilient—Powered by the Science of Games*. New York: Penguin, 2015.

McGonigal, Jane. "This Might Be a Game: Ubiquitous Play and Performance at the Turn of the Twenty-First Century." PhD diss., University of California, Berkeley, 2006.

McGregor, Douglas. *The Human Side of Enterprise*. New York: McGraw-Hill, 1960.

McKnight, Jenna. "Clive Wilkinson Suggests 'Carpet Bombing' London with a Co-Working Office in the Sky." *Dezeen*, December 16, 2015. http://www.dezeen .com/2015/12/16/clive-wilkinson-architects-endless-workplace-london-open -plan-office-in-sky-coworking/.

McRobbie, Angela. *Be Creative: Making a Living in the New Culture Industries*. Cambridge, UK: Polity, 2015.

Mead, Lawrence M. *Beyond Entitlement: The Social Obligations of Citizenship*. New York: Free Press, 1986.

Mead, Lawrence M. *From Prophecy to Charity: How to Help the Poor*. Washington, DC: AEI, 2011.

Melville, Herman. *Bartleby, the Scrivener: A Story of Wall-Street*. N.p.: SMK Books, 2012.

Merkel, Janet. "Coworking in the City." *Ephemera: Theory and Politics in Organization* 15, no. 1 (2015): 121–39.

Miles, Steven. "The Neoliberal City and the Pro-Active Complicity of the Citizen Consumer." *Journal of Consumer Culture* 12, no. 2 (July 2012): 216–30.

Miles, Steven. *Spaces for Consumption: Pleasure and Placelessness in the Post-Industrial City*. London: SAGE, 2010.

Miller, Dan. *48 Days to the Work You Love*. Nashville: B&H, 2010.

Miller, Jody Greenstone, and Matt Miller. "The Rise of the Supertemp." *Harvard Business Review*, May 1, 2012. https://hbr.org/2012/05/the-rise-of-the-supertemp.

Miller, Peter. "Psychotherapy of Work and Unemployment." In *The Power of Psychiatry*, edited by Peter Miller and Nikolas Rose, 143–76. Oxford: Polity, 1986.

Miller, Rex, Mabel Casey, and Mark Konchar. *Change Your Space, Change Your Culture: How Engaging Workspaces Lead to Transformation and Growth*. Hoboken, NJ: Wiley, 2014.

Mills, Charles Wright. *The Sociological Imagination*. Oxford: Oxford University Press, 2000.

Mills, Charles Wright. *White Collar: The American Middle Classes*. New York: Oxford University Press, 1953.

Mirowski, Philip, and Edward Nik-Khah. *The Knowledge We Have Lost in Information: The History of Information in Modern Economics*. Oxford: Oxford University Press, 2017.

Montgomery, James D. "Job Search and Network Composition: Implications of the Strength-of-Weak-Ties Hypothesis." *American Sociological Review* 57, no. 5 (October 1992): 586–96.

Morgenstern, Joe. "'In the Air': Up, Up and Away." *Wall Street Journal*, December 4, 2009. http://www.wsj.com/articles/SB10001424052748704107104574571753931267892.

Morrison, Melissa S. *Unstick Your Stuck: How to Find Your Passion, Gain Clarity, and Play Bigger in Your Life*. New York: Morgan James, 2018.

Mortensen, Dale T. "Unemployment Insurance and Job Search Decisions." *ILR Review* 30, no. 4 (July 1977): 505–17.

Mozilla Foundation, Peer 2 Peer University, and MacArthur Foundation. "Open Badges for Lifelong Learning" (working document). Last updated August 27, 2012. https://wiki.mozilla.org/images/5/59/OpenBadges-Working-Paper _012312.pdf.

Mozingo, Louise A. *Pastoral Capitalism: A History of Suburban Corporate Landscapes*. Cambridge, MA: MIT Press, 2014

Murphy, Michelle. *The Economization of Life*. Durham, NC: Duke University Press, 2017.

Murthy, Vivek H. *Connecting at Work*. Brighton, MA: Harvard Business Review, 2017.

Murthy, Vivek H. *Together: The Healing Power of Human Connection in a Sometimes Lonely World*. New York: Harper Wave, 2020.

Nakamura, Jeanne, and Mihály Csíkszentmihályi. "The Concept of Flow." In *The Oxford Handbook of Positive Psychology*, edited by Shane J. Lopez and C. R. Snyder, 89–105. Oxford: Oxford University Press, 2002.

National Employment Law Project. "Hiring Discrimination against the Unemployed." July 12, 2011. https://s27147.pcdn.co/wp-content/uploads/2015/03/unemployed.discrimination.7.12.2011.pdf.

Neff, Gina. *Venture Labor: Work and the Burden of Risk in Innovative Industries.* Cambridge, MA: MIT Press, 2012.

Neuberg, Brad. "The Start of Coworking." Keynote address at the 2015 Global Coworking Unconference Conference (GCUC) on the Roots of Coworking. May 7, 2015. Video, 25:02. https://vimeo.com/127201764.

Newport, Cal. *So Good They Can't Ignore You: Why Skills Trump Passion in the Quest for Work You Love.* New York: Business Plus, 2012.

Newport, Cal. "Solving Gen Y's Passion Problem." *Harvard Business Review,* September 18, 2012. https://hbr.org/2012/09/solving-gen-ys-passion-problem.

Ngai, Sianne. *Our Aesthetic Categories: Zany, Cute, Interesting.* Cambridge, MA: Harvard University Press, 2012.

Ngai, Sianne. *Ugly Feelings.* Cambridge, MA: Harvard University Press, 2005.

Niles, Mary Cushing Howard. *Middle Management: The Job of the Junior Administrator.* Harper, 1941.

Noble, David F. *Forces of Production: A Social History of Industrial Automation.* New Brunswick, NJ: Transaction, 2011.

North, Paul. *The Problem of Distraction.* Stanford, CA: Stanford University Press, 2012.

Nouvel, Sergio. "Why Gamification Is Broken (and How to Fix It)." The Next Web, October 17, 2015. http://thenextweb.com/dd/2015/10/16/why-gamification-is-broken-and-how-to-fix-it/.

Nussbaum, Martha Craven. *Political Emotions: Why Love Matters for Justice.* Cambridge, MA: Belknap Press of Harvard University Press, 2013.

O'Connor, Brendan. "The Workers behind WeWork." The Awl, July 2, 2015. https://www.theawl.com/2015/07/the-workers-behind-wework/.

Ogata, Amy F. *Designing the Creative Child: Playthings and Places in Midcentury America.* Minneapolis: University of Minnesota Press, 2013.

Oksala, Johanna. "Affective Labor and Feminist Politics." *Signs: Journal of Women in Culture and Society* 41, no. 2 (2016): 281–303.

Oldenburg, Ray. *The Great Good Place: Cafes, Coffee Shops, Bookstores, Bars, Hair Salons, and Other Hangouts at the Heart of a Community.* 3rd ed. New York: Marlowe, 1999.

O'Neill, Bruce. *The Space of Boredom: Homelessness in the Slowing Global Order.* Durham, NC: Duke University Press, 2017.

Opodz. "Build It Together." Accessed July 26, 2021. https://web.archive.org/web/20160314084456/http://www.opodz.com/

Oren.S. [Oren Saloman]. "Infuriating Article on the 'High Premiums' Charged by Coworking Spaces in Bloomberg." Global Coworking Forum, February 15, 2015. https://forum.coworking.org/t/infuriating-article-on-the-high-premiums-charged-by-coworking-spaces-in-bloomberg/5442/24.

Osnowitz, Debra. *Freelancing Expertise: Contract Professionals in the New Economy.* Ithaca, NY: ILR Press, 2010.

O'Toole, James, Elisabeth Hansot, William Herman, Neal Herrick, Elliot Liebow, Bruce Lusignan, Harold Richman, Harold Sheppard, Ben Shephansky, and James Wright, eds. *Work in America.* Cambridge, MA: MIT Press, 1973.

Paharia, Rajat. *Loyalty 3.0: How to Revolutionize Customer and Employee Engagement with Big Data and Gamification.* New York: McGraw-Hill Education, 2013.

Pan, J. C. "Our Summer of Financial Ruin." *New Republic,* June 23, 2020. https://newrepublic.com/article/158257/summer-financial-ruin.

Parry, Liz. "Is Freelancing a Lonely Business?" *Guardian,* July 22, 2014. http://www.theguardian.com/money/work-blog/2014/jul/22/freelancing-lonely-business.

Peck, Jamie. "The Cult of Urban Creativity." In *Leviathan Undone? Towards a Political Economy of Scale,* edited by Roger Keil and Rianne Mahon, 159–76. Vancouver: University of British Columbia Press, 2009.

Peck, Jamie. "Struggling with the Creative Class." *International Journal of Urban and Regional Research* 29, no. 4 (December 2005): 740–70.

Pedwell, Carolyn. "Digital Tendencies: Intuition, Algorithmic Thought and New Social Movements." *Culture, Theory and Critique* 60, no. 2 (2019): 123–38.

Penenberg, Adam L. "How Video Games Are Infiltrating—and Improving—Every Part of Our Lives." *Fast Company,* December 13, 2010. https://www.fastcompany.com/1702209/how-video-games-are-infiltrating-and-improving-every-part-our-lives.

Penenberg, Adam L. *Play at Work: How Games Inspire Breakthrough Thinking.* New York: Portfolio, 2013.

Perlin, Ross. *Intern Nation: How to Earn Nothing and Learn Little in the Brave New Economy.* London: Verso, 2012.

Pfaller, Robert. 2017. *Interpassivity: The Aesthetics of Delegated Enjoyment.* Edinburgh: Edinburgh University Press, 2017.

Pomeroy, Claire. "Loneliness Is Harmful to Our Nation's Health." *Observations* (blog), *Scientific American,* March 20, 2019. https://blogs.scientificamerican.com/observations/loneliness-is-harmful-to-our-nations-health/.

Popsugar. "Buzz Interview: Jason Reitman Talks Clooney and *Up in the Air.*" November 30, 2009. https://web.archive.org/web/20091201193818/http://www.buzzsugar.com/6465092.

Potts, Tracey. "Life Hacking and Everyday Rhythm." In *Geographies of Rhythm: Nature, Place, Mobilities and Bodies,* edited by Tim Edensor, 33–44. Farnham, UK: Ashgate, 2010.

Pratt, Andy C. "Creative Cities: The Cultural Industries and the Creative Class." *Geografiska Annaler: Series B, Human Geography* 90, no. 2 (November 2016): 107–17.

Price, Brian. *A Theory of Regret.* Durham, NC: Duke University Press, 2017.

Rabinbach, Anson. *The Eclipse of the Utopias of Labor*. New York: Fordham University Press, 2018.

Ramesh, Randeep. "Does Getting Tough on the Unemployed Work?" *Guardian*, June 16, 2010. https://www.theguardian.com/society/2010/jun/16/lawrence -mead-tough-us-welfare-unemployed.

Randstad. "The Art of the Job Hunt." Randstad's Workforce360. Last accessed May 20, 2020. https://web.archive.org/web/20200502132224/http://www .randstadusa.com/jobs/career-resources/career-advice/the-art-of-the-job-hunt /631/.

Raventós, Daniel, and Julie Wark. *Against Charity*. Chico, CA: AK Press, 2018.

Reddy, William M. "Against Constructionism: The Historical Ethnography of Emotions." *Current Anthropology* 38, no. 3 (1997): 327–51.

Reddy, William M. *The Navigation of Feeling: A Framework for the History of Emotions*. New York: Cambridge University Press, 2001.

Reeves, Byron, and J. Leighton Read. *Total Engagement: How Games and Virtual Worlds Are Changing the Way People Work and Businesses Compete*. Boston: Harvard Business Review Press, 2009.

Regester, Alice. "The Passion Industry Was Having a Moment, but Now It's Booming." The Drum, April 14, 2020. https://www.thedrum.com/opinion/2020 /04/14/the-passion-industry-was-having-moment-now-its-booming.

Reich, Charles A. *The Greening of America*. Harmondsworth, UK: Penguin Books, 1972.

Rice, Andrew. "Is This the Office of the Future or a $5 Billion Waste of Space?" Bloomberg, May 21, 2015. http://www.bloomberg.com/news/features/2015-05 -21/wework-real-estate-empire-or-shared-office-space-for-a-new-era-.

Richmond, Scott C. "Vulgar Boredom, or What Andy Warhol Can Teach Us about Candy Crush." *Journal of Visual Culture* 14, no. 1 (April 2015): 21–39.

Riesman, David, Nathan Glazer, and Reuel Denney. *The Lonely Crowd: A Study of the Changing American Character*. New Haven, CT: Yale University Press, 2001.

Riskin, Jessica. *The Restless Clock: A History of the Centuries-Long Argument over What Makes Living Things Tick*. Reprint ed. Chicago: University of Chicago Press, 2018.

Robertson, Margaret. "Can't Play, Won't Play." Kotaku, October 11, 2010. https:// kotaku.com/cant-play-wont-play-5686393.

Robinett, Judy. *How to Be a Power Connector: The 5 + 50 + 100 Rule for Turning Your Business Network into Profits*. New York: McGraw-Hill Education, 2014.

Roethlisberger, Fritz Jules. *The Elusive Phenomena: An Autobiographical Account of My Work in the Field of Organizational Behavior at the Harvard Business School*. Cambridge, MA: Harvard Business School, 1977.

Rorty, Amélie Oksenberg. "From Passions to Emotions and Sentiments." *Philosophy* 57, no. 220 (April 1982): 159–72.

Rose, Nikolas. *Governing the Soul: The Shaping of the Private Self.* 2nd ed. London: Free Association, 1999.

Rose, Nikolas, and Filippa Lentzos. "Making Us Resilient: Responsible Citizens for Uncertain Times." In *Competing Responsibilities,* edited by Susanna Trnka and Catherine Trundle, 27–48. Durham, NC: Duke University Press, 2017.

Rosenblat, Alex. *Uberland: How Algorithms Are Rewriting the Rules of Work.* Oakland: University of California Press, 2018.

Rosenwein, Barbara. *Emotional Communities in the Early Middle Ages.* Ithaca, NY: Cornell University Press, 2007.

Ross, Andrew. *No Collar: The Humane Workplace and Its Hidden Costs.* Philadelphia: Temple University Press, 2003.

Roszak, Theodore. *The Making of a Counter Culture: Reflections on the Technocratic Society and Its Youthful Opposition.* New York: Anchor, 1969.

Rugaber, Christopher. "U.S. Unemployment Rate Falls to 50-Year Low." *PBS NewsHour,* October 4, 2019. https://www.pbs.org/newshour/economy/u-s -unemployment-rate-falls-to-50-year-low.

Samuel, Lawrence. *The American Dream: A Cultural History.* Syracuse, NY: Syracuse University Press, 2012.

Scannell, Paddy. *Television and the Meaning of "Live": An Enquiry into the Human Situation.* Cambridge, UK: Polity, 2014.

Schachter, Hindy L. *Frederick Taylor and the Public Administration Community: A Reevaluation.* Albany: State University of New York Press, 1989.

Schawbel, Dan. *Promote Yourself: The New Rules for Career Success.* New York: St. Martin's, 2013.

Scheiber, Noam. "How Uber Uses Psychological Tricks to Push Its Drivers' Buttons." *New York Times,* April 2, 2017. https://www.nytimes.com/interactive/2017 /04/02/technology/uber-drivers-psychological-tricks.html.

Schell, Erwin Haskell. *The Technique of Executive Control.* 5th ed. New York: McGraw-Hill, 1942.

Schell, Erwin Haskell, and Frank Forester Gilmore. *Manual for Executives and Foremen.* New York: McGraw-Hill, 1939.

Schell, Jesse. *The Art of Game Design: A Book of Lenses.* 3rd ed. Boca Raton, FL: CRC, 2019.

Schell, Jesse. "When Games Invade Real Life." Filmed February 2010 at the DICE Summit in Las Vegas. TED video, 28:17. https://www.ted.com/talks/jesse_schell _when_games_invade_real_life.

Schepp, Brad, and Debra Schepp. *How to Find a Job on LinkedIn, Facebook, Twitter and Google+.* New York: McGraw-Hill, 2012.

Schepp, Brad, and Debra Schepp. *The Telecommuter's Handbook: How to Earn a Living without Going to the Office.* New York: McGraw-Hill, 1995.

Schram, Sanford. "In the Clinic: The Medicalization of Welfare." *Social Text* 18, no. 1 (2000): 81–107.

Schüll, Natasha Dow. *Addiction by Design: Machine Gambling in Las Vegas*. Repr. ed. Princeton, NJ: Princeton University Press, 2014.

Schwartz, Nelson D. "Poorest Areas Have Missed out on Boons of Recovery, Study Finds." *New York Times*, February 24, 2016. http://www.nytimes.com /2016/02/25/business/economy/poorest-areas-have-missed-out-on-boons-of -recovery-study-finds.html.

Seitzinger, Joyce. "Open Badges." Filmed March 2015 in Bendigo, Australia. TEDx Talks video, 26:48. https://www.youtube.com/watch?v =DiTHIuqAocc.

Seligman, Martin E. P., and Mihály Csíkszentmihályi. "Positive Psychology: An Introduction." *American Psychologist* 55, no. 1 (January 2000): 5–14.

Seligman, Martin E. P., and Mihály Csíkszentmihályi. "Reply to Comments." *American Psychologist* 56, no. 1 (January 2001): 89–91.

Sennett, Richard. *The Craftsman*. New Haven, CT: Yale University Press, 2009.

Sennett, Richard. *The Fall of Public Man*. New York: Norton, 1996.

Sharma, Sarah. *In the Meantime: Temporality and Cultural Politics*. Durham, NC: Duke University Press, 2014.

Sharone, Ofer. *Flawed System/Flawed Self: Job Searching and Unemployment Experiences*. Chicago: University of Chicago Press, 2013.

Sharone, Ofer, David L. Blustein, and Carl E. Van Horn. "Long-Term Unemployment in the United States." In *The Cambridge Handbook of Social Problems*, 551–66. Cambridge, UK: Cambridge University Press, 2018.

Shavell, Steven, and Laurence Weiss. "The Optimal Payment of Unemployment Insurance Benefits over Time." *Journal of Political Economy* 87, no. 6 (December 1979): 1347–62.

Sheppard, Harold, and Neal Q. Herrick. *Where Have All the Robots Gone? Worker Dissatisfaction in the '70s*. New York: Free Press, 1972.

Shimer, Robert, and Iván Werning. "Reservation Wages and Unemployment Insurance." *Quarterly Journal of Economics* 122, no. 3 (August 2007): 1145–85.

Sicart, Miguel. "Playing the Good Life: Gamification and Ethics." In *The Gameful World: Approaches, Issues, Applications*, edited by Steffen P. Walz and Sebastian Deterding, 225–44. Cambridge, MA: MIT Press, 2014

Silva, Jennifer M. *Coming Up Short: Working-Class Adulthood in an Age of Uncertainty*. Oxford: Oxford University Press, 2015.

Silver-Greenberg, Jessica, and Michael Corkery. "Start-Ups Embrace Arbitration to Settle Workplace Disputes." *New York Times*, May 14, 2016. http://www .nytimes.com/2016/05/15/business/dealbook/start-ups-embrace-arbitration-to -settle-workplace-disputes.html.

Sin, Yuen. "Technology Kills Jobs? It Can Also Create Interesting Ones." *Straits Times*, March 26, 2017. http://www.straitstimes.com/singapore/technology-kills -jobs-it-can-also-create-interesting-ones.

Skeates, Richard. "The Infinite City." *City* 2, no. 8 (1997): 6–20.

SkillsYouNeed. "Employability Skills: The Skills You Need to Get a Job." Accessed January 1, 2020. https://www.skillsyouneed.com/general/employability-skills.html.

Skipper, Clay. "The Most Important Survival Skill for the Next 50 Years Isn't What You Think." *GQ*, September 30, 2018. https://www.gq.com/story/yuval -noah-harari-tech-future-survival.

Sloterdijk, Peter. *You Must Change Your Life: On Anthropotechnics.* Translated by Wieland Hoban. Cambridge, UK: Polity, 2013.

Smith, Adam. *The Theory of Moral Sentiments.* Indianapolis: Library Fund, 1984.

Smith, Matt. "Amazon Retaliation: Workers Striking Back." CounterPunch, April 7, 2020. https://www.counterpunch.org/2020/04/07/amazon-retaliation -workers-striking-back/.

Snider, Emma. "Answers to 4 Pressing Gamification Faqs." HubSpot, October 22, 2014. https://web.archive.org/web/20141025015407/http://blog.hubspot.com /sales/answers-to-gamification-faq.

Sobel, Dava. "Interview: Mihaly Csikszentmihalyi." *Omni* 17, no. 5 (January 1995): 73–94.

Solman, Paul. "Selling Office Space and Happy Hour to a Rising Economy of Freelancers." *PBS NewsHour.* November 5, 2015. Audio, 8:49. http://www .pbs.org/newshour/bb/selling-office-space-happy-hour-rising-economy -freelancers/.

Somers, Margaret R., and Fred Block. "From Poverty to Perversity: Ideas, Markets, and Institutions over 200 Years of Welfare Debate." *American Sociological Review* 70, no. 2 (April 2005): 260–87.

Sophie. "Getting Rid of the 'Co-Working' Hyphen." Google Groups, September 1, 2011. https://groups.google.com/forum/?fromgroups=#!searchin/coworking /hyphen/coworking/AyZVba1lSs/GRfpfQv9JCkJ.

Spates, Thomas G. *Human Values Where People Work.* New York: Harper, 1960.

Spencer, Laura. "29 Easy Ways That Freelancers Can Feel Less Lonely." FreelanceM.ag, February 6, 2013. http://freelancem.ag/freelancing-basics/lonely/.

Spreitzer, Gretchen. "'Coworking' Grows amid Search for New Office Lifestyle." *Inquirer*, February 14, 2016. http://business.inquirer.net/207073/coworking -grows-amid-search-for-new-office-lifestyle.

Spreitzer, Gretchen, Peter Bacevice, and Lyndon Garrett. "Why People Thrive in Coworking Spaces." *Harvard Business Review*, May 13, 2015. https://hbr.org /2015/05/why-people-thrive-in-coworking-spaces.

Stauffer, Jill. *Ethical Loneliness: The Injustice of Not Being Heard.* New York: Columbia University Press, 2015.

Steckle, Lynde C. *The Man in Management: A Manual for Managers.* New York: Harper, 1958.

Stewart, Kathleen. *Ordinary Affects.* Durham, NC: Duke University Press, 2007.

Storper, Michael, and Anthony J. Venables. "Buzz: Face-to-Face Contact and the Urban Economy." *Journal of Economic Geography* 4, no. 4 (August 2004): 351–70.

Streeter, Thomas. "Steve Jobs, Romantic Individualism, and the Desire for Good Capitalism." *International Journal of Communication* 9 (2015): 3106–24.

Suarez, Ramon. *The Coworking Handbook: The Guide for Owners and Managers.* North Charleston, SC: CreateSpace, 2014.

Suriano, Jason. *Office Arcade: Gamification, Byte-Size Learning, and Other Wins on the Way to Productive Human Resources.* [Austin, TX?]: Lioncrest, 2017.

Svendsen, Lars. *A Philosophy of Loneliness.* London: Reaktion, 2017.

Szalavitz, Maia. "Pain and Isolation Are Driving America's Lockdown Overdose Surge." Vice, February 20, 2021. https://www.vice.com/en/article/88a3a4/pain -and-isolation-are-driving-americas-lockdown-overdose-surge.

Tafuri, Manfredo. *Architecture and Utopia: Design and Capitalist Development.* Translated by Barbara Luigia La Penta. Cambridge, MA: MIT Press, 1976.

Tassier, Troy. "Labor Market Implications of Weak Ties." *Southern Economic Journal* 72, no. 3 (January 2006): 704–19.

Taylor, Bill. "Why Amazon Is Copying Zappos and Paying Employees to Quit." *Harvard Business Review,* April 14, 2014. https://hbr.org/2014/04/why-amazon -is-copying-zappos-and-paying-employees-to-quit.

Taylor, Charles. *Modern Social Imaginaries.* Durham, NC: Duke University Press, 2004.

Tead, Ordway. *The Art of Leadership.* New York: McGraw-Hill, 1935.

Tead, Ordway. *Human Nature and Management.* New York: Arno, 1977.

Terada, Rei. *Feeling in Theory: Emotion after the "Death of the Subject."* Cambridge, MA: Harvard University Press, 2001.

Terada, Rei. *Looking Away: Phenomenality and Dissatisfaction, Kant to Adorno.* Cambridge, MA: Harvard University Press, 2009.

Terada, Rei. "Passion and Mental Work." PMLA 114, no. 1 (January 1999): 99.

Terkel, Studs. *Working: People Talk about What They Do All Day and How They Feel about What They Do.* New York: Avon, 1975.

Terranova, Tiziana. "Free Labor." In *Digital Labor: The Internet as Playground and Factory,* edited by Trebor Scholz, 33–57. New York: Routledge, 2013.

Terranova, Tiziana. "Free Labor: Producing Culture for the Digital Economy." *Social Text* 18, no. 2 (2000): 33–58.

Thompson, Anne. "20 Questions for *Up in the Air*'s Jason Reitman." IndieWire, November 29, 2009. http://www.indiewire.com/2009/11/20-questions-for-up -in-the-airs-jason-reitman-239297/.

Thompson, Nicholas. "Stanford and Its Startups." *New Yorker,* September 11, 2013. https://www.newyorker.com/business/currency/stanford-and-its-start-ups.

Thrift, Nigel. *Non-Representational Theory: Space, Politics, Affect.* New York: Routledge, 2007.

Tokumitsu, Miya. *Do What You Love and Other Lies about Success and Happiness.* New York: Regan Arts, 2015.

Tokumitsu, Miya. "In the Name of Love." *Jacobin,* January 12, 2014. https://www .jacobinmag.com/2014/01/in-the-name-of-love/.

Tolentino, Jia. "The Gig Economy Celebrates Working Yourself to Death." *New Yorker*, March 22, 2017. https://www.newyorker.com/culture/jia-tolentino/the -gig-economy-celebrates-working-yourself-to-death.

Tone, Andrea. *The Business of Benevolence: Industrial Paternalism in Progressive America*. Ithaca, NY: Cornell University Press, 1997.

Trahair, Richard C. S. *Elton Mayo: The Humanist Temper*. New Brunswick, NJ: Transaction, 2006.

Trzebiatowski, Tiffany M., Connie R. Wanberg, and Karyn Dossinger. "Unemployed Needn't Apply: Unemployment Status, Legislation, and Interview Requests." *Journal of Management* 46, no. 8 (January 2019): 1380–1407.

Tsing, Anna Lowenhaupt. *The Mushroom at the End of the World: On the Possibility of Life in Capitalist Ruins*. Princeton, NJ: Princeton University Press, 2017.

Tsotsis, Alexia. "TaskRabbit Turns Grunt Work into a Game." *Wired*, July 15, 2011. https://www.wired.com/2011/07/mf-taskrabbit/.

Turner, Fred. *The Democratic Surround: Multimedia and American Liberalism from World War II to the Psychedelic Sixties*. Chicago: University of Chicago Press, 2013.

Turnstone. "Why Coworking." May 4, 2016. Video, 2:30. https://www.youtube.com /watch?v=iXYUXFg14Xc.

Tyner, James. *Dead Labor: Toward a Political Economy of Premature Death*. Minneapolis: University of Minnesota Press, 2019.

Upwork. "Freelancing in America: 2019." SlideShare presentation, September 23, 2019. https://www.slideshare.net/upwork/freelancing-in-america-2019/1.

Urban Institute. "Urban Institute—How Place Matters." August 12, 2016. Video, 4:27. https://www.youtube.com/watch?v=rkU795f4fv4&feature=emb_logo.

Virno, Paolo. "The Ambivalence of Disenchantment." In *Radical Thought in Italy: A Potential Politics*, edited by Paolo Virno and Michael Hardt, 12–33. Minneapolis: University of Minnesota Press, 1996.

Vogel, Lise. *Marxism and the Oppression of Women: Toward a Unitary Theory*. Leiden, Netherlands: Brill, 2013.

Vogler, Candace. "Much of Madness and More of Sin: Compassion, for Ligeia." In *Compassion: The Culture and Politics of an Emotion*, edited by Lauren Berlant, 29–58. New York: Routledge, 2004.

Vough, Clair F. *Tapping the Human Resource: A Strategy for Productivity*. New York: AMACOM, 1975.

Walker, Rob. "Hiring a Coach to Spark the Job Hunt." *New York Times*, March 7, 2015. http://www.nytimes.com/2015/03/08/jobs/hiring-a-coach-to-spark-the -job-hunt.html.

Walters, William. "The Demise of Unemployment?" *Politics and Society* 24, no. 3 (September 1, 1996): 197–219.

Walters, William. *Unemployment and Government: Genealogies of the Social*. Cambridge, UK: Cambridge University Press, 2000.

Wark, McKenzie. *Gamer Theory*. Cambridge, MA: Harvard University Press, 2007.

Wayfinding Academy. "Wayfinding Academy." Accessed February 28, 2017. https://wayfindingacademy.org/home/.

Weber, Max. *The Protestant Ethic and the Spirit of Capitalism*. New York: Scribner's, 1958.

Weeks, Kathi. *The Problem with Work: Feminism, Marxism, Antiwork Politics, and Postwork Imaginaries*. Durham, NC: Duke University Press, 2011.

Wells, Nicholas. "Government Says Unemployment Is at 5%—But Here's the Bigger Picture." CNBC, Yahoo! Sports. October 8, 2016. http://sports.yahoo.com/news/government-says-unemployment-5-heres-125241102.html.

Welshman, John. "The Concept of the Unemployable." *Economic History Review* 59, no. 3 (August 2006): 578–606.

Werbach, Kevin, and Dan Hunter. *For the Win: How Game Thinking Can Revolutionize Your Business*. Philadelphia: Wharton Digital, 2012.

Westley, William A., and Margaret W. Westley. *The Emerging Worker: Equality and Conflict in the Mass Consumption Society*. Montreal: McGill-Queen's University Press, 1971.

White, Gillian B. "The Racial Gaps in America's Recovery." *Atlantic*, August 7, 2015. http://www.theatlantic.com/business/archive/2015/08/jobs-numbers-racial-gap-recovery/400685/.

Whitebrook, M. "Love and Anger as Political Virtues." In *The Politics of Compassion*, edited by Michael Ure and Mervyn Frost, 21–36. New York: Routledge, 2014.

Whyte, William H. *The Organization Man*. Philadelphia: University of Pennsylvania Press, 1956.

Williams, Raymond. *Marxism and Literature*. Oxford: Oxford University Press, 1978.

Williams, Raymond. *Politics and Letters: Interviews with New Left Review*. London: Verso, 1979.

Willis, Paul E. *Learning to Labor: How Working Class Kids Get Working Class Jobs*. Farnborough, UK: Saxon House, 1977.

Wilson, Everett B. *Getting Things Done in Business*. New York: McGraw-Hill, 1937.

Woodward, Kathleen. "Calculating Compassion." In *Compassion: The Culture and Politics of an Emotion*, edited by Lauren Berlant, 59–86. New York: Routledge, 2004.

Wren, Daniel A., and Arthur G. Bedeian. *The Evolution of Management Thought*. 7th ed. Hoboken, NJ: Wiley, 2017.

Yate, Martin John. *Knock 'em Dead*. Boston, MA: Bob Adams, Inc., 1985.

Yate, Martin John. *Knock 'em Dead*. Holbrook, MA: Bob Adams, Inc., 1994.

Yate, Martin John. *Knock 'em Dead*. Holbrook, MA: Adams Media, 2000.

Zaleznik, Abraham, ed. "Foreword: The Promise of Elton Mayo." In *Elton Mayo: The Humanist Temper*, 1–14. New Brunswick, NJ: Transaction, 2009.

Zichermann, Gabe, and Joselin Linder. *The Gamification Revolution: How Leaders Leverage Game Mechanics to Crush the Competition*. New York: McGraw-Hill Education, 2013.

Zuboff, Shoshana. *The Age of Surveillance Capitalism: The Fight for a Human Future at the New Frontier of Power*. New York: PublicAffairs, 2019.

Zukin, Sharon. *Naked City: The Death and Life of Authentic Urban Places*. Oxford: Oxford University Press, 2011.

INDEX

www.ingramcontent.com/pod-product-compliance
Lightning Source LLC
Chambersburg PA
CBHW071737270326
41928CB00013B/2717